AF575357

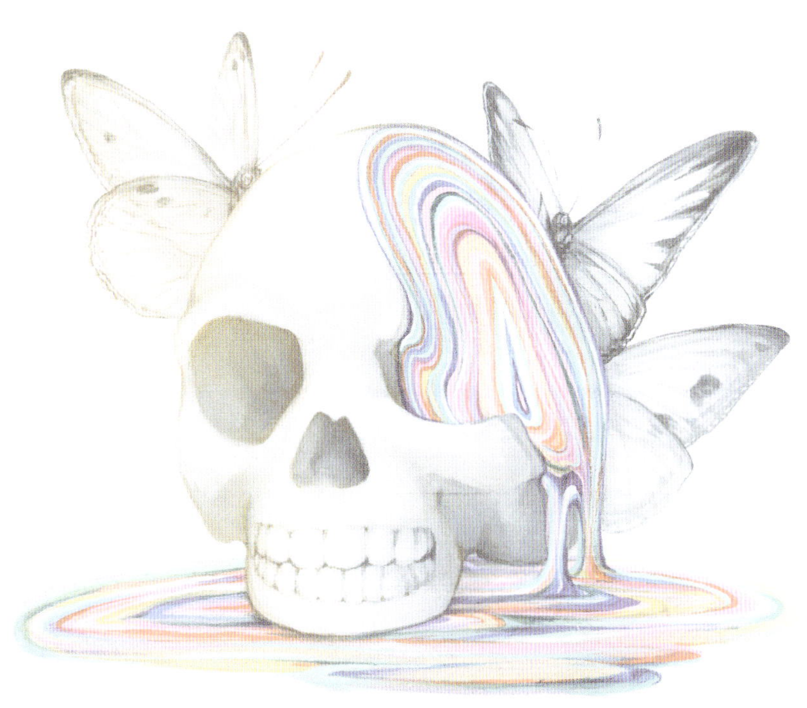

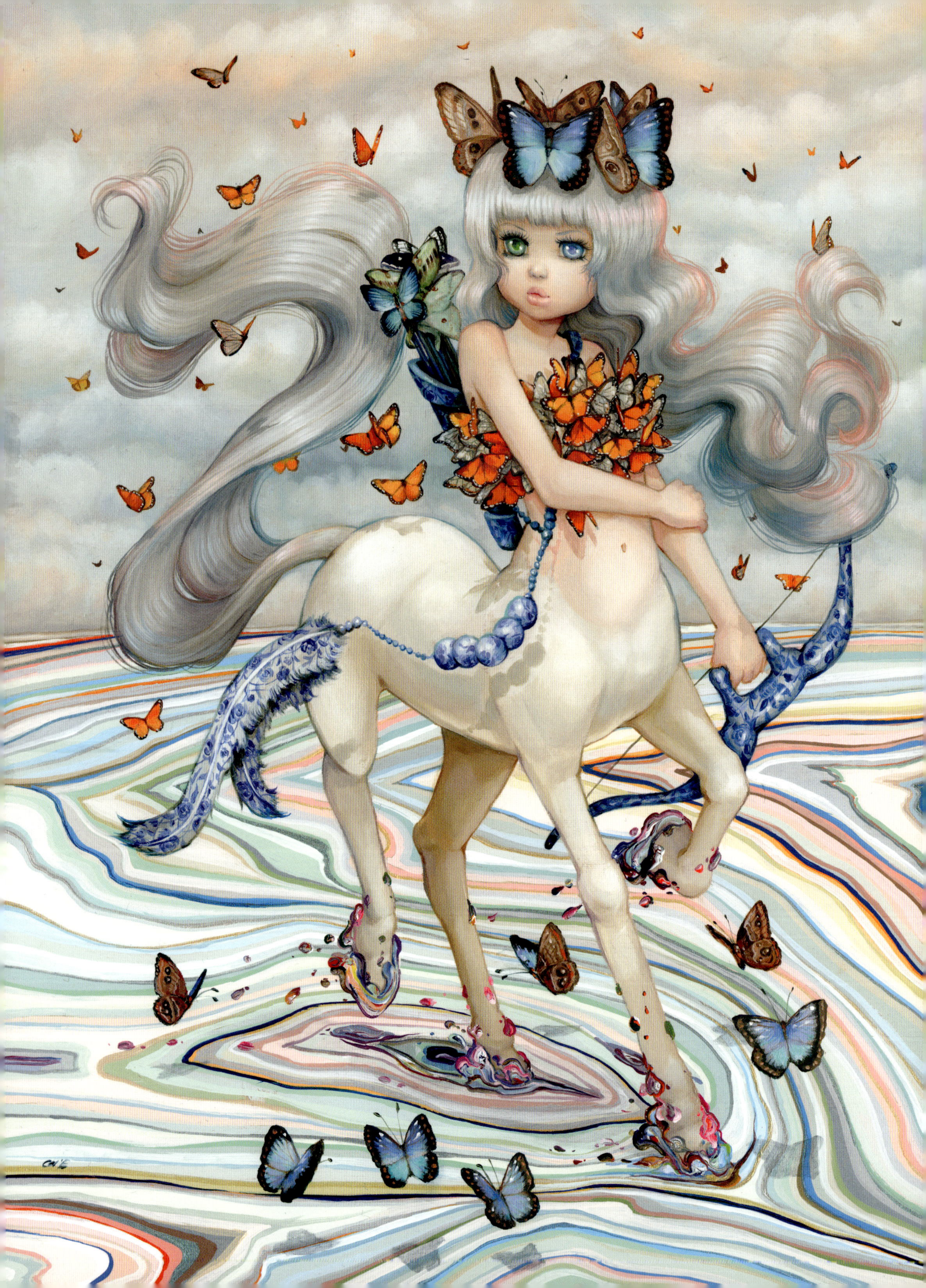

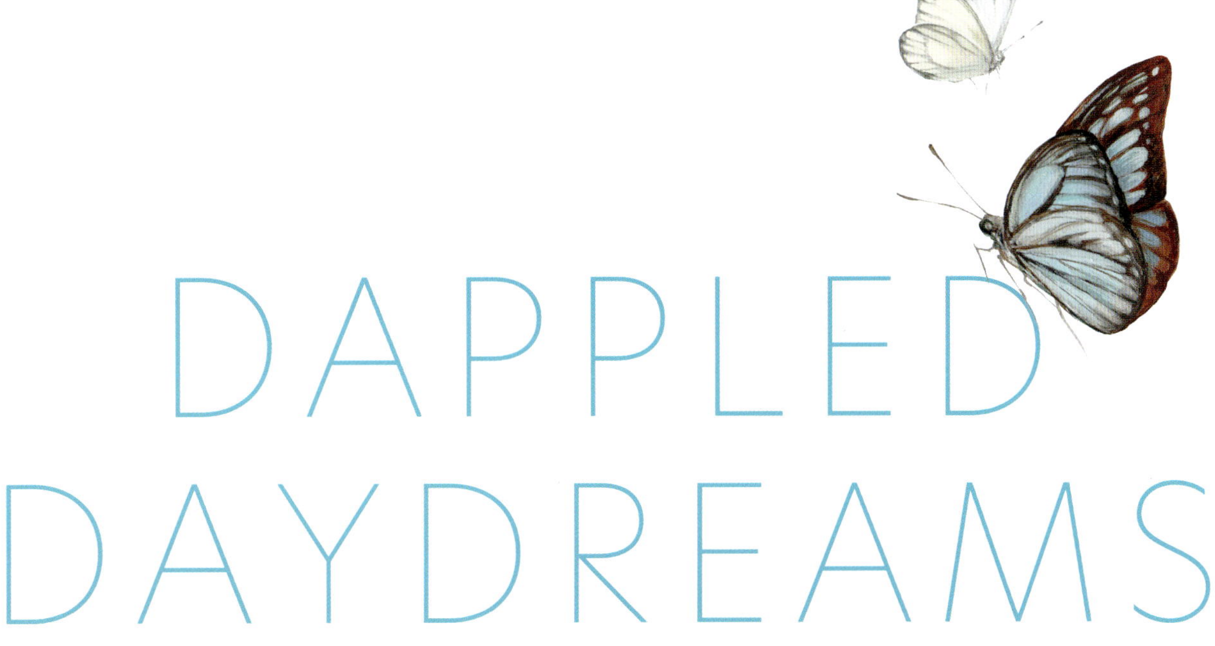

DAPPLED DAYDREAMS

The Art of Camilla d'Errico

DARK HORSE BOOKS

Dedication

This book is dedicated to my friends and family who put up with me being a social hermit while I worked. If it wasn't for your patience and understanding, I wouldn't have created half of what is in this book. And to my constant companion Loki who is the reason that I've completed half of what I could have if he wasn't such a needy little furry potato.

PRESIDENT AND PUBLISHER
Mike Richardson

EDITOR
Rachel Roberts

ASSOCIATE EDITOR
Jenny Blenk

ASSISTANT EDITOR
Anastacia Ferry

DESIGNER
Stephen Reichert

DIGITAL ART TECHNICIAN
Chris Horn

DAPPLED DAYDREAMS: THE ART OF CAMILLA d'ERRICO

Dark Horse Books
A division of Dark Horse Comics LLC
10956 S.E. Main Street
Milwaukie OR 97222

darkhorse.com
camilladerrico.com

First edition: May 2022
Ebook ISBN 978-1-50671-957-3
Hardcover ISBN 978-1-50671-959-7

10 9 8 7 6 5 4 3 2 1

Printed in China

Library of Congress Cataloging-in-Publication Data

Names: D'Errico, Camilla, artist.
Title: Dappled daydreams : the art of Camilla d'Errico / Camilla d'Errico.
Description: First edition. | Milwaukie, OR : Dark Horse Books, [2020]
Identifiers: LCCN 2019054953 (print) | LCCN 2019054954 (ebook) | ISBN 9781506719573 (ebook) | ISBN 9781506719597 (hardback)
Subjects: LCSH: D'Errico, Camilla--Themes, motives.
Classification: LCC N6549.D485 (ebook) | LCC N6549.D485 A4 2020 (print) | DDC 709.2--dc23
LC record available at https://lccn.loc.gov/2019054953

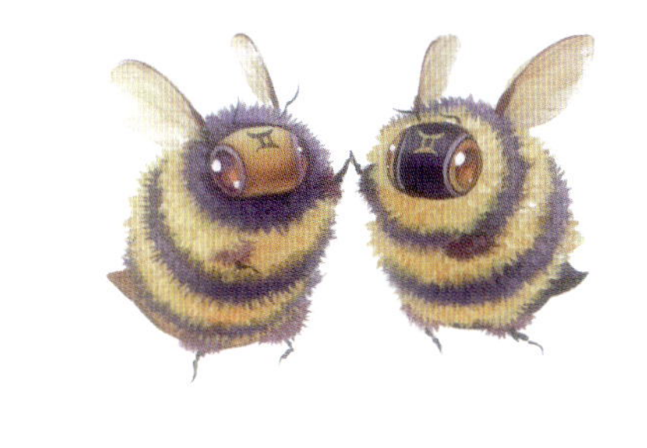

CONTENTS

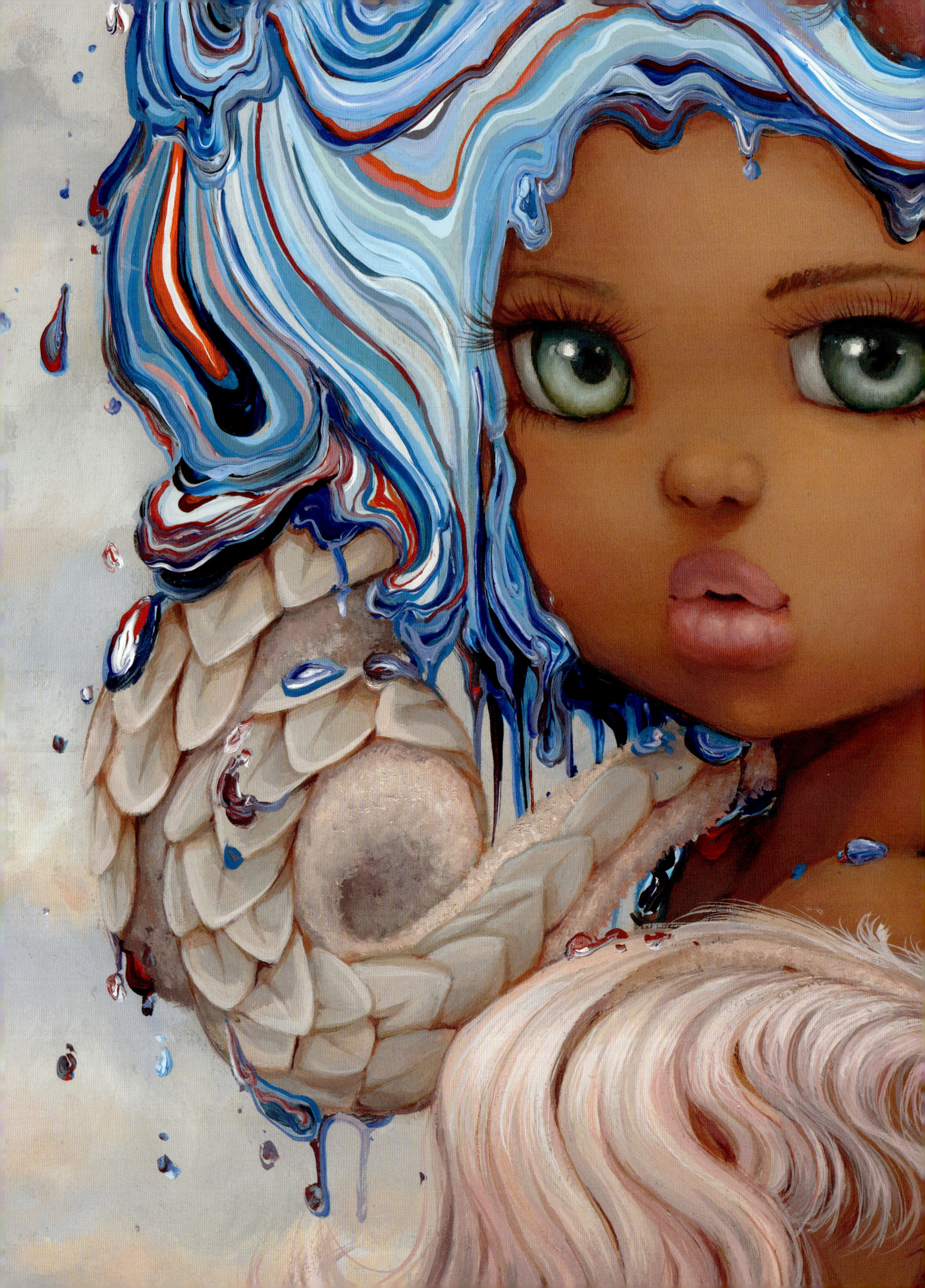

FOREWORD

The whimsical work of Camilla d'Errico caught my eye many years ago through the worlds of art magazines and social media, and I became instantly obsessed. Camilla gracefully takes on overtly feminine subject matter and pop surrealism, with a touch of dreamy darkness that has been fascinating to watch morph and grow over the years. She has masterfully stretched, bent, and explored her unique style in a way that always stays fresh, while still referencing her older works. With their very '90s manga feel, the large, glistening eyes and small heart-shaped faces of her subjects are a callback to the nostalgia of childhood: toys, plush baby animals, dragons, unicorns, candies, ice cream, fashion, and cartoons.

In this collection, I was immediately gripped by the soft rainbow witchy women and their familiars. Covered in dripping pastel swirls, antlers, and flowers, they are seemingly caught off guard by the viewer, and their confrontational yet intimate gazes submerge you in otherworldly stories of life, love, sorrow, death, and sin. Camilla's recent work focuses on representations of the feminine, divine goddesses, and fauns being overwhelmed and drowned in soft melancholy, embraced by the vibrant, loving warmth of adorable critters such as baby bunnies, fluffy lambs, kittens, foxes, mice, puffy snakes, butterflies, moths, and baby dragons. Camilla also tastefully embraces natural physical rarities like albinism, heterochromia, and vitiligo, which have been common themes in her work throughout her career. She masterfully continues to make the overall theme of the unusual into powerful symbols of ethereal beauty.

Camilla has taken mythological concepts even further in her zodiac series, one of the collections featured in this book. Embodying deep mythological and maternal roots, her characters are depicted with their familiars in their arms in a symbiotic relationship of comfort and protection. The creatures are seen embracing their protectors snugly around their heads like elaborate crowns, exploding with color and activity, protecting their innocent goddess-like hosts, and daring you to get closer.

In juxtaposition with the goddesses, Camilla also creates a sickeningly sweet, cuteness-aggression-inducing body of work featuring chunky, colorful zodiac bumblebees cuddling, playing, and being mischievous. Camilla is, hands down, the master of "cute." I'm personally obsessed with the adorable blue bumblebee-mermaid in a tiny pink shell bra, titled "Aquaribuzz." It just brings me a sense of pure joy, as do so many of her pieces. They're so sweet, I think Camilla's bees might've taken a few years off of my life. Proceed with caution through that whole section.

In summation, I hope you enjoy the colorful cotton candy journey that is Camilla d'Errico's beautiful book *Dappled Daydreams: The Art of Camilla d'Errico*. Your eyes are in for a sweet treat.

—Lauren Marx
September 2021

Facing page:
Little Miss Goo | 16" X 20" | OIL | 2018

INTRODUCTION

Do you ever get inspiration from your dreams? Or is it our inspiration that creates our dreams? I've often wondered this over the years as I sat in front of my easel painting or my drawing table sketching wild things with my pen and paper.

The number one question I am asked is, "Where do you get your inspiration?" to which I answer . . . I have no idea. This is a truth that I wish I could have an answer for. An elaborate equation of hot chilies, mixed with the sounds of swans singing and The Beatles playing in the background.

But there is no simple answer. I do feel, however, that my dreams are creative gateways into my subconscious mind. Where I play with purple dinosaurs and web-sling from Manhattan into an Ewok forest (these are actual dreams I've had, believe it or not). Though I don't know where my dreams or inspiration come from, I can say this: I am moved by life. The human struggle to find answers not only about the universe and the meaning to our existence but by the emotional journeys we all go through daily. Love, passion, sadness, anger, defiance, and gentility are fascinating facets of our being. With each drawing, painting, or story I create, I try to decipher the meaning of who one individual is within this maelstrom of human existence. I try to unthread the quilt that is life and remake it into a visual puzzle.

If my art resembles a dreamlike state, then I have successfully transported you to the world of fantasies. I hope you enjoy the art within these pages and that it perhaps inspires you.

—Camilla d'Errico

Facing page:
Polina | 16" X 20" | OIL | 2018

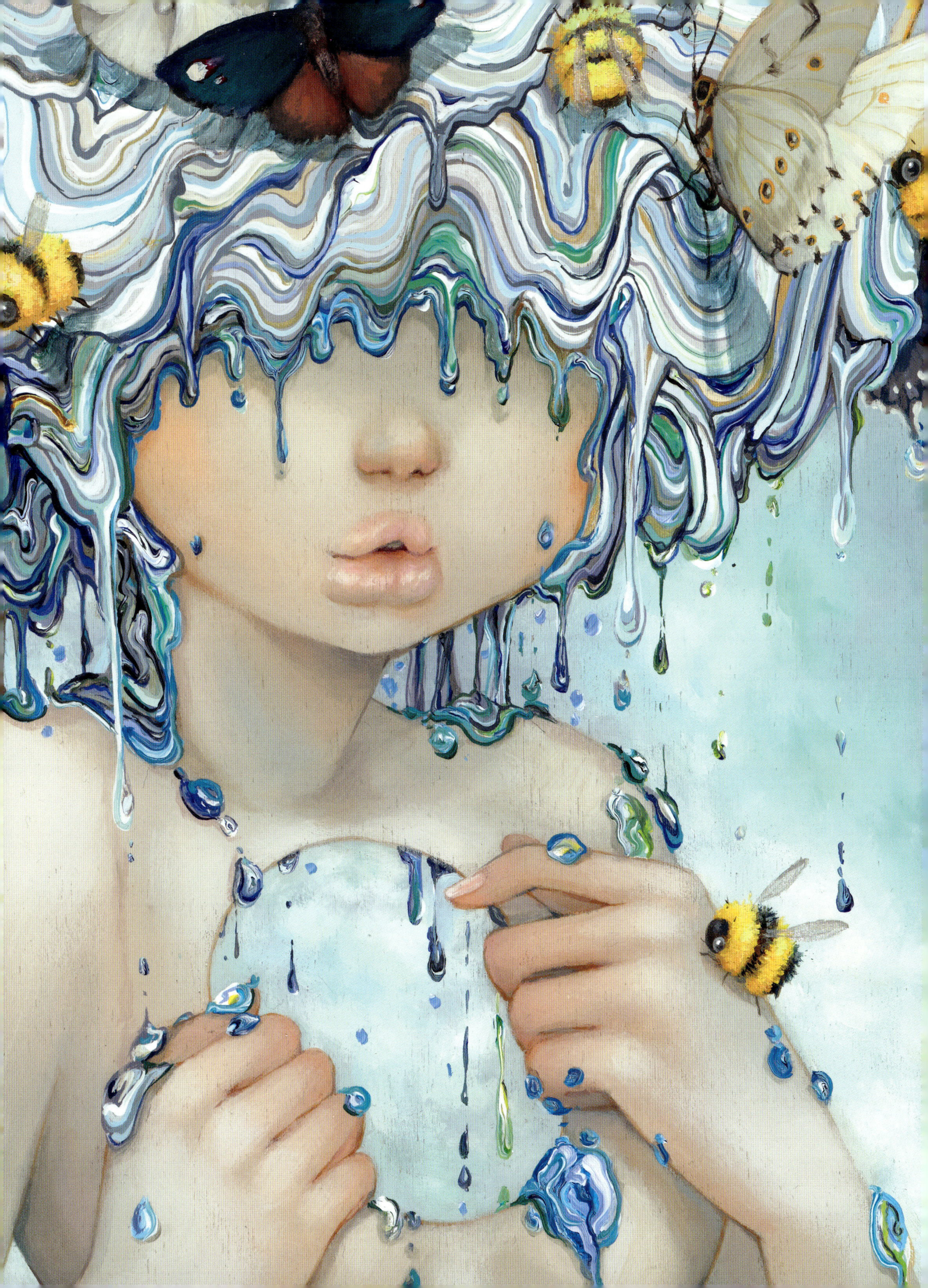

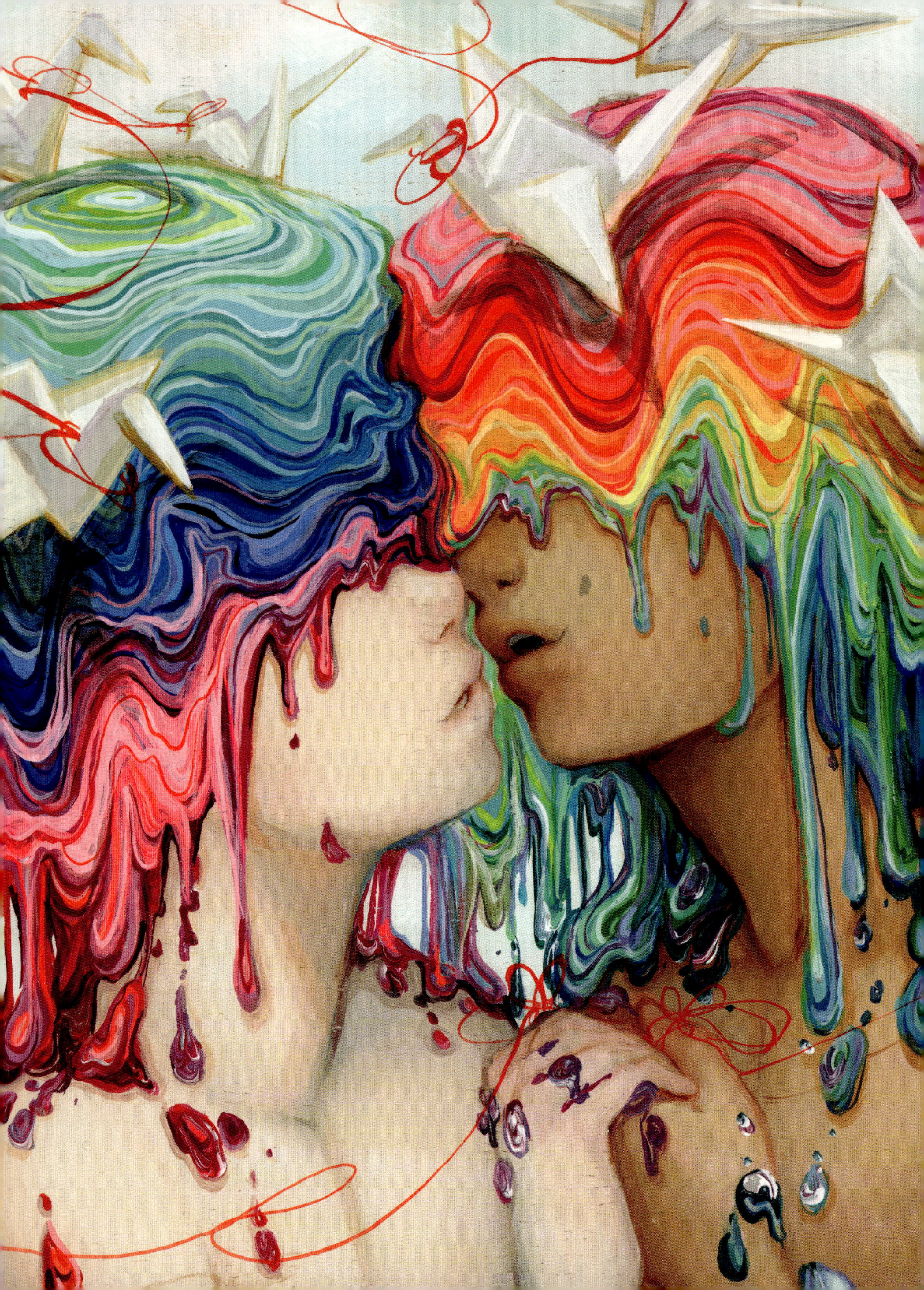

RAINBOW REVELRY

Facing page:
A Wish Upon a String | 11" X 14" | OIL | 2018

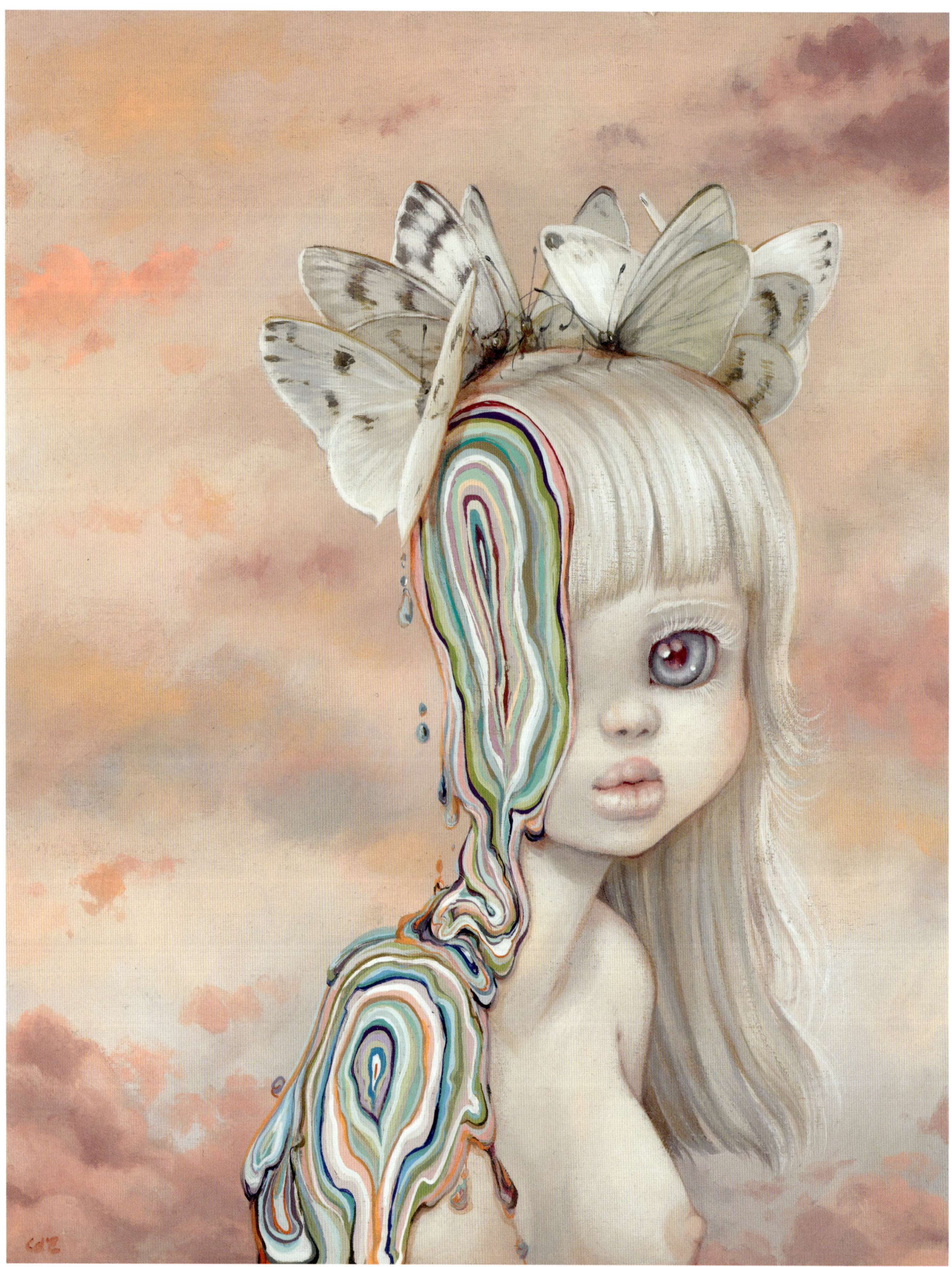

Bianca | 11" X 14" | OIL | 2018

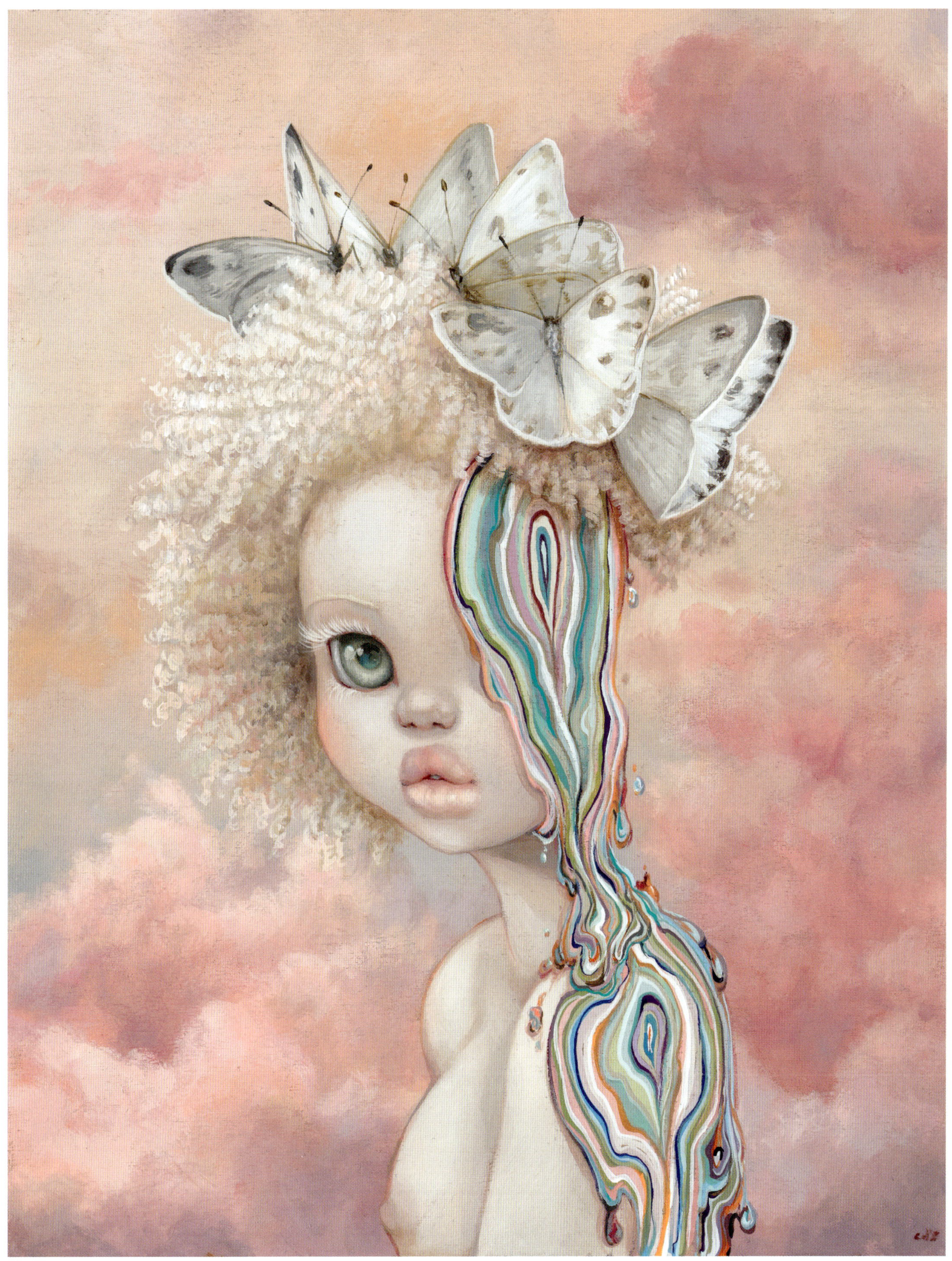

Umoja | 11" X 14" | OIL | 2018

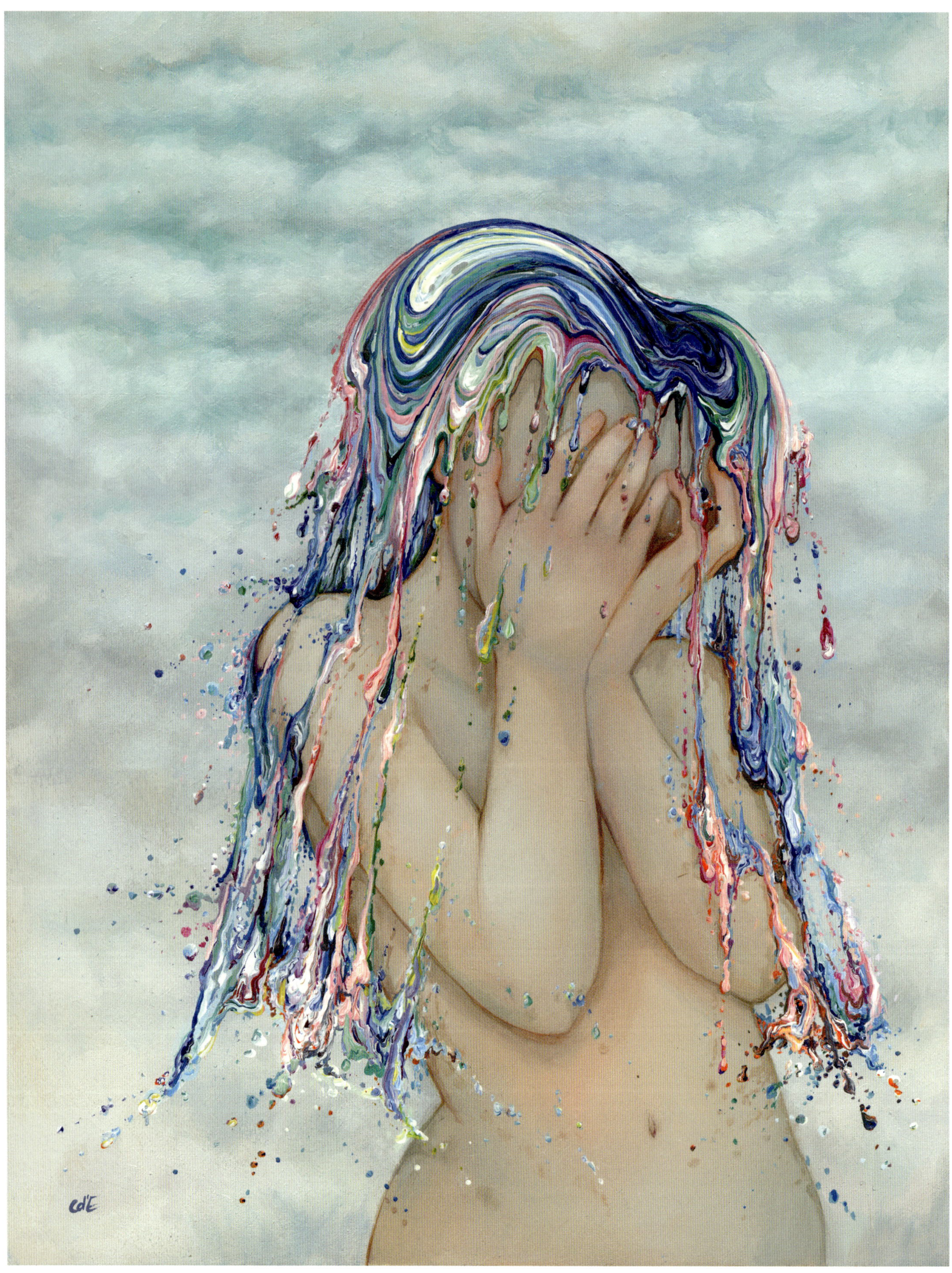

Ebb and Flow | 12" X 16" | OIL | 2018

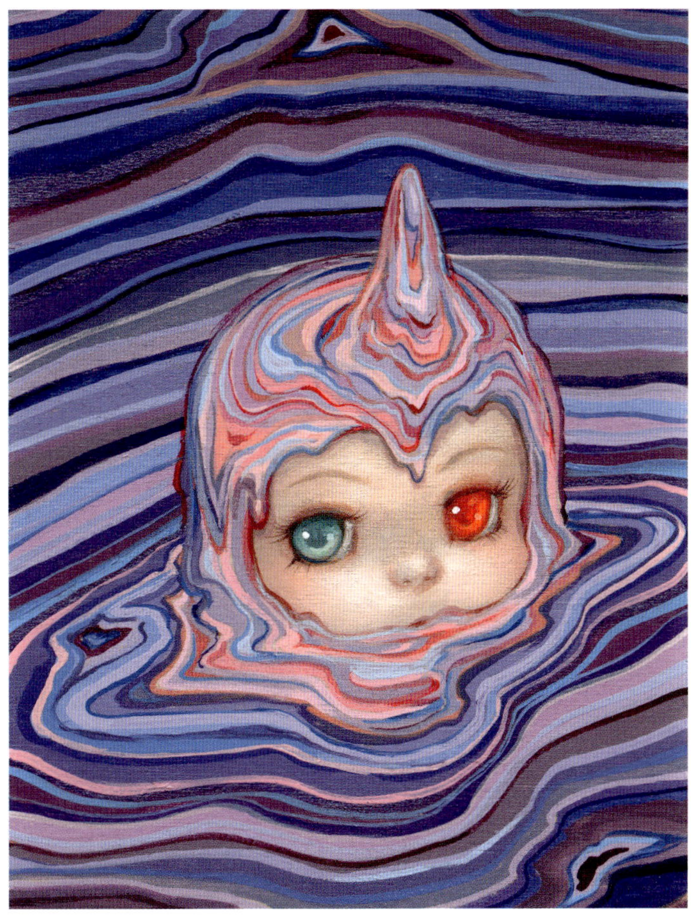

Ribbon Candy | 5" X 7" | OIL and ACRYLIC | 2019

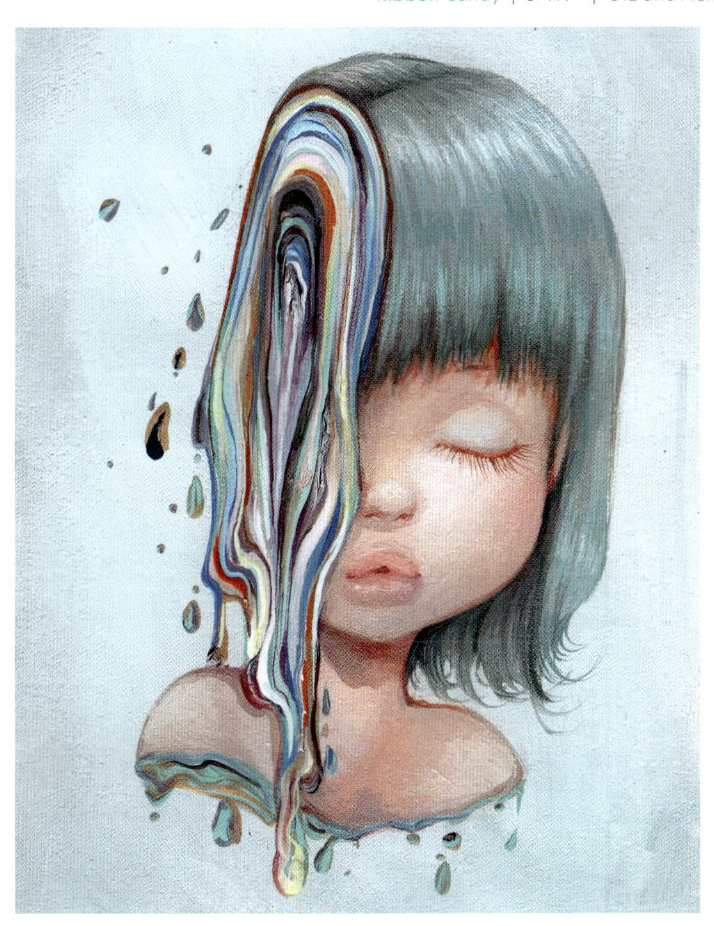

Sweet Dreams | 5" X 7" | OIL and ACRYLIC | 2019

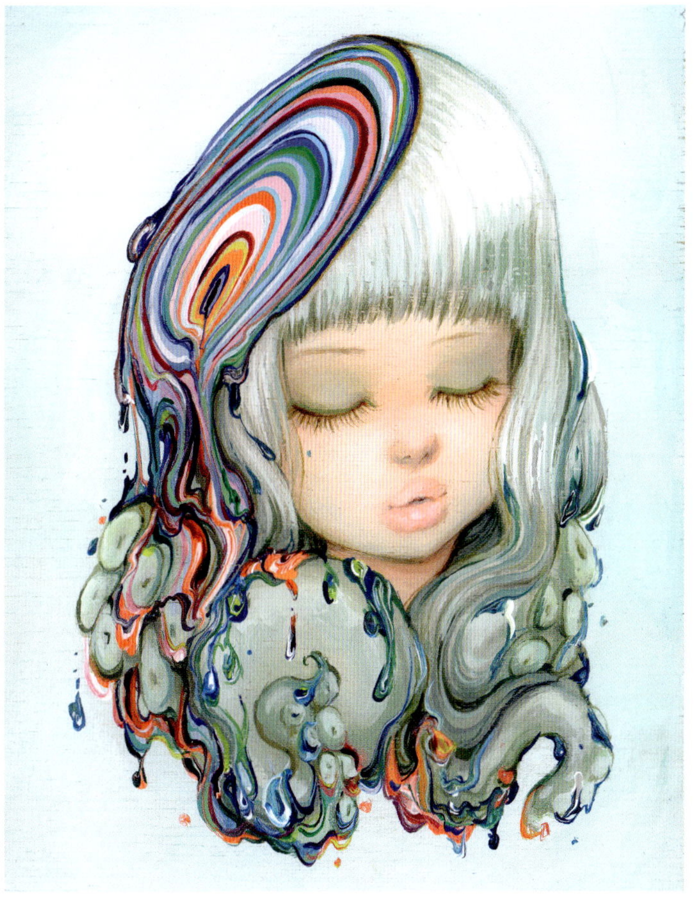

Inside and Out | 5" X 7" | OIL and ACRYLIC | 2018

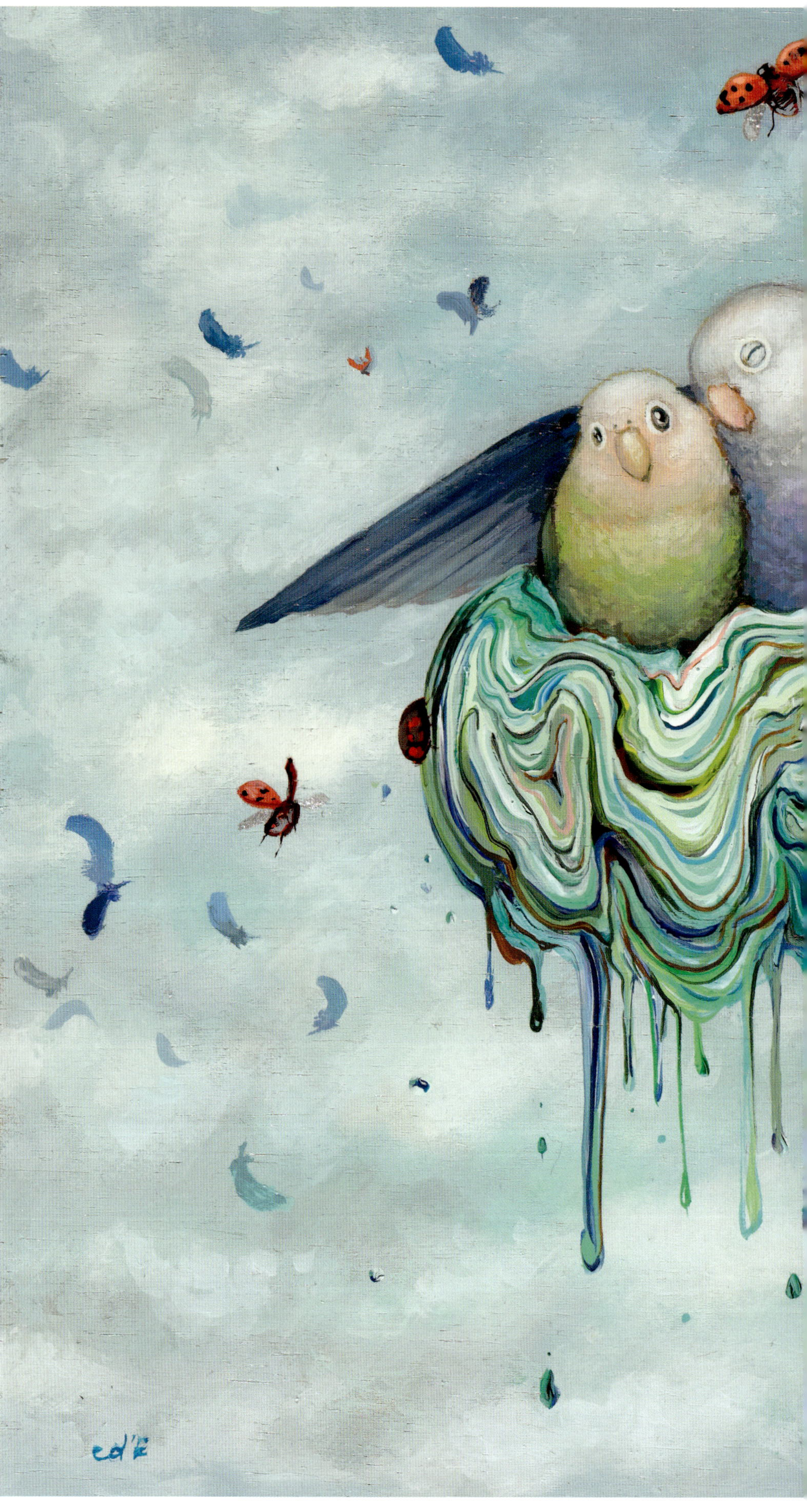

Lovebug | 11" X 14" | OIL | 2018

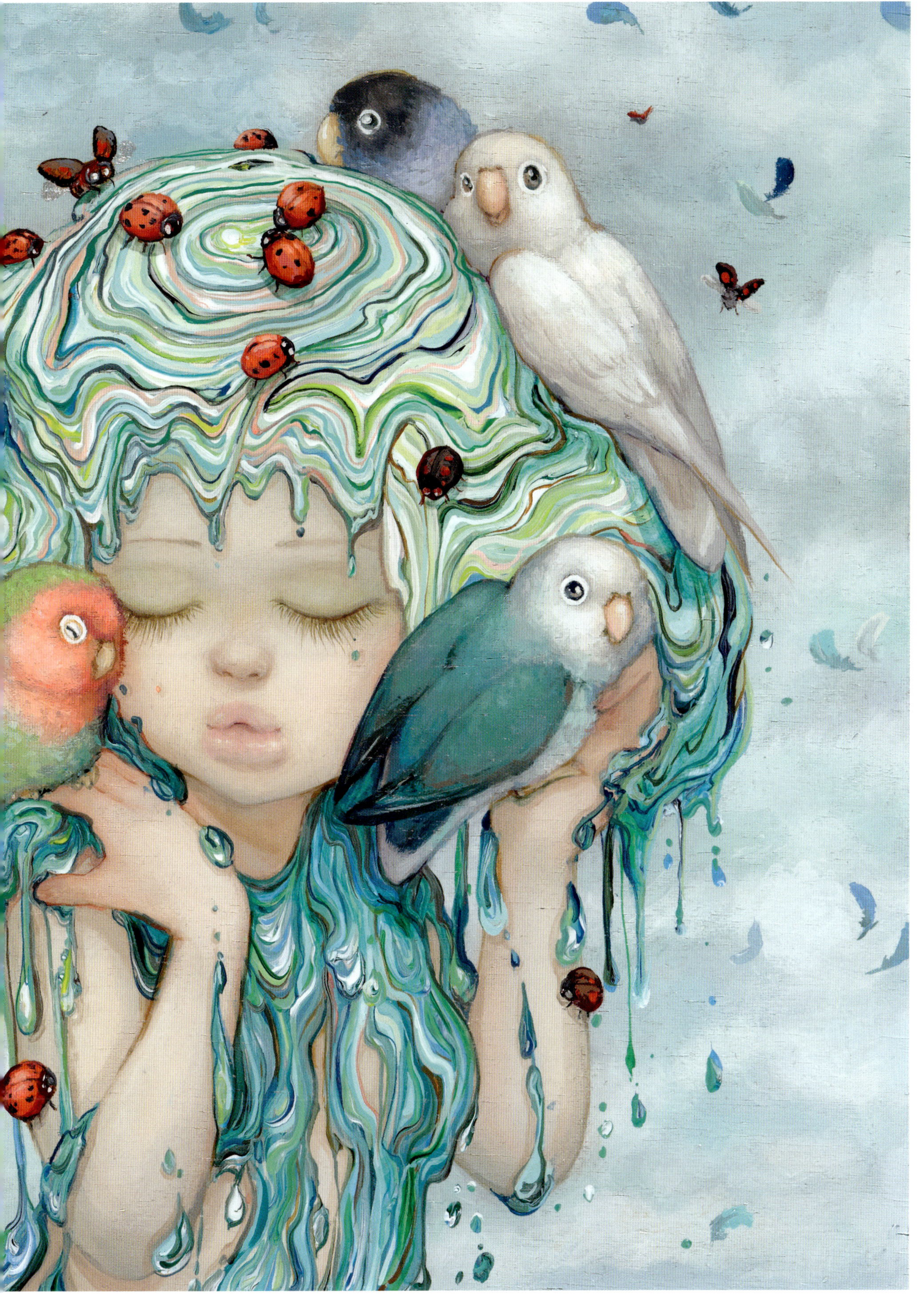

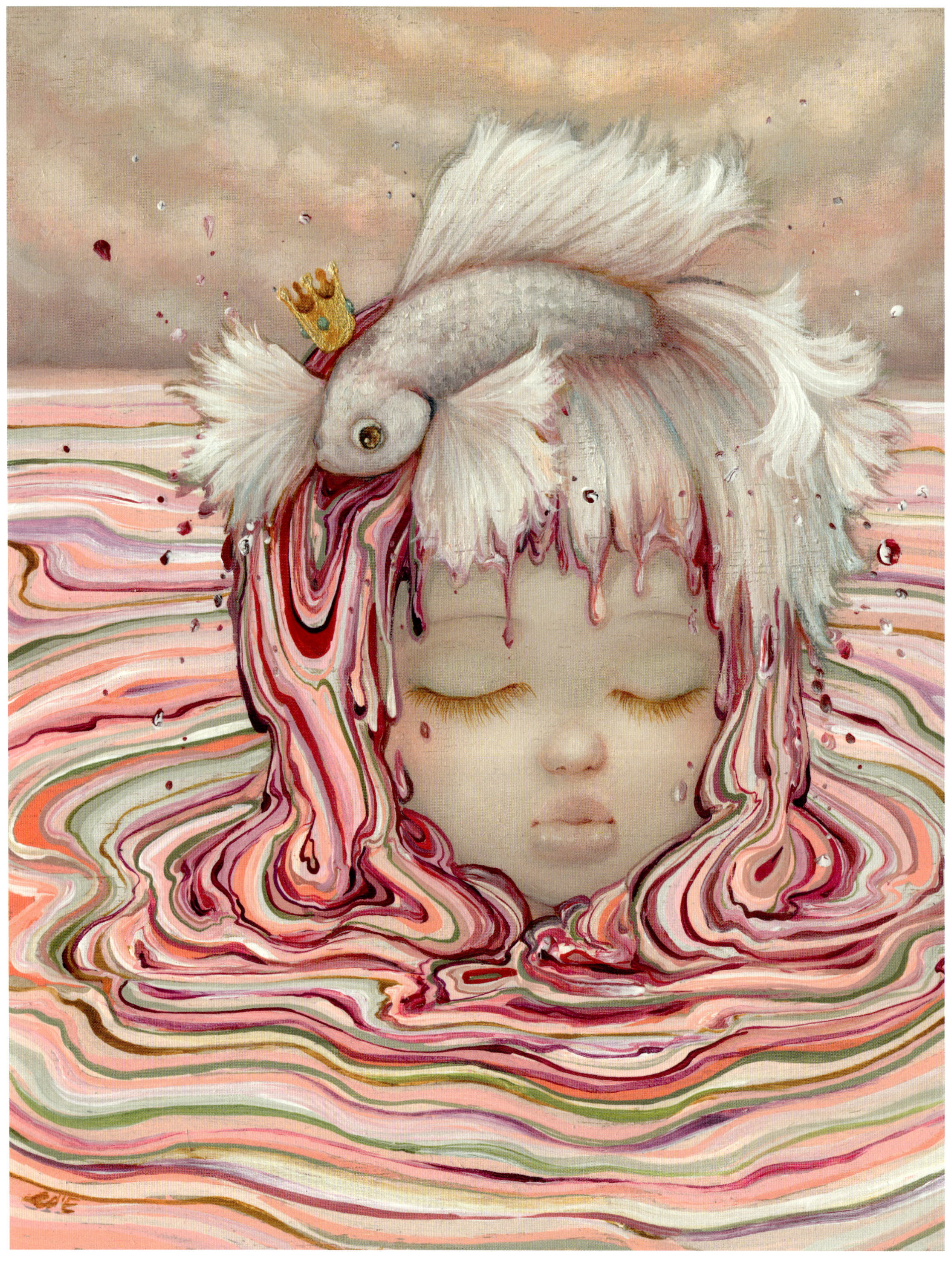

Queen Sakana | 8" X 10" | OIL | 2018

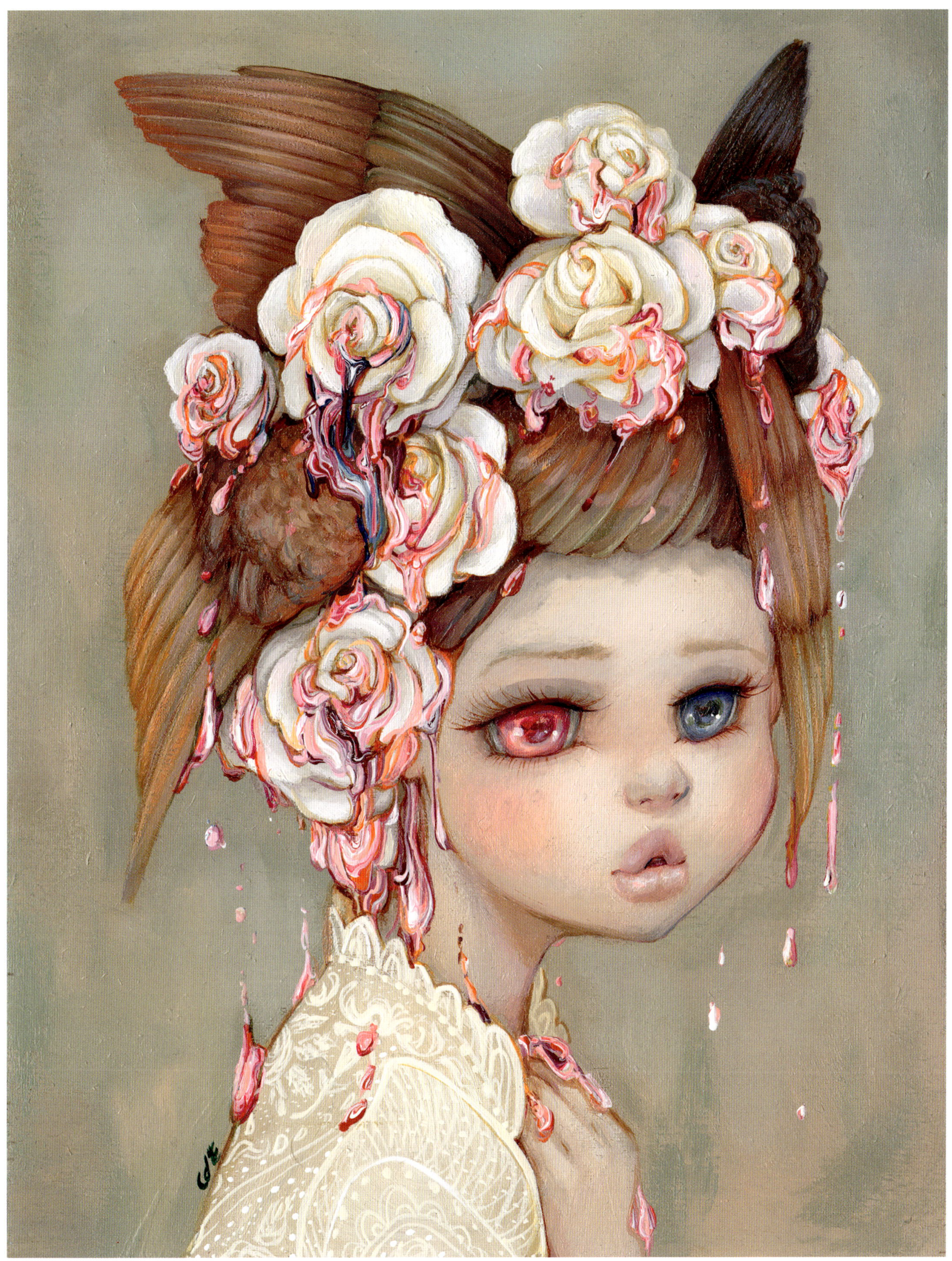

Rosa | 6.5" X 8.5" | OIL | 2018

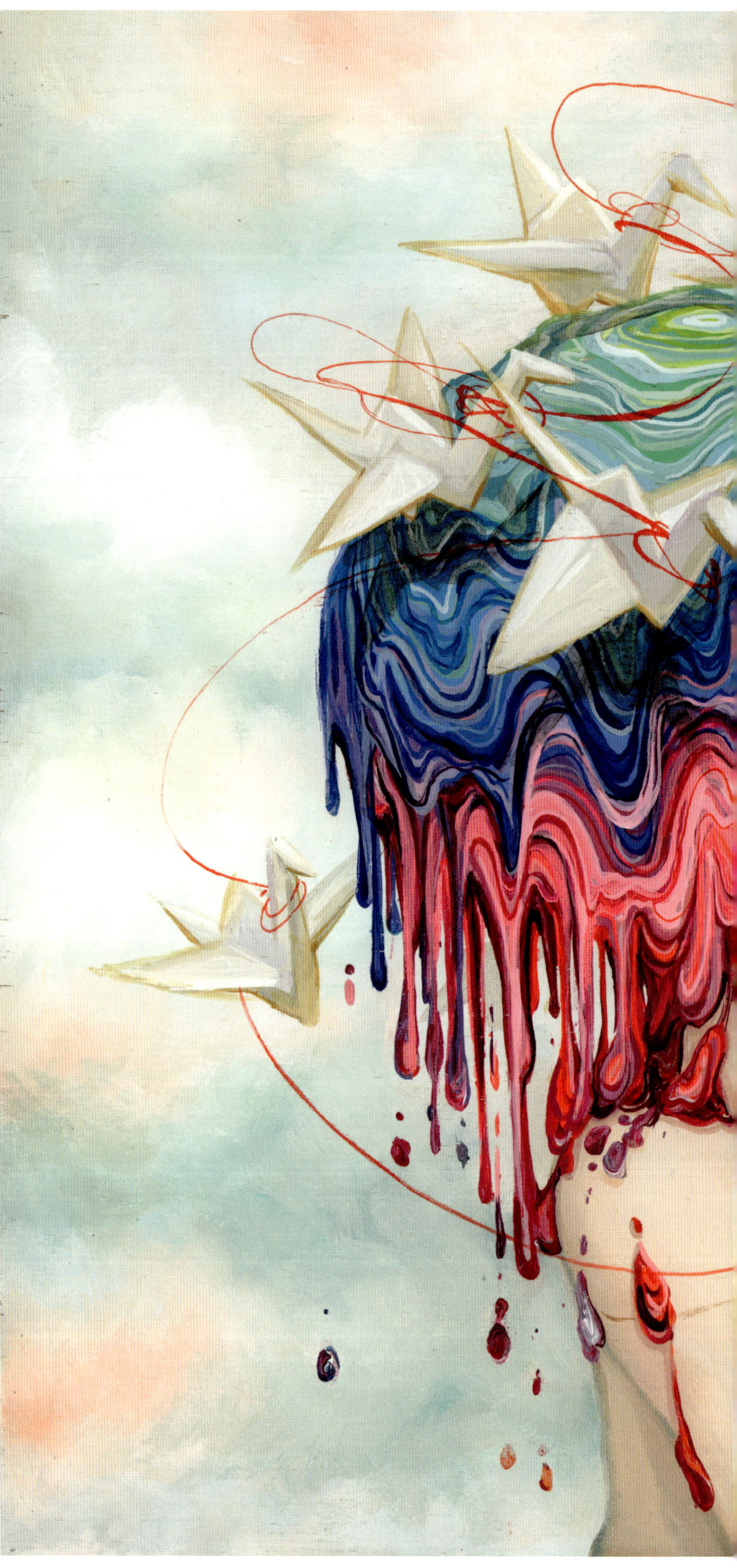

A Wish Upon a String | 11" X 14" | OIL | 2018

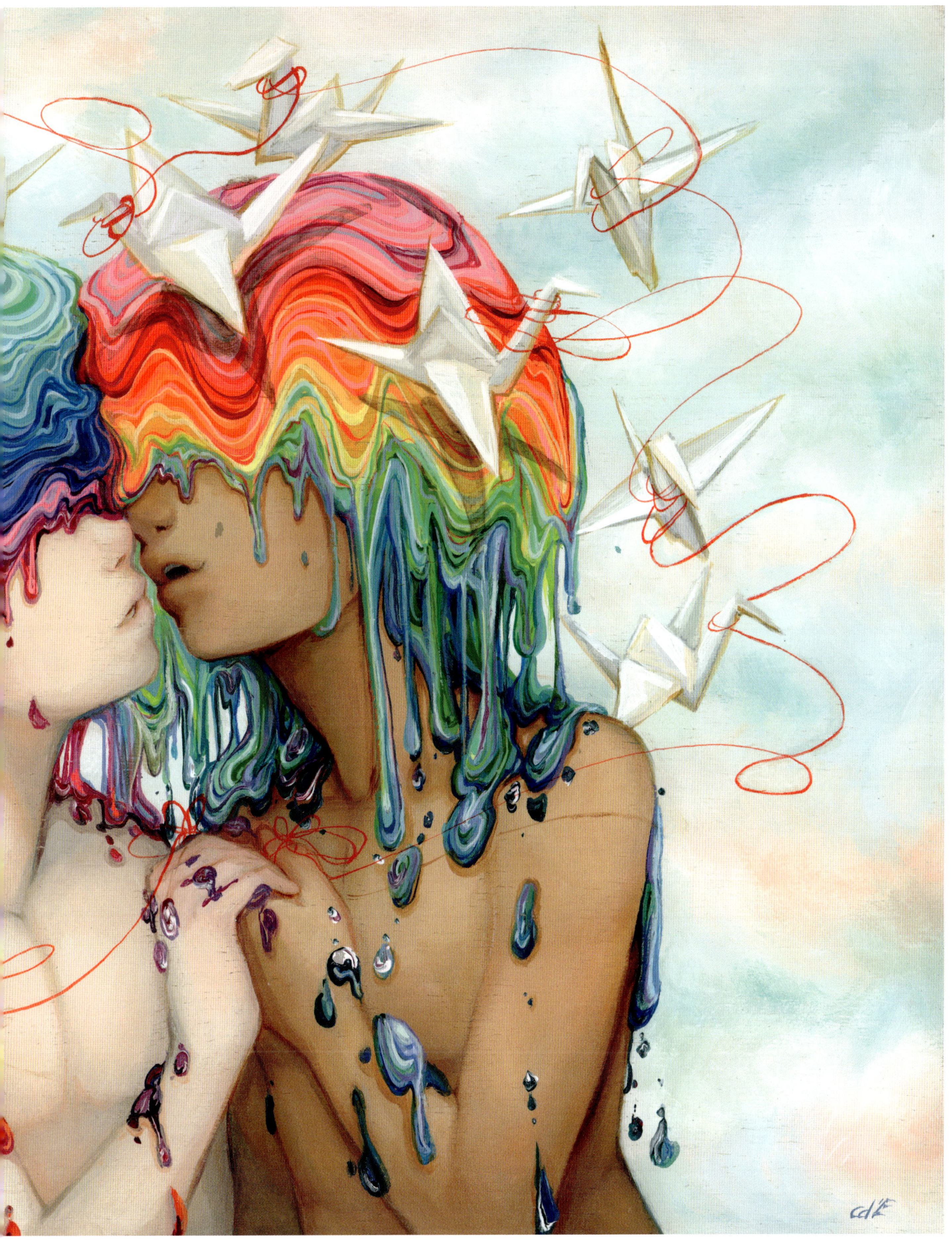

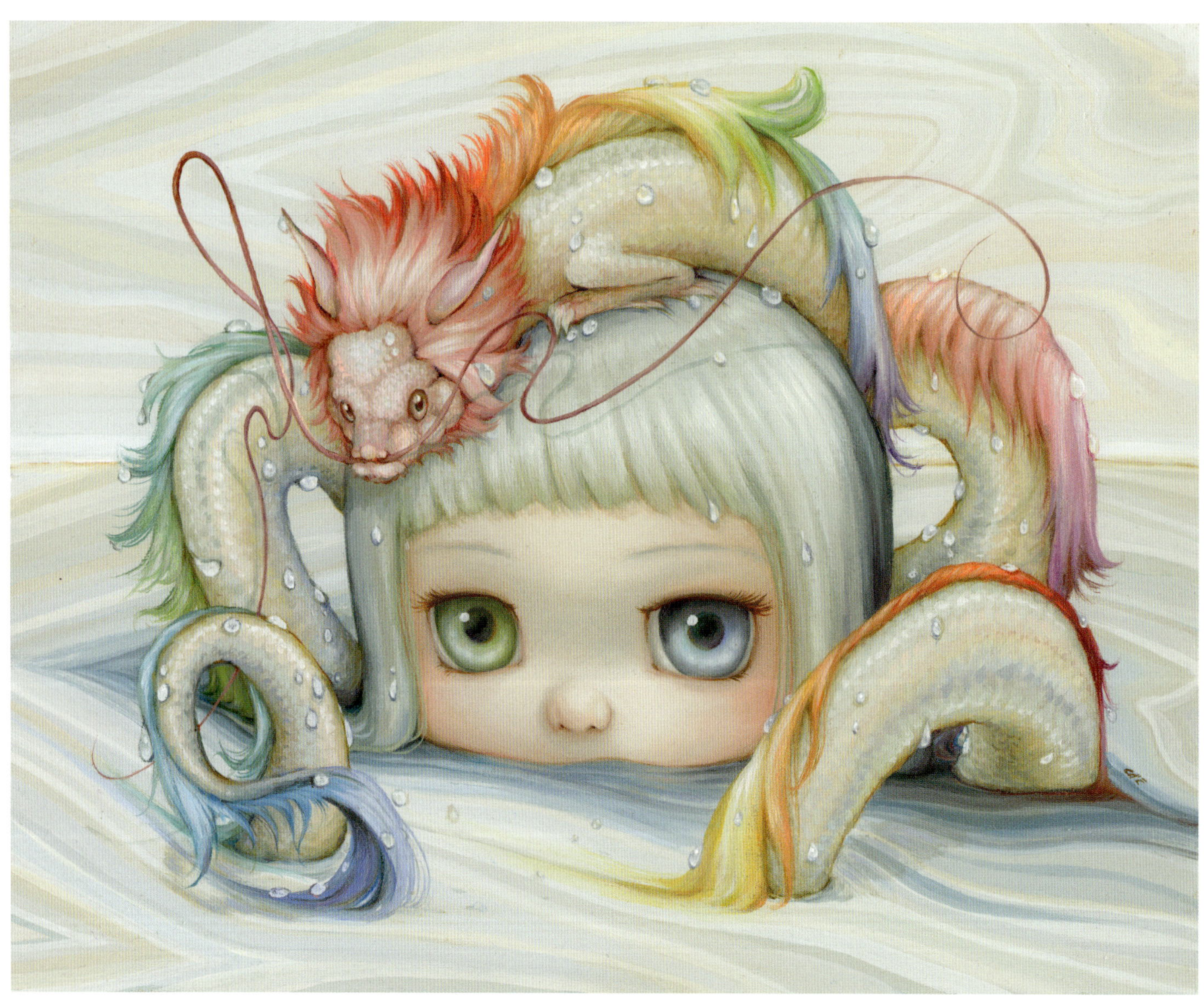

Pop Goes the Weasel | 11" X 14" | OIL | 2017

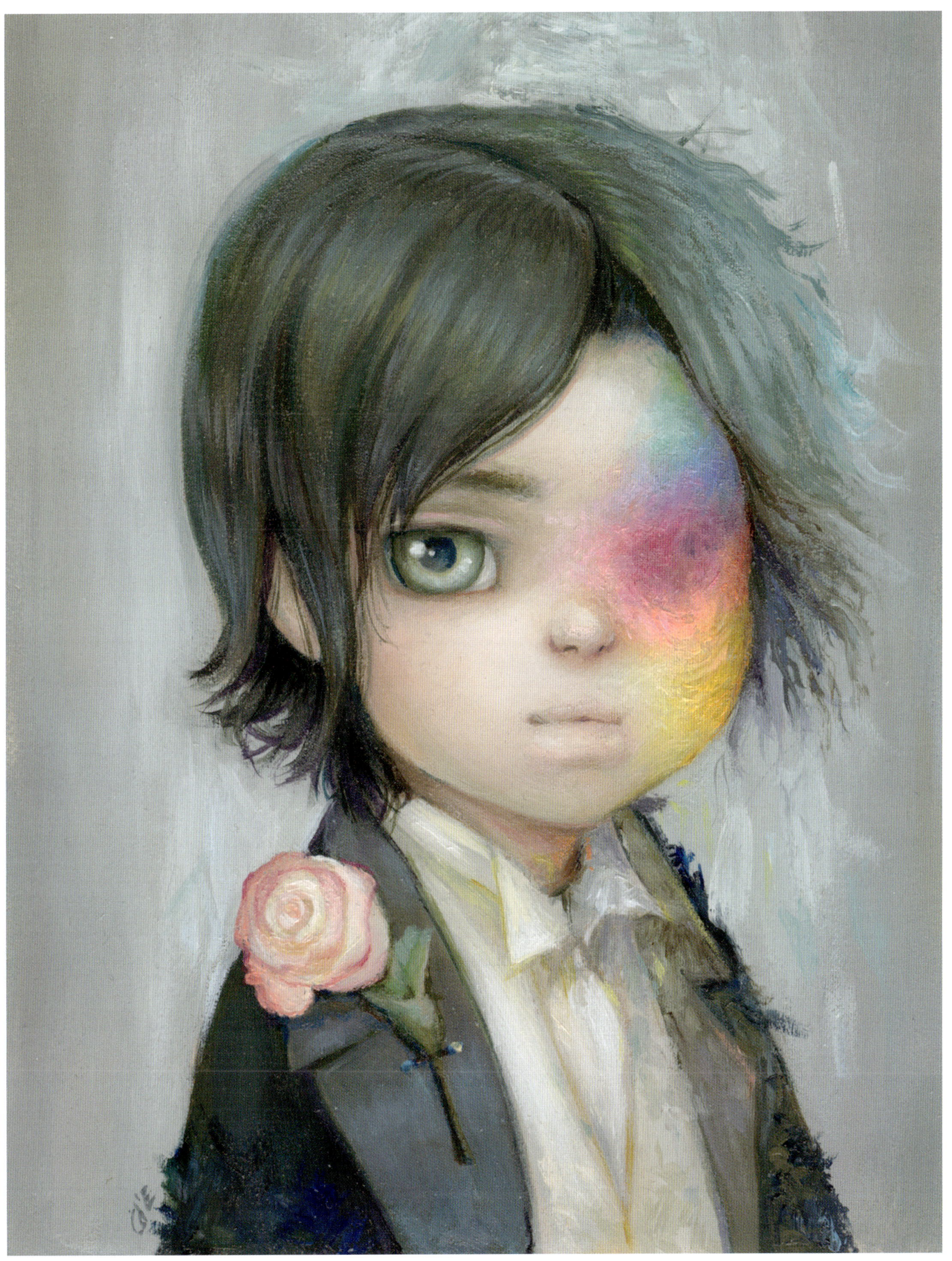

Dorian Gray | 5" X 7" | OIL | 2017

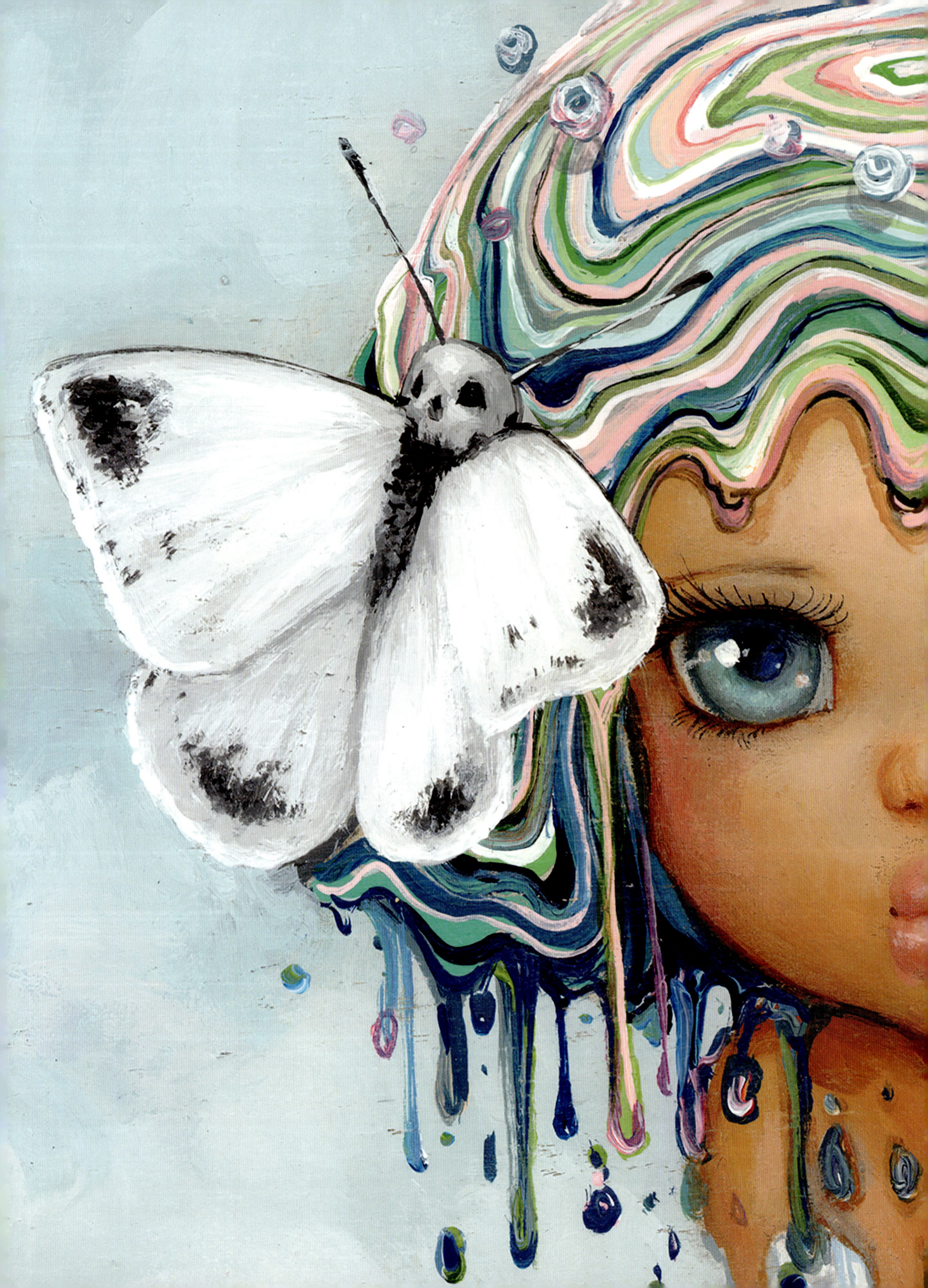

PAPILIONIDAE PRISMATICA

Facing page:
Silence | 8" X 10" | OIL | 2018

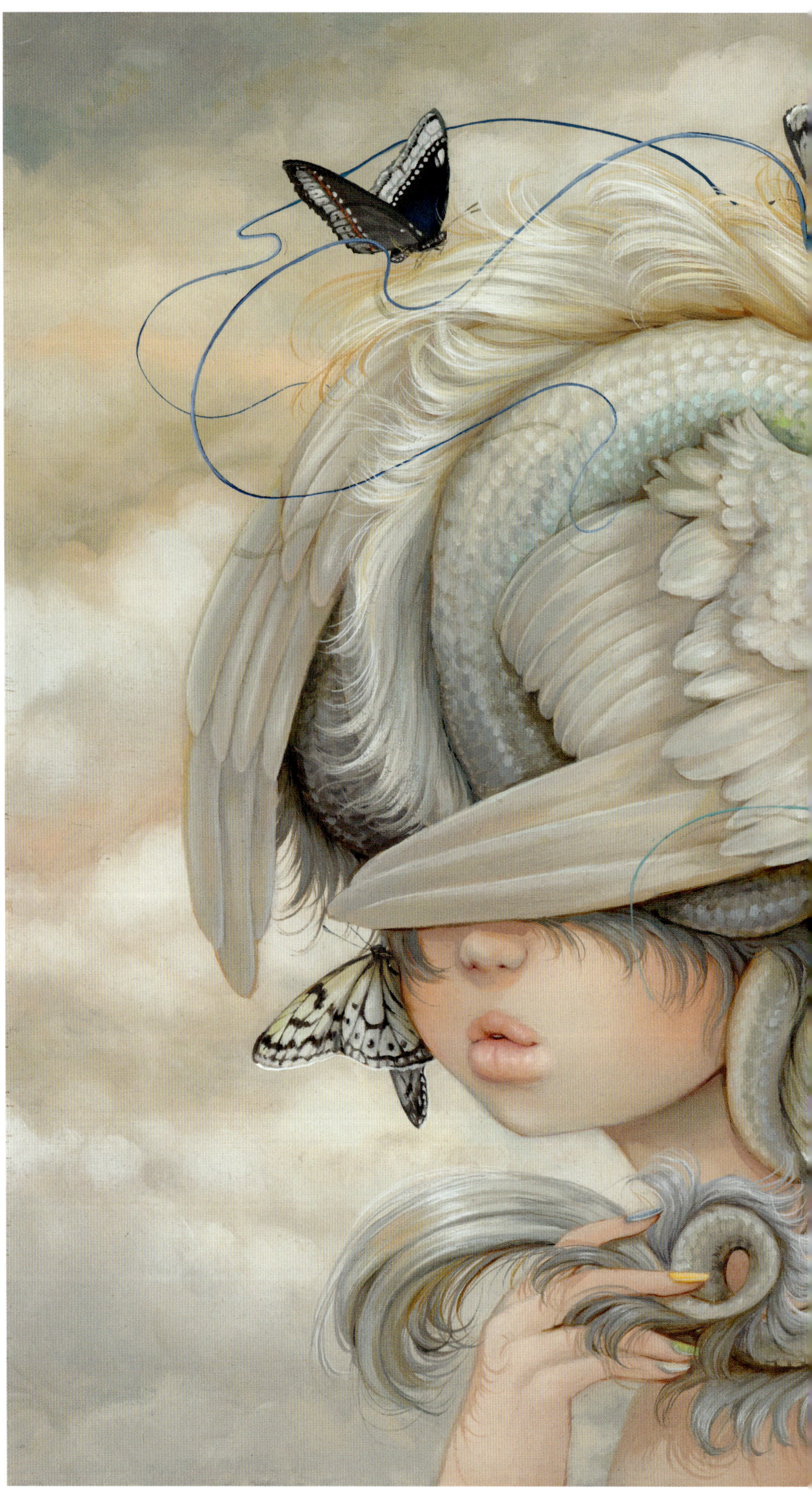

Hydie | 20" X 24" | OIL | 2018

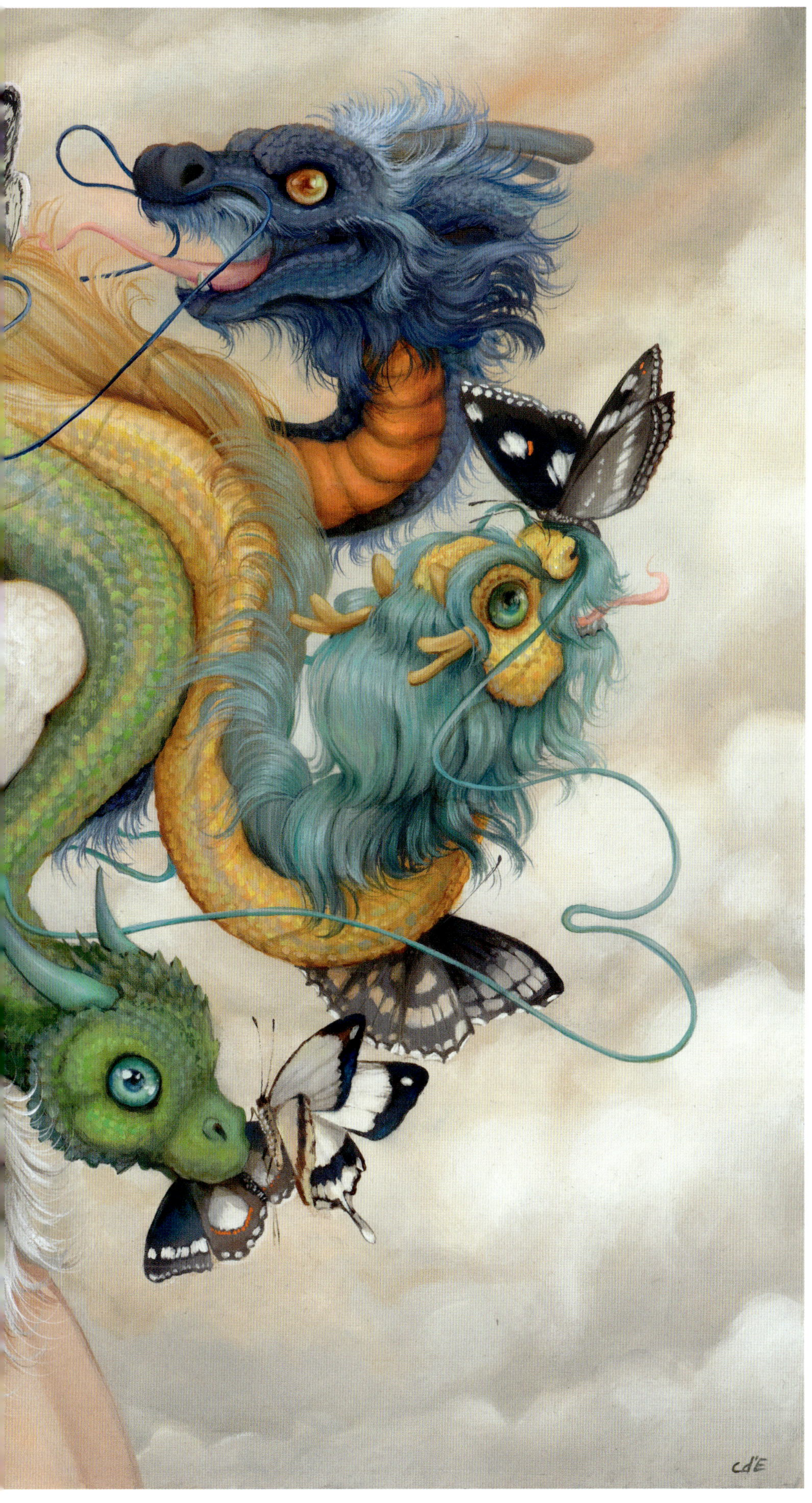
cd'E

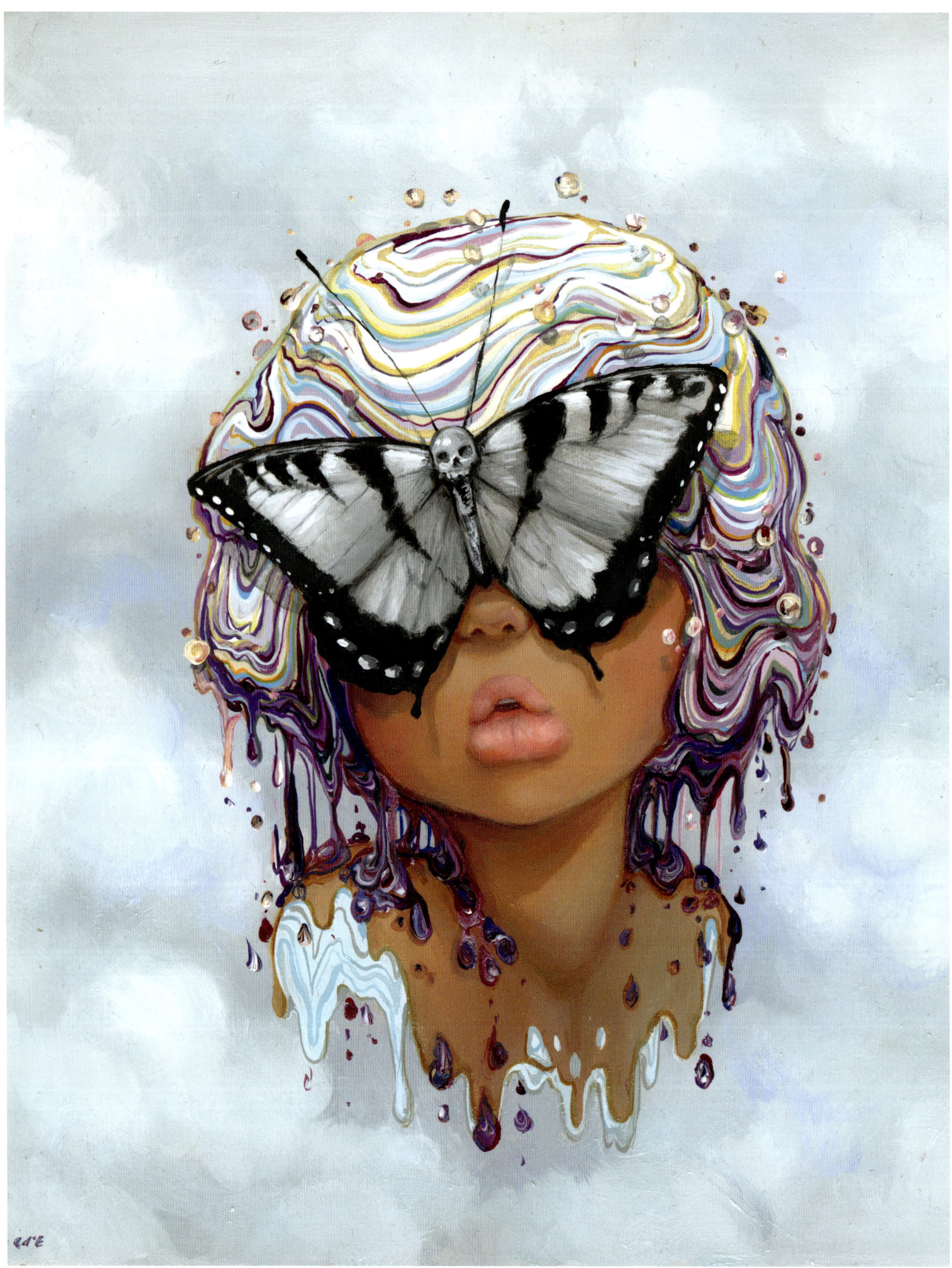

Sightless | 8.5" X 10.5" | OIL | 2018

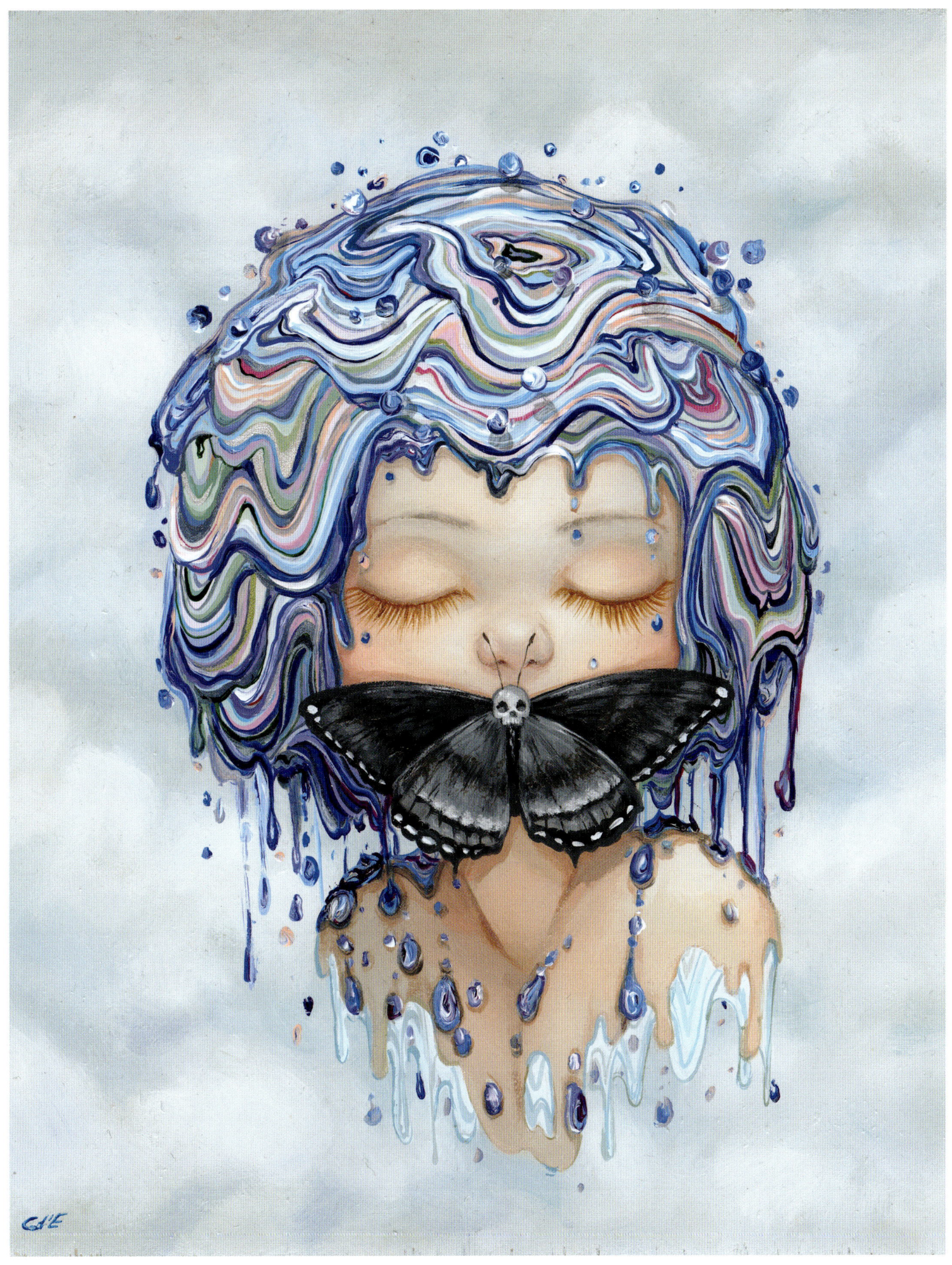

Soundless | 8.5" X 10" | OIL | 2018

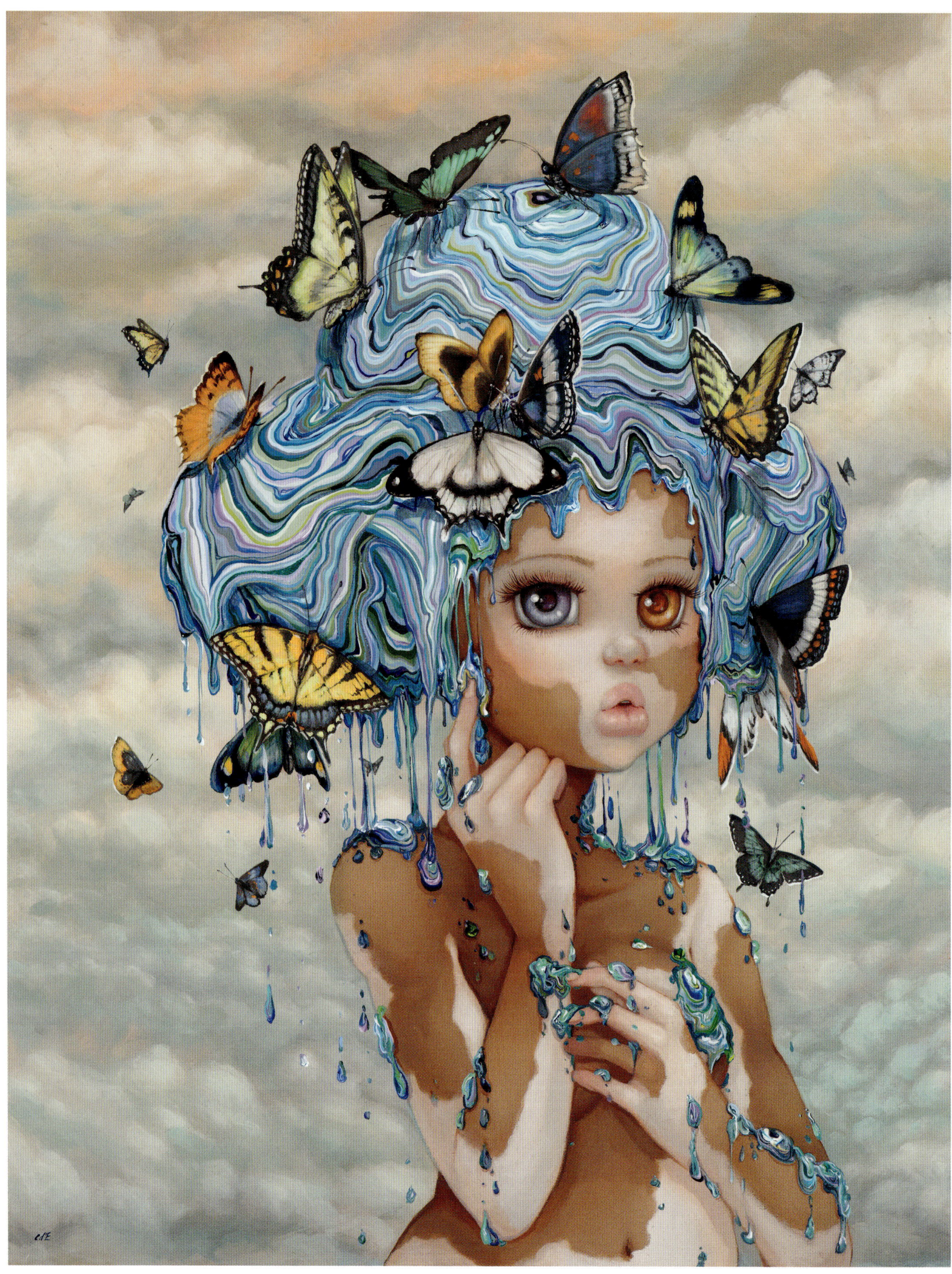

Miss Duplexity | 18" X 24" | OIL | 2018

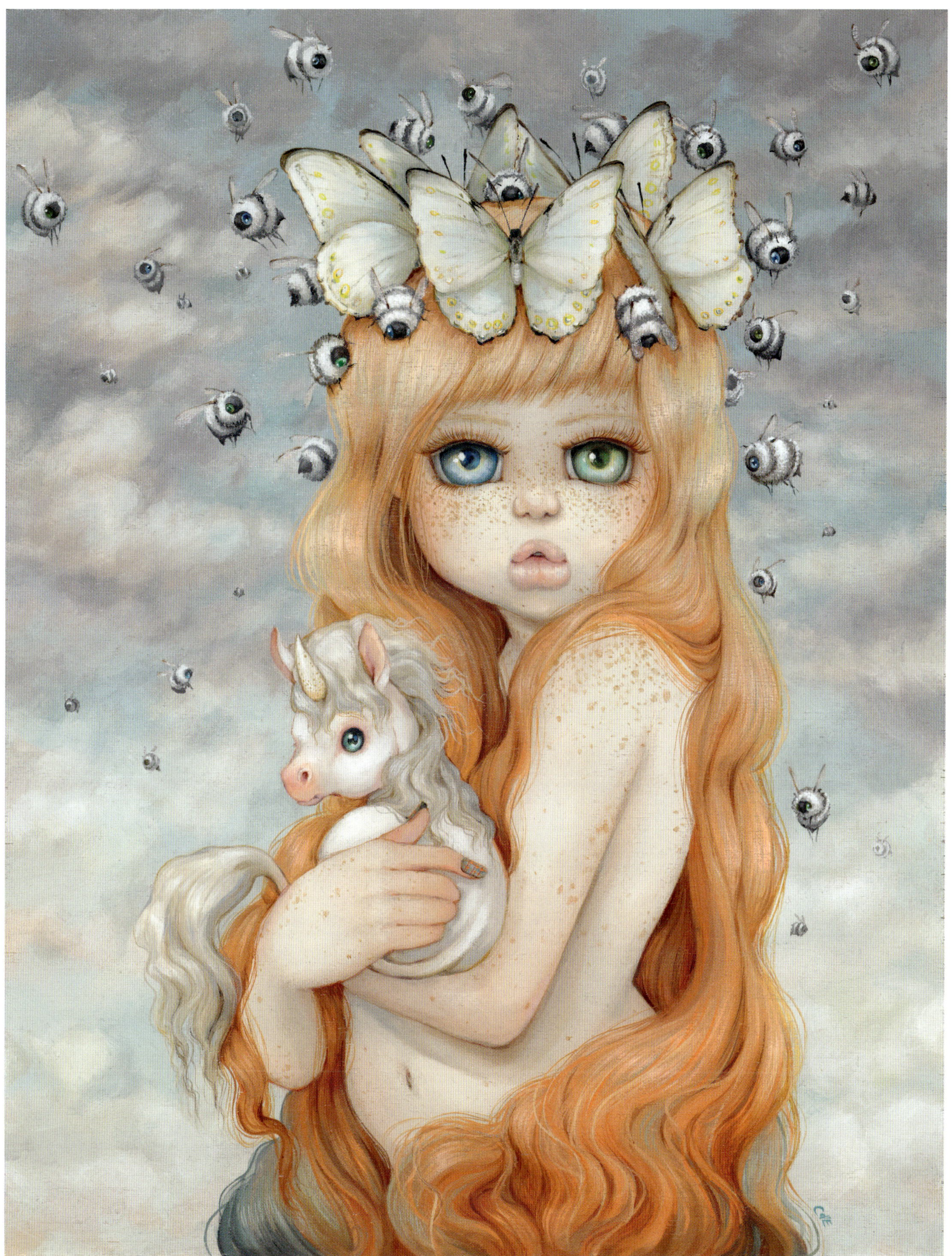

Sun Kisses | 14" X 18" | OIL | 2018

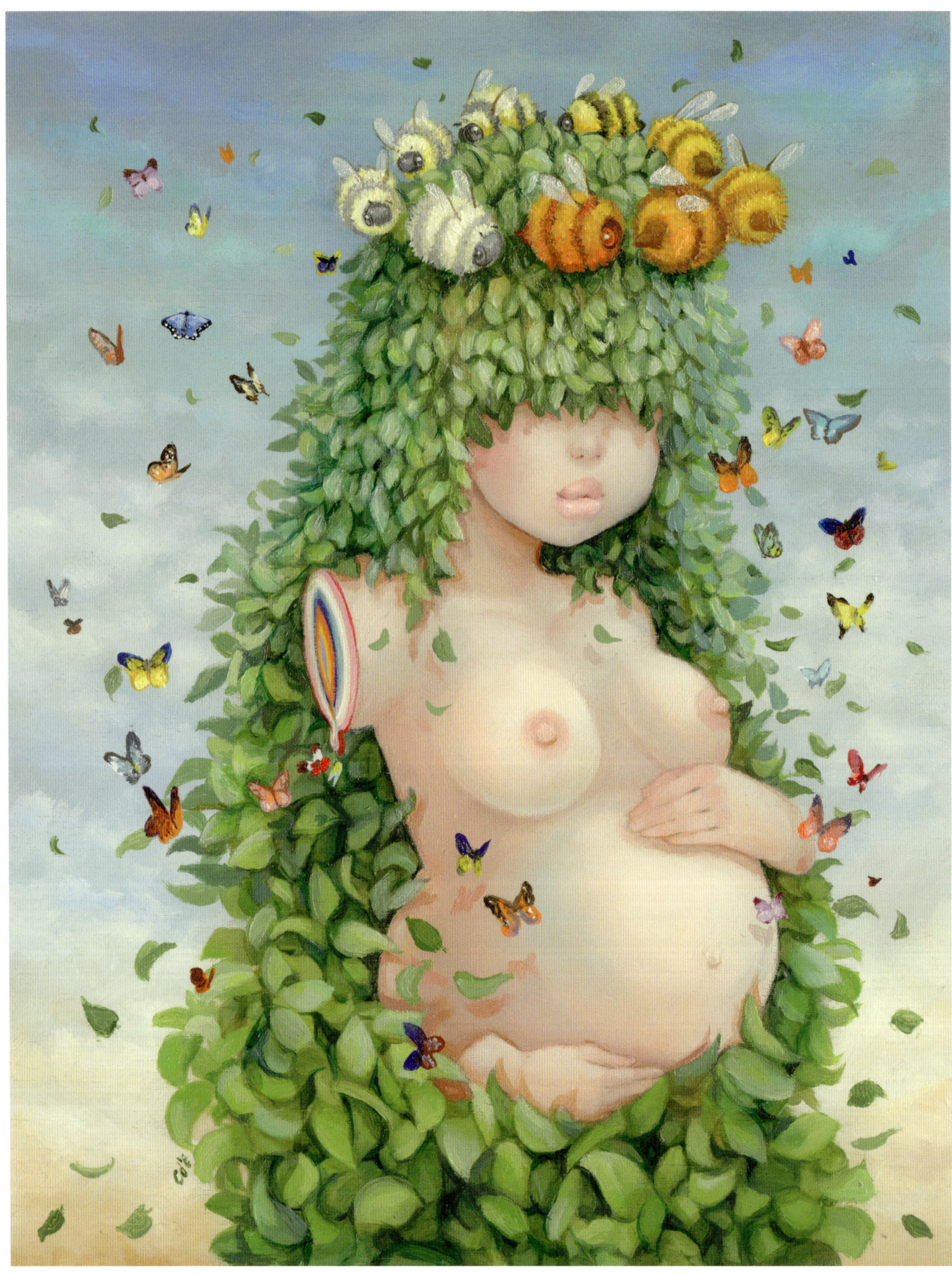

Gaia | 8" X 10" | OIL | 2019

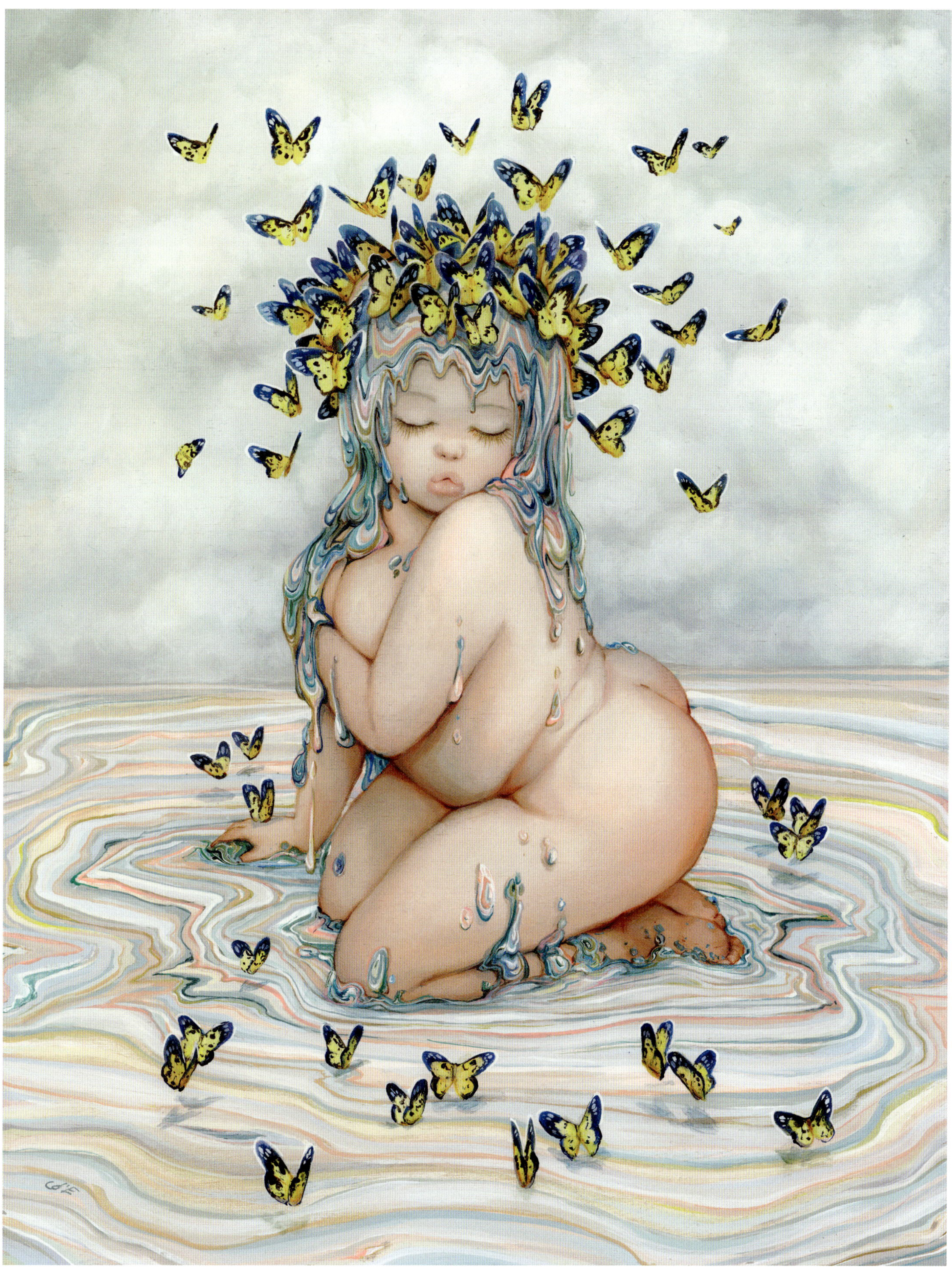

Godiva | 14" X 18" | OIL | 2018

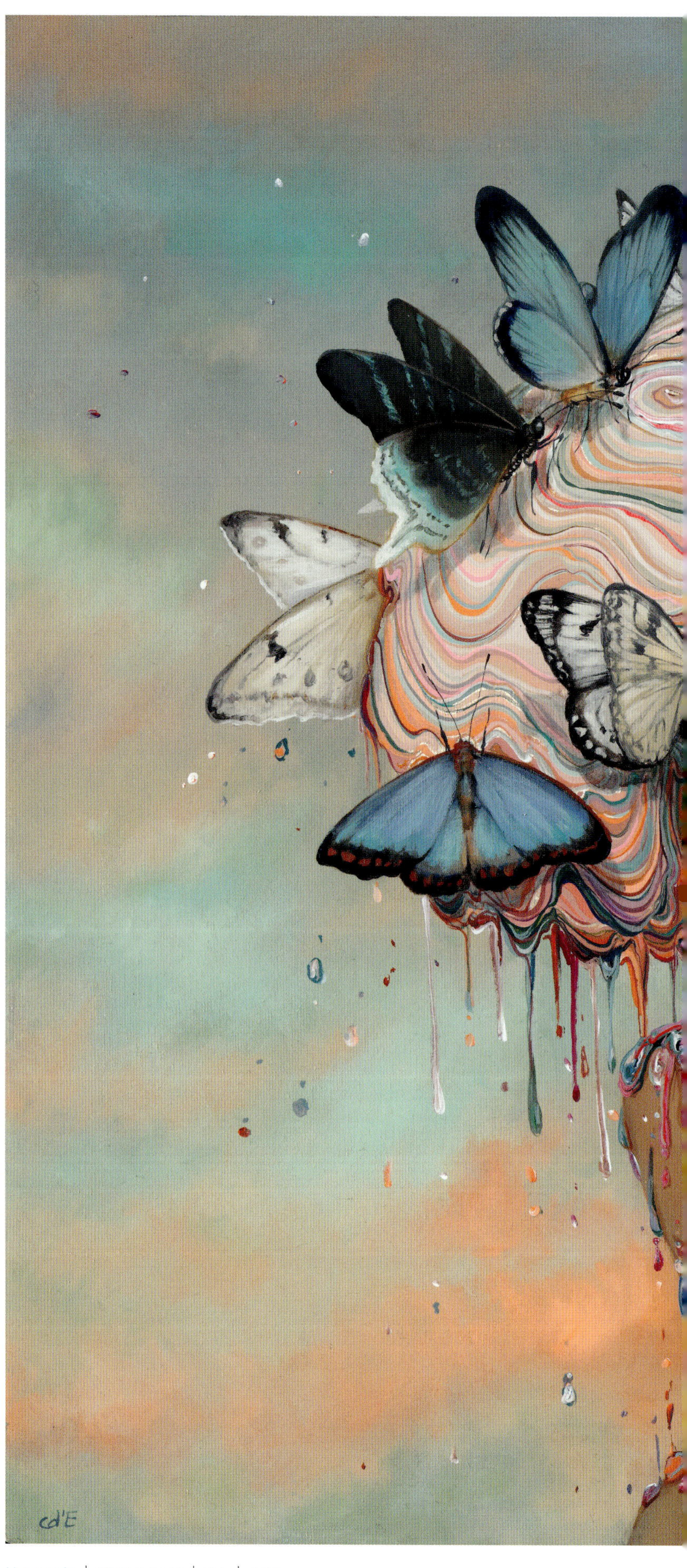

Harmonie | 18.5" X 24.5" | OIL | 2018

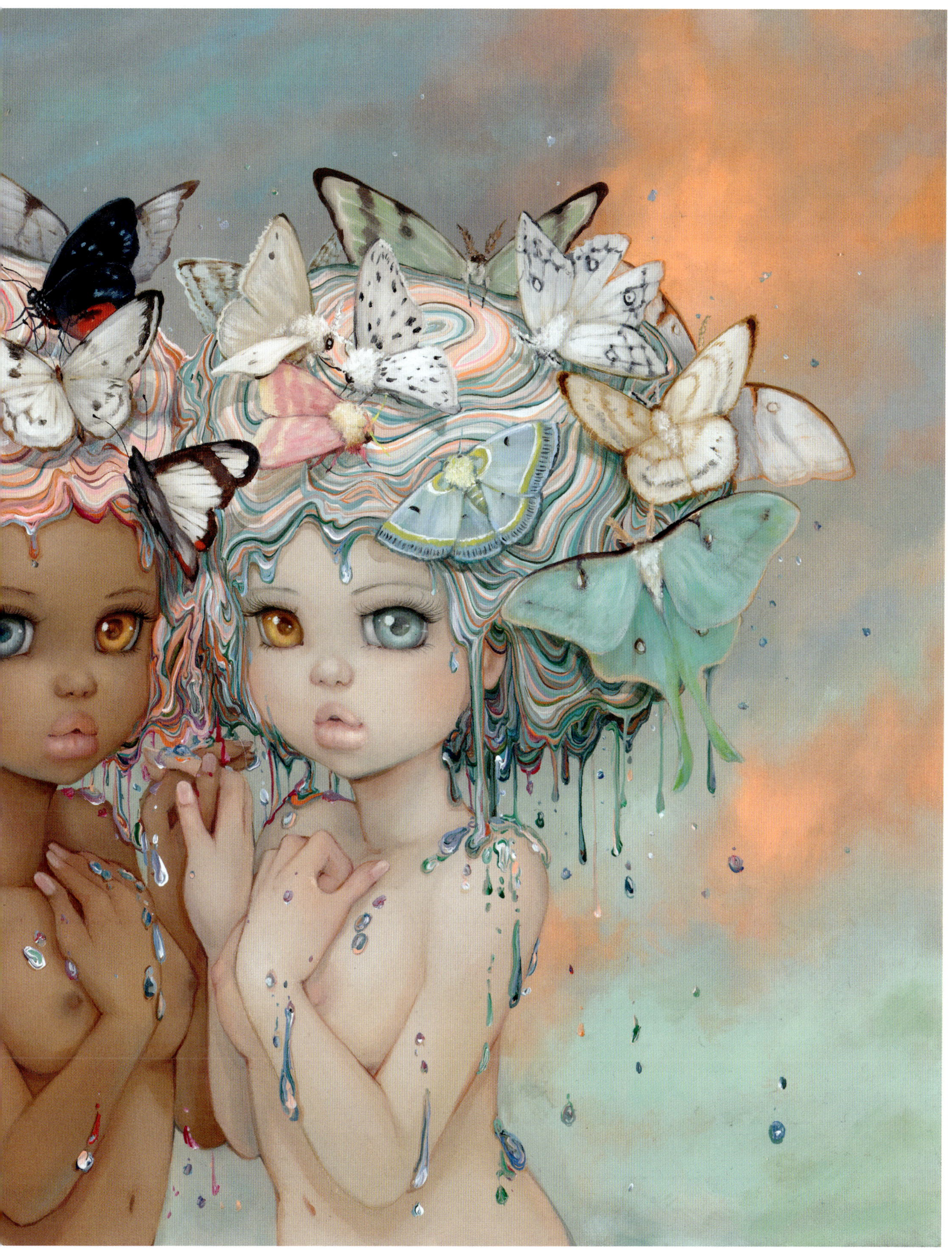

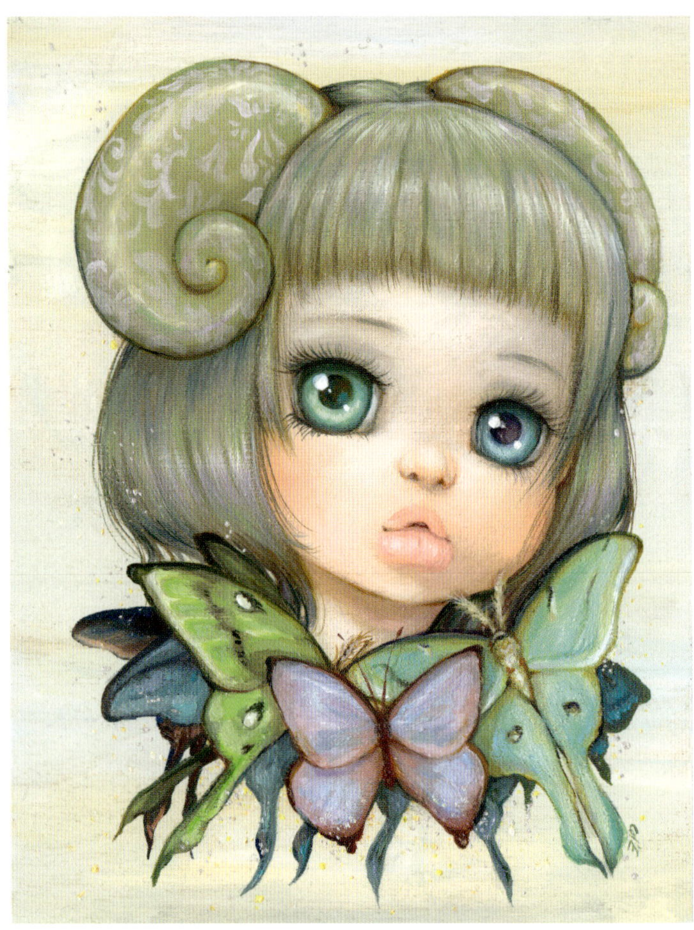

Princess Papalia | 6" X 8" | OIL | 2017

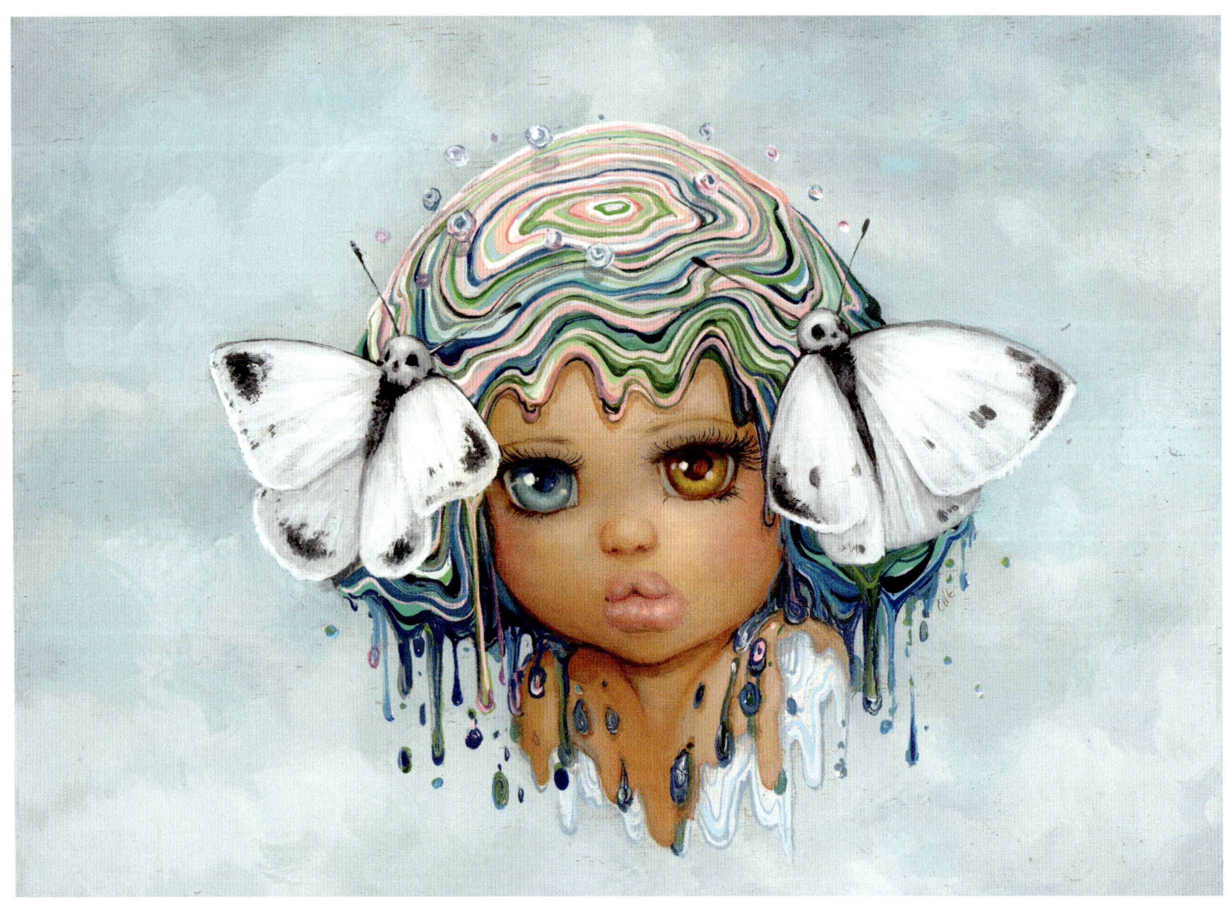

Silence | 8" X 10" | OIL | 2018

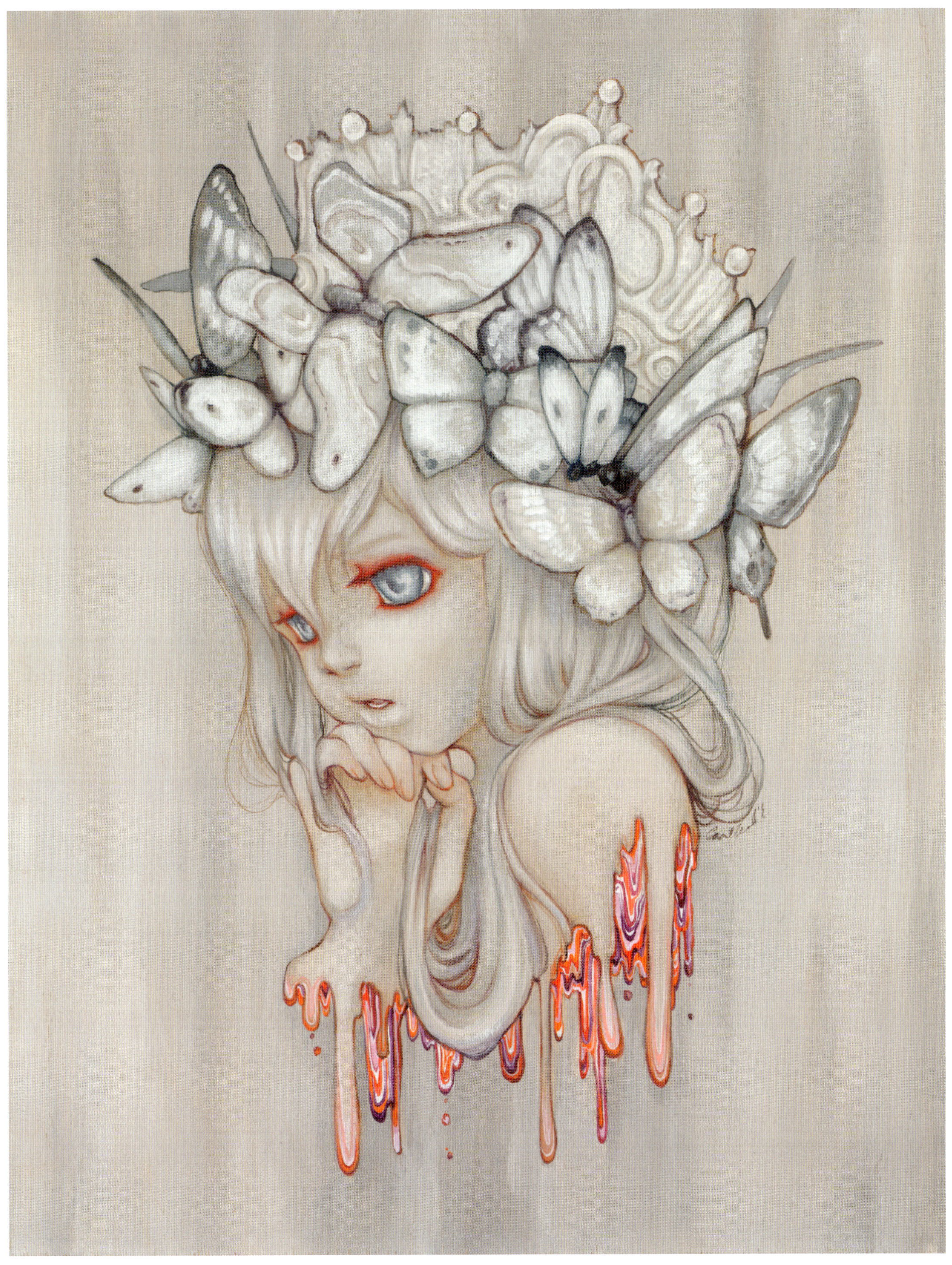

Strawberry Whispers | 11" X 14" | OIL | 2012

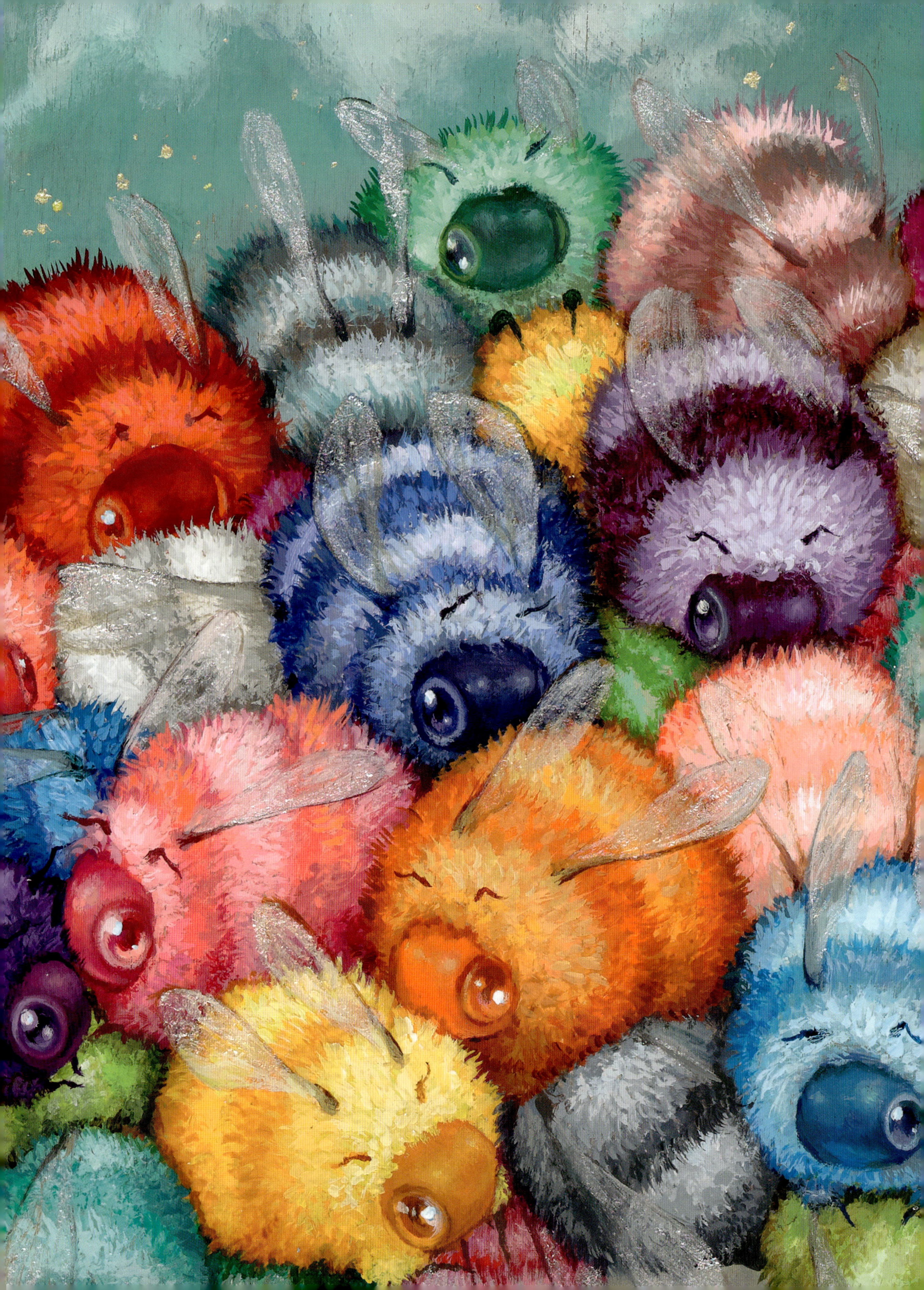

NECTARIVOROUS NATURE

Facing page:

Bonnie Bonnet | 16" X 20" | OIL | 2018

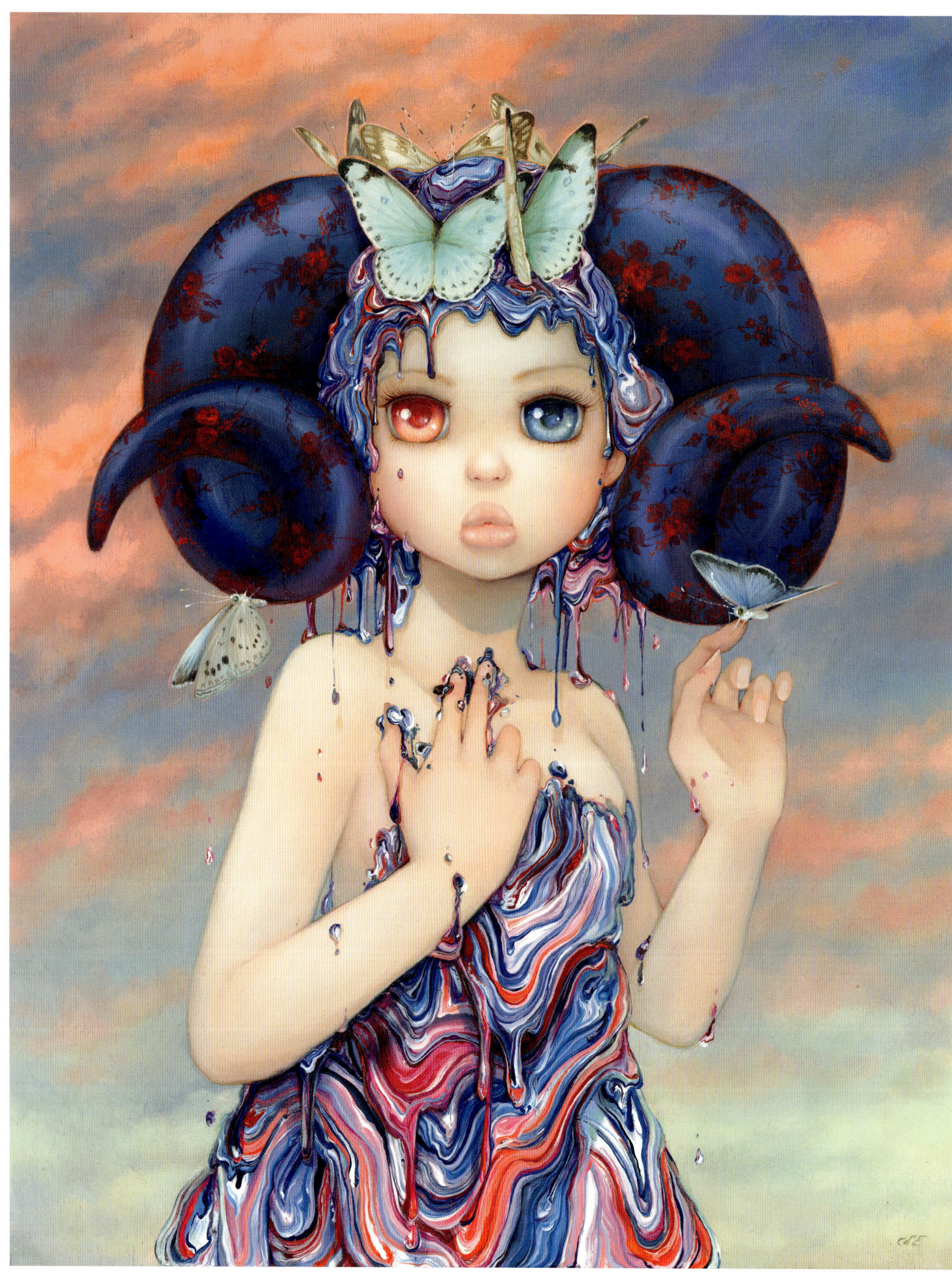

The Migrator | 16" X 20" | OIL | 2019

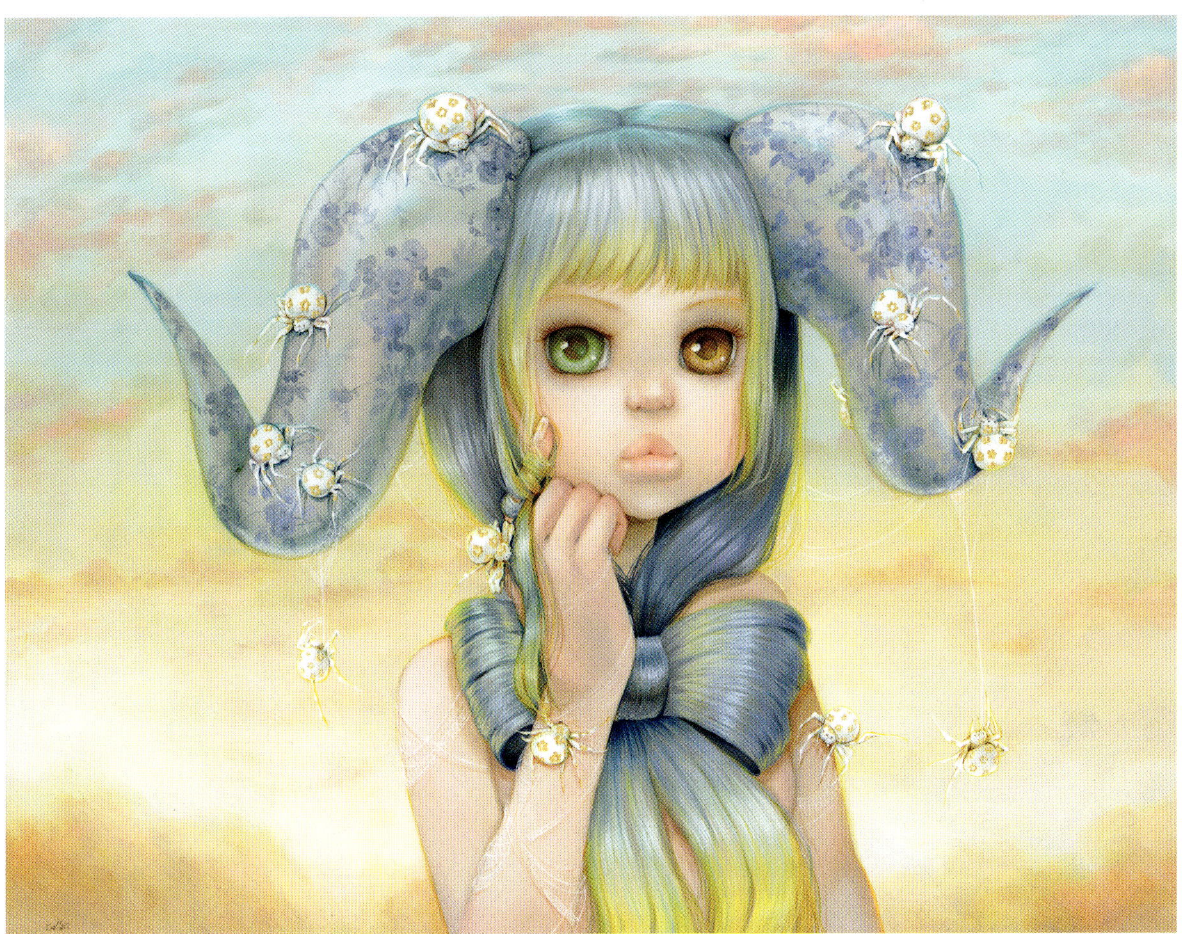

The Protector | 16" X 20" | OIL | 2019

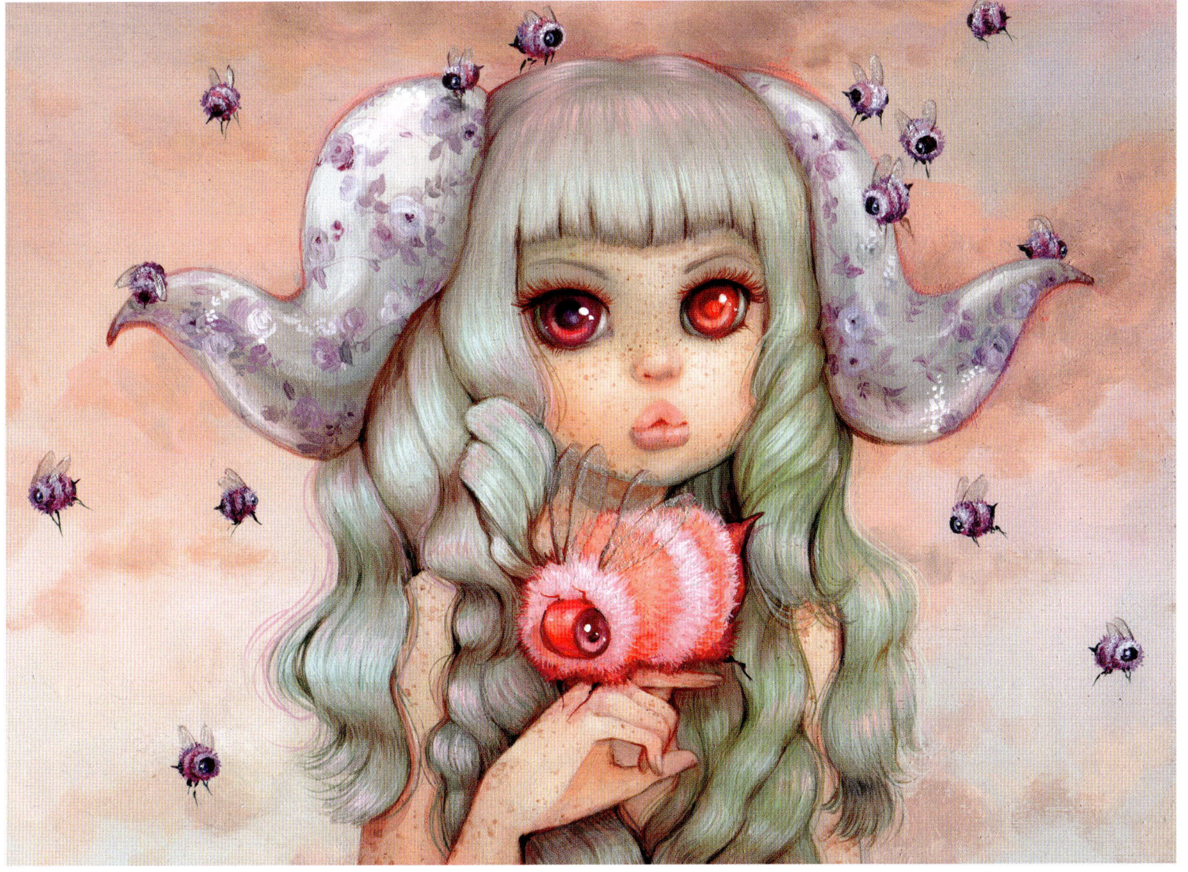

The Pollinator | 8" X 10" | OIL | 2019

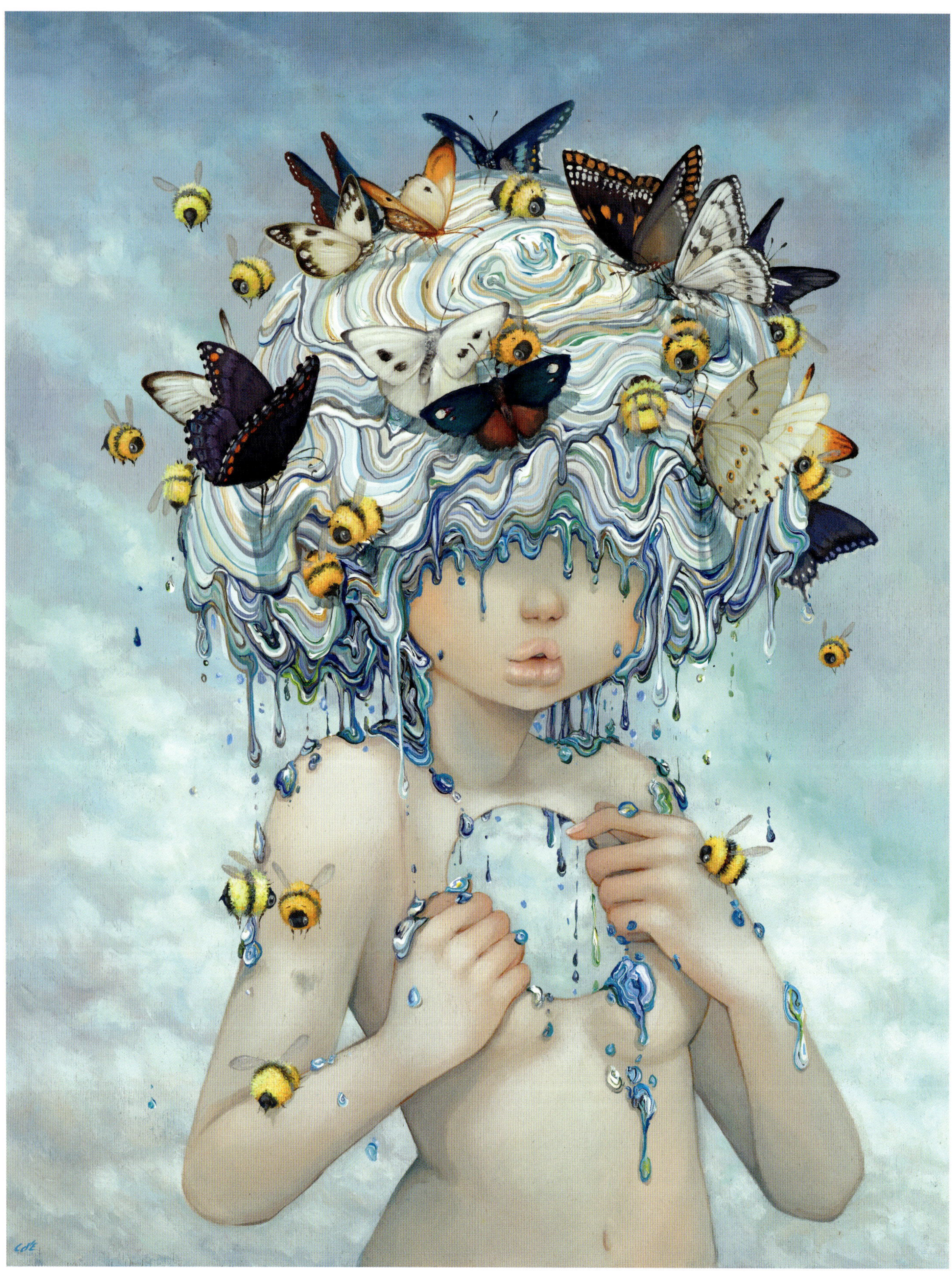

Polina | 16" X 20" | OIL | 2018

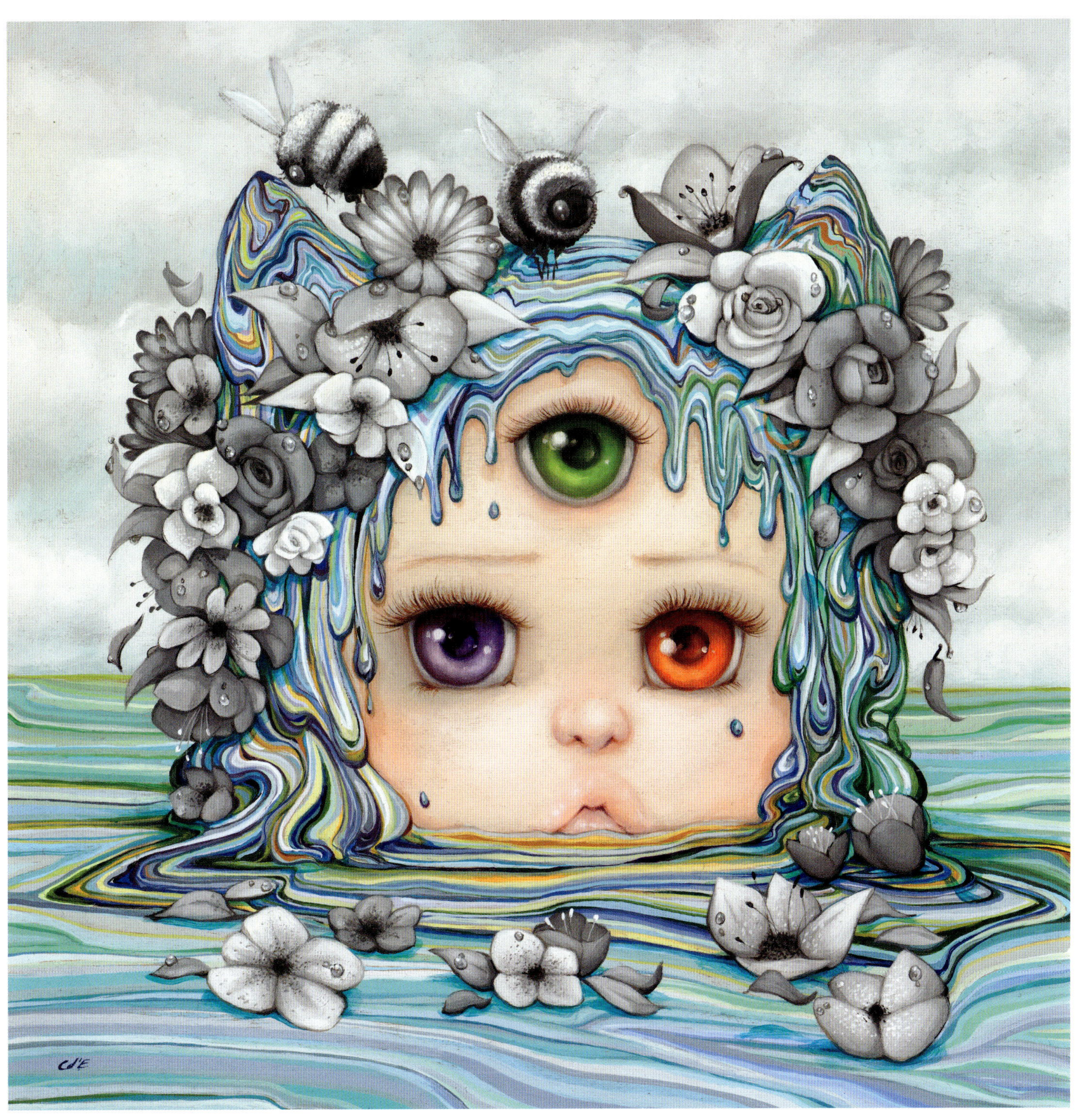

Ajna | 12" X 12" | OIL | 2017

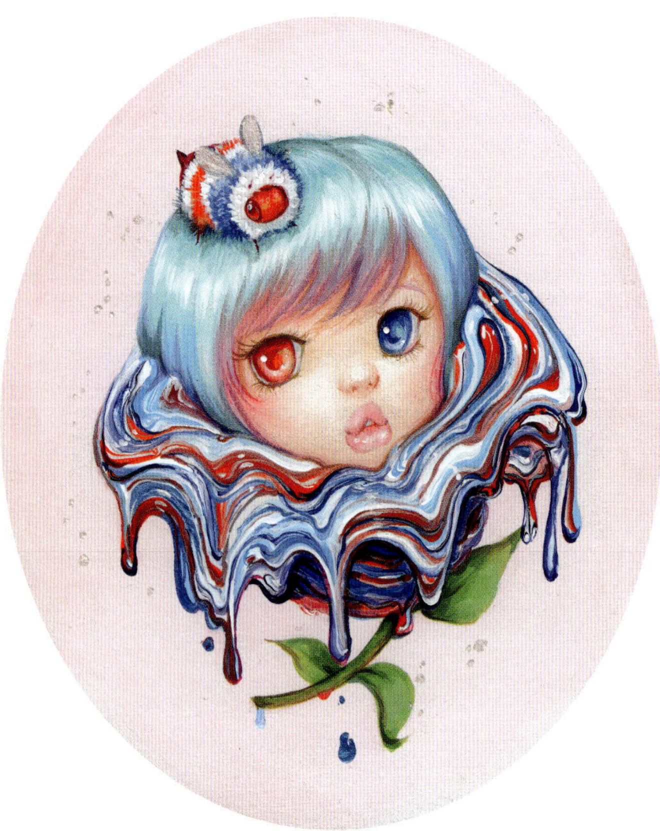

Salt Water Taffy | 5" X 7" | OIL and ACRYLIC | 2019

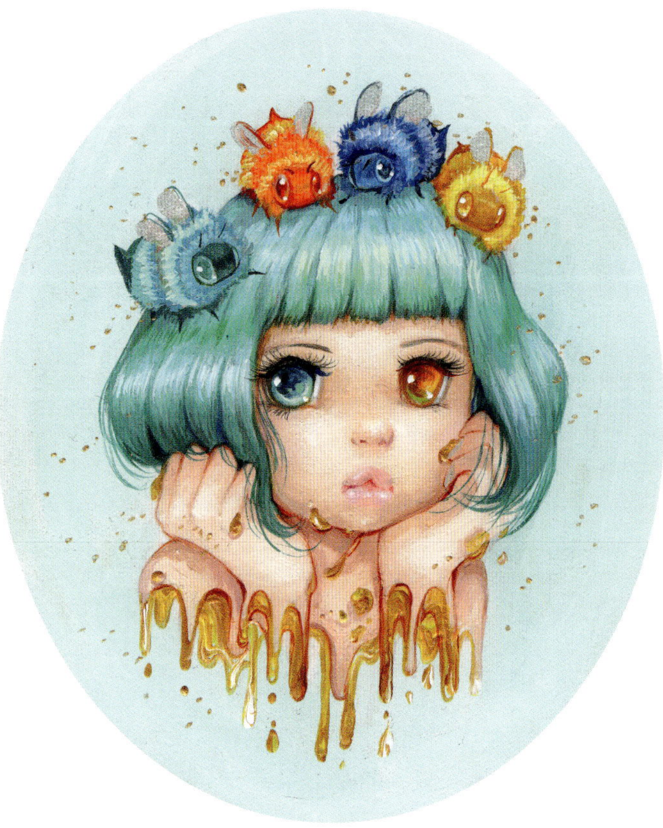

Jujubees | 5" X 7" | OIL and ACRYLIC | 2019

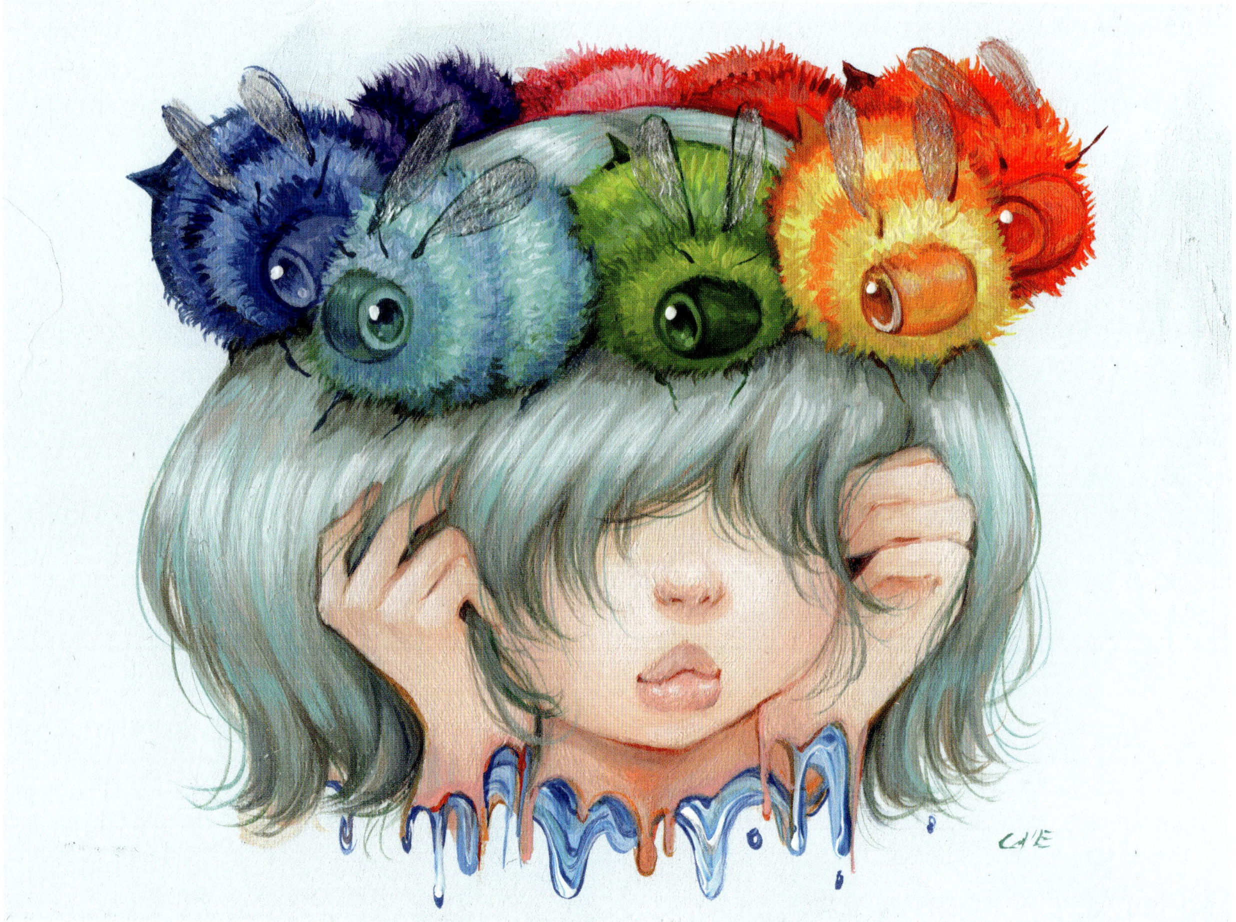

Thinking Out Loud | 5" X 7" | OIL and ACRYLIC | 2019

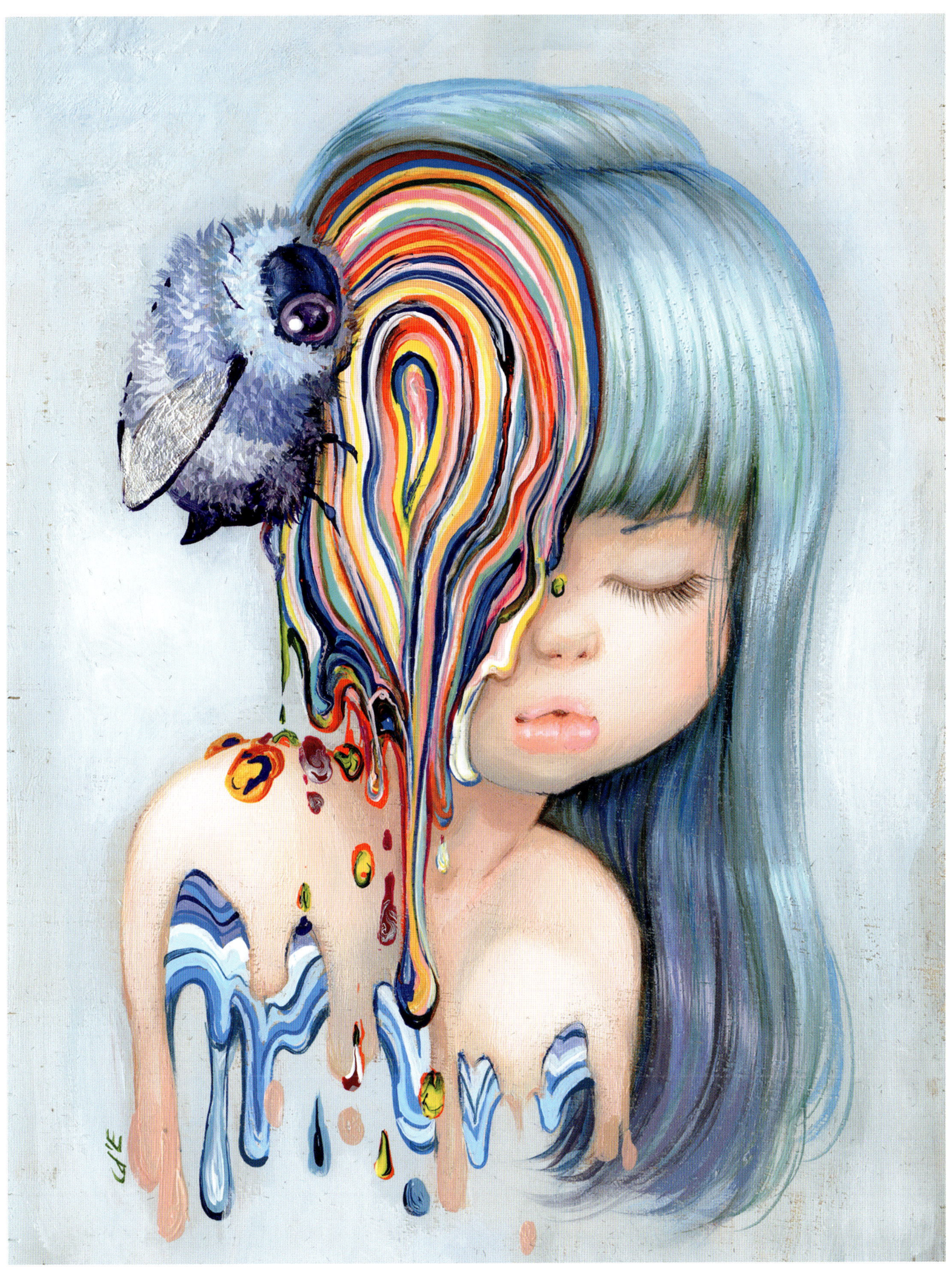

Hachi Hive | 5" X 7" | OIL and ACRYLIC | 2019

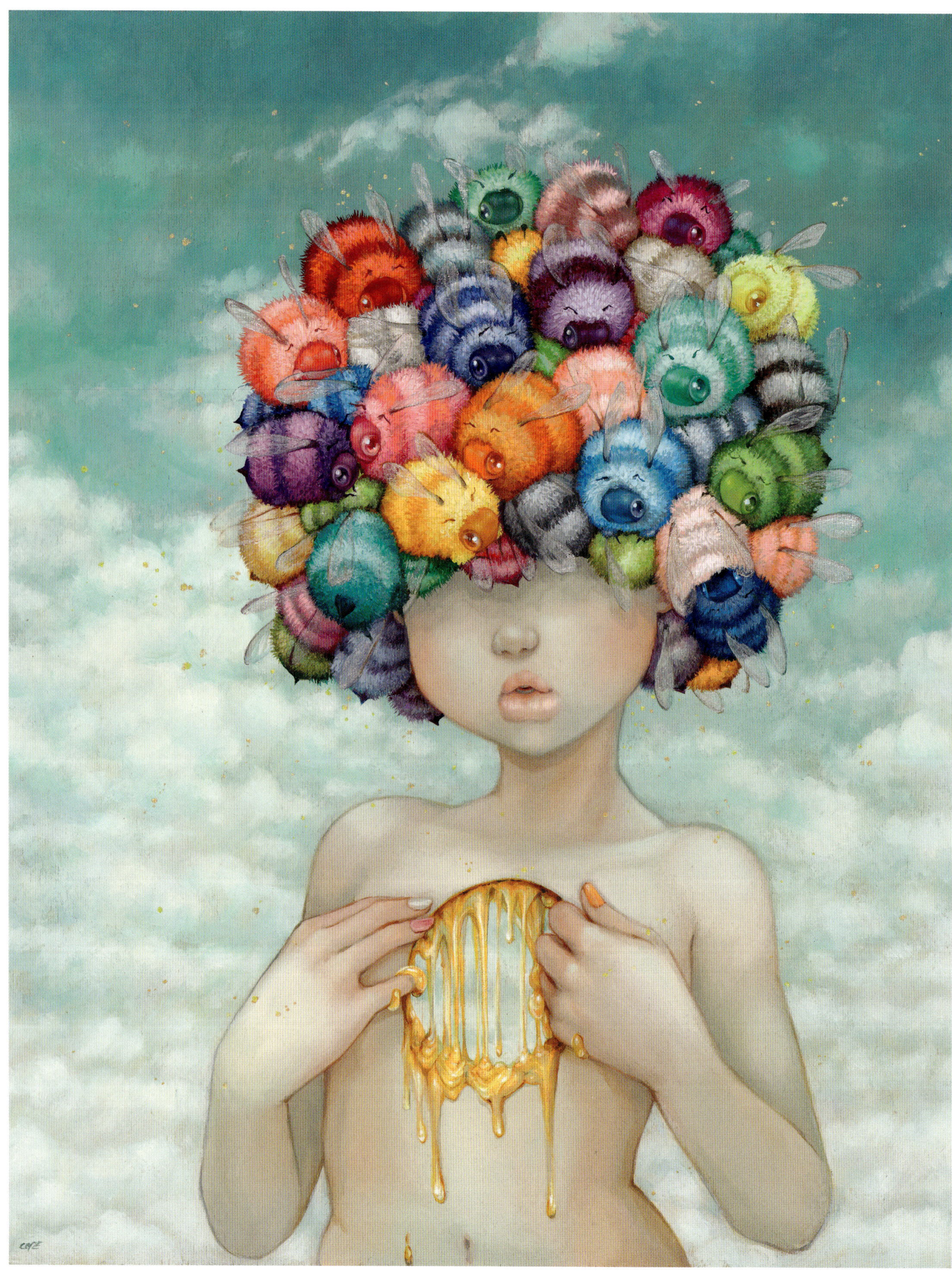

Bonnie Bonnet | 16" X 20" | OIL | 2018

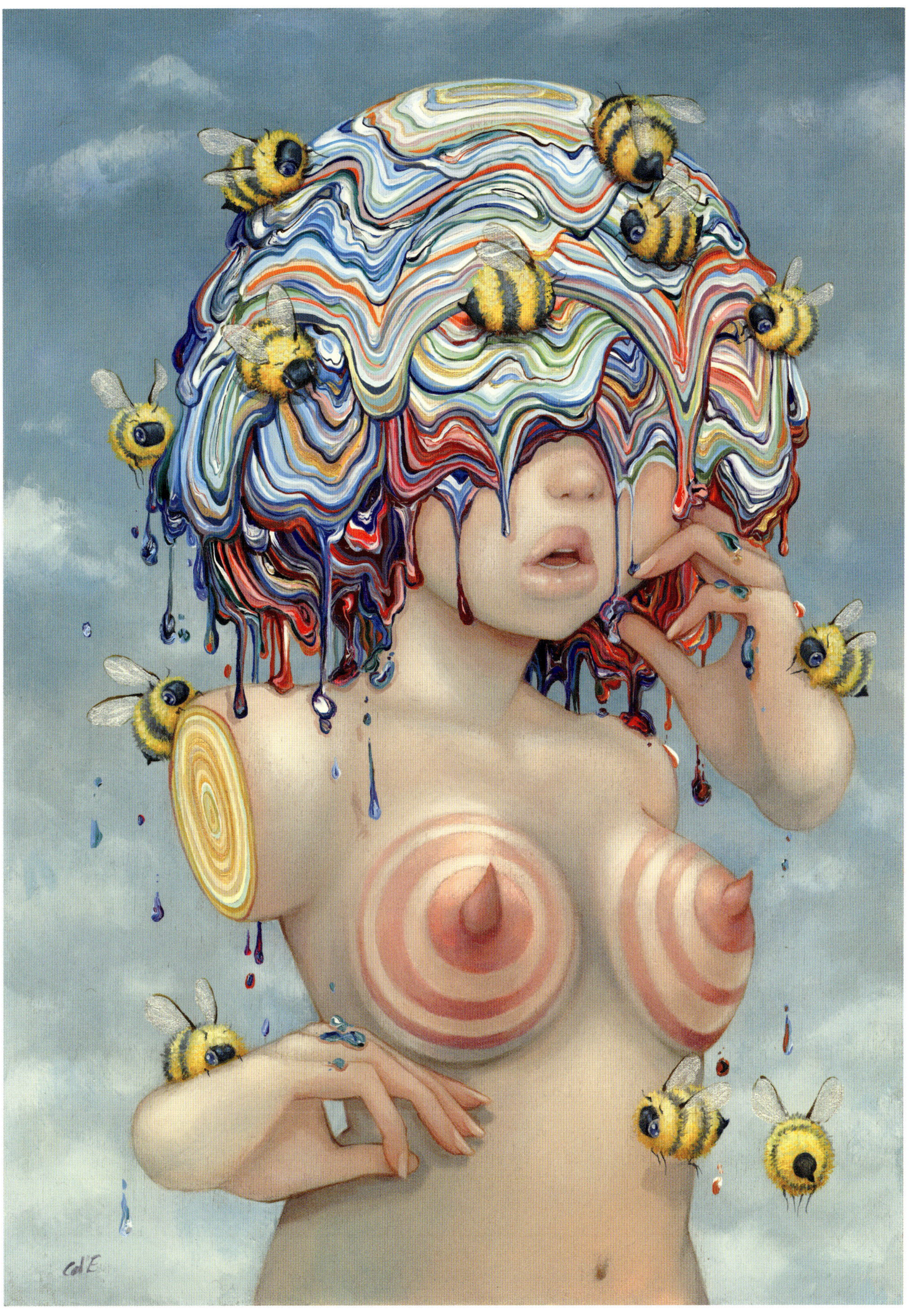

Boobees | 10" X 14" | OIL | 2019

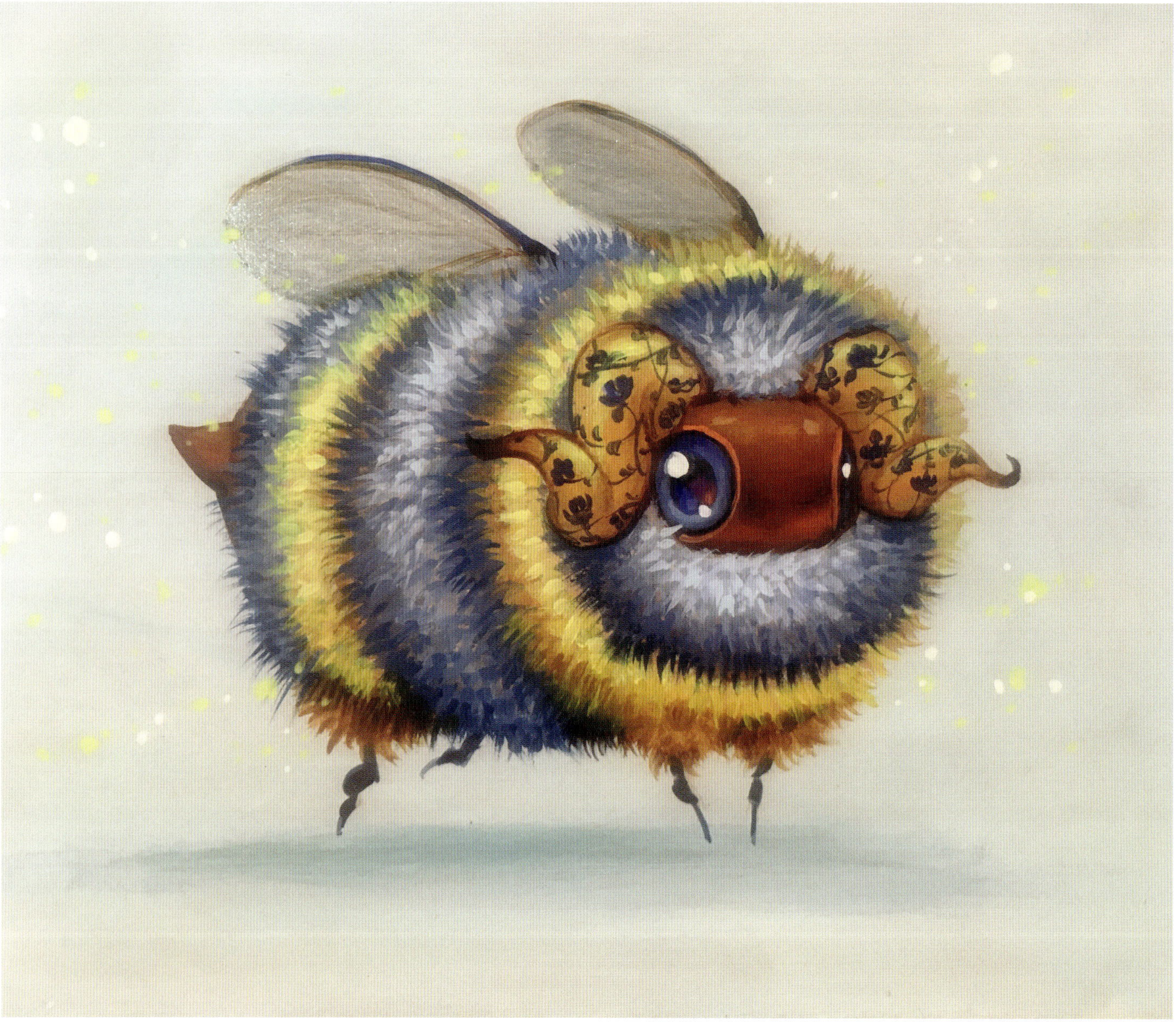

Arbees | 5" X 7" | OIL and ACRYLIC | 2019

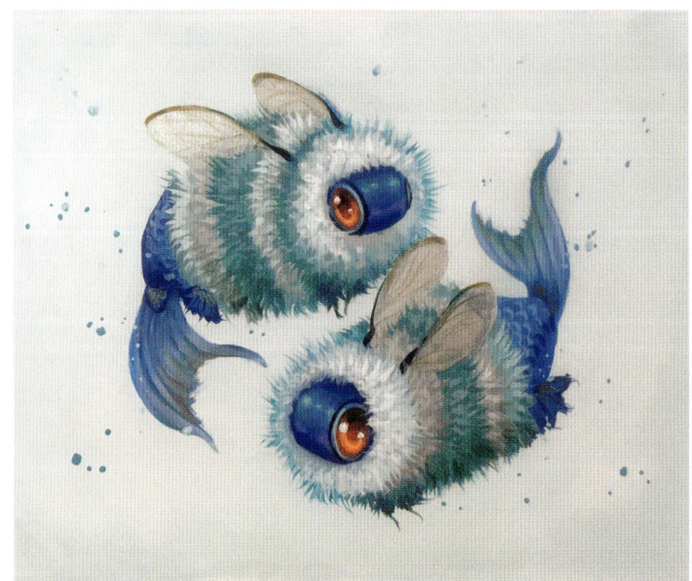

Buzzces | 5" X 7" | OIL and ACRYLIC | 2019

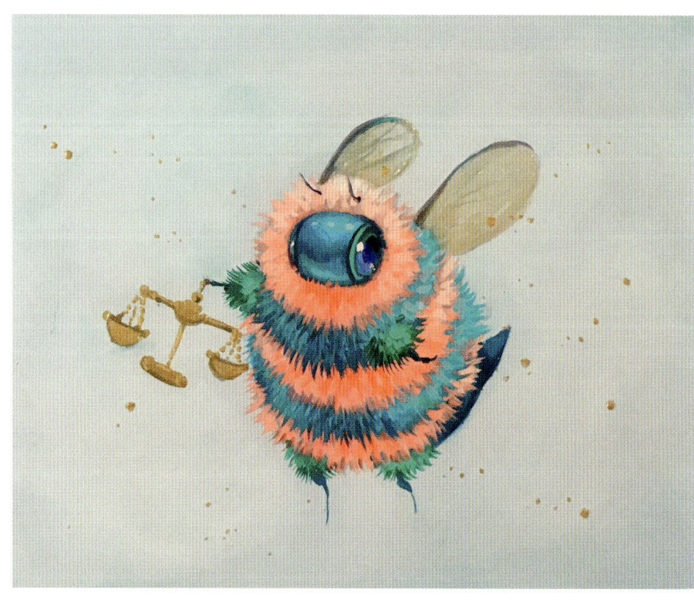

Beera | 5" X 7" | OIL and ACRYLIC | 2019

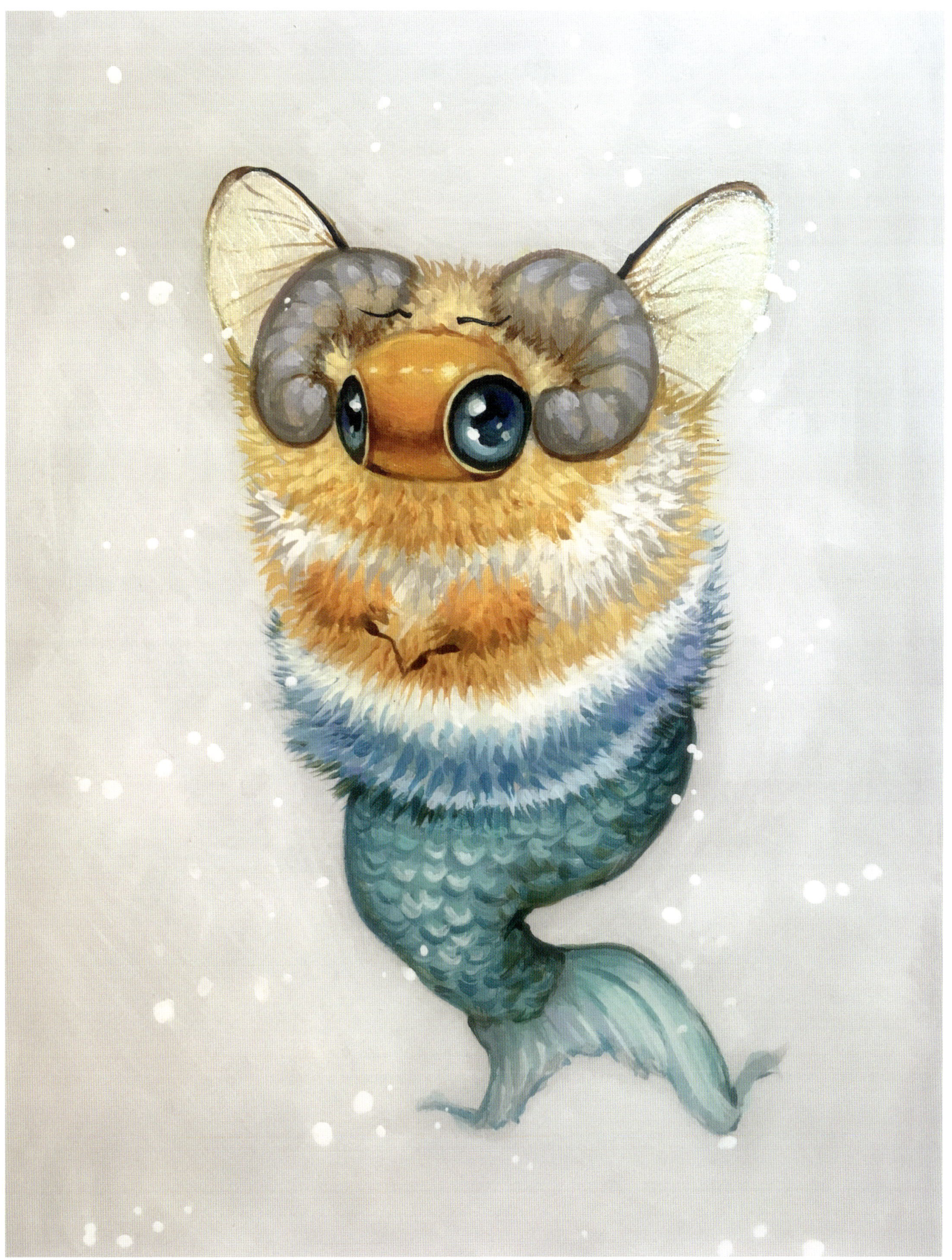

Buzzicorn | 5" X 7" | OIL and ACRYLIC | 2019

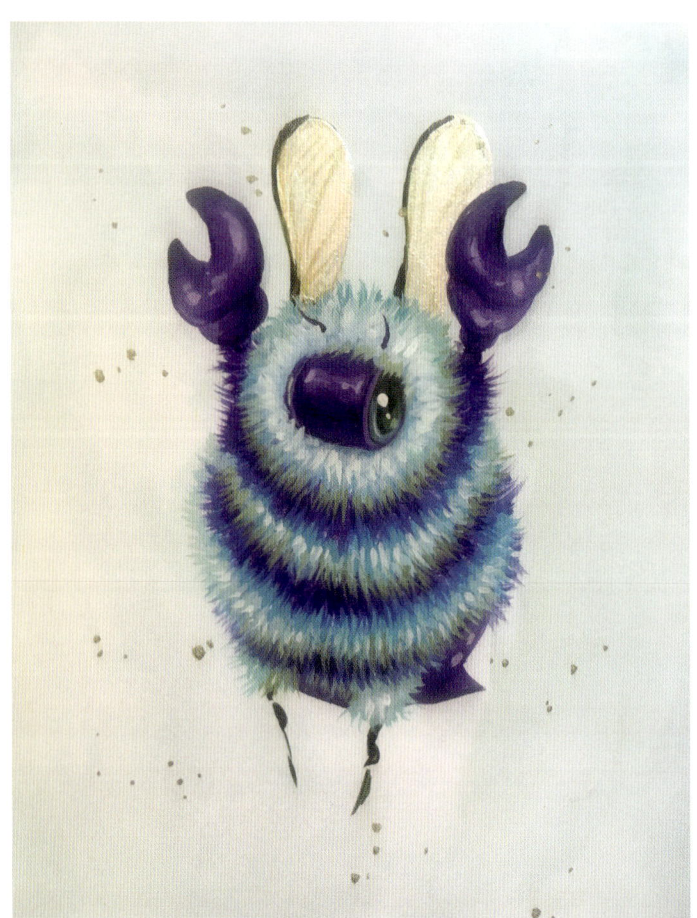

Buzzcer | 5" X 7" | OIL and ACRYLIC | 2019

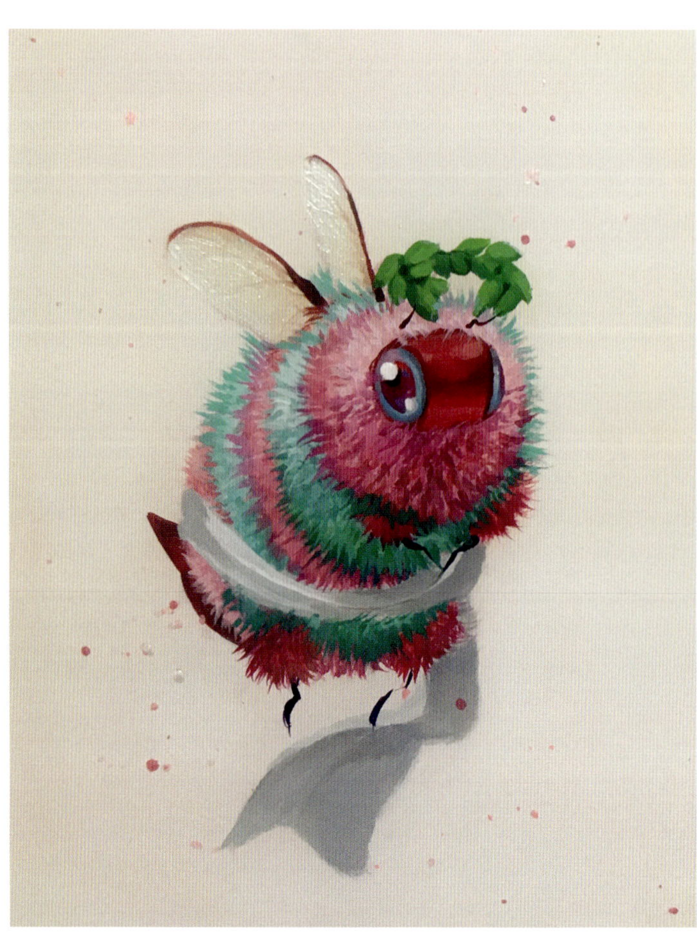

Stingro | 5" X 7" | OIL and ACRYLIC | 2019

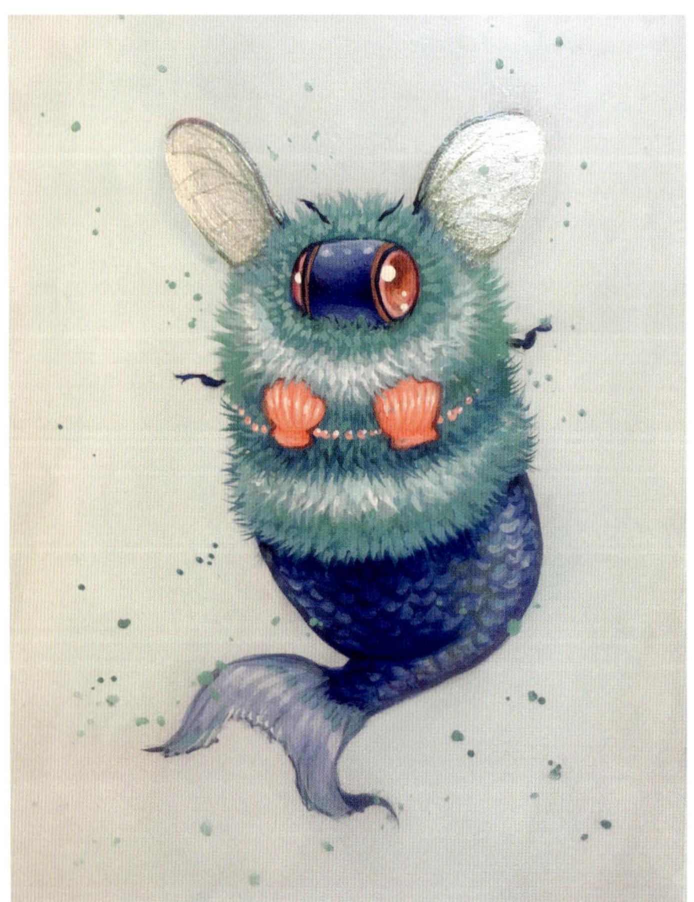

Aquaribuzz | 5" X 7" | OIL and ACRYLIC | 2019

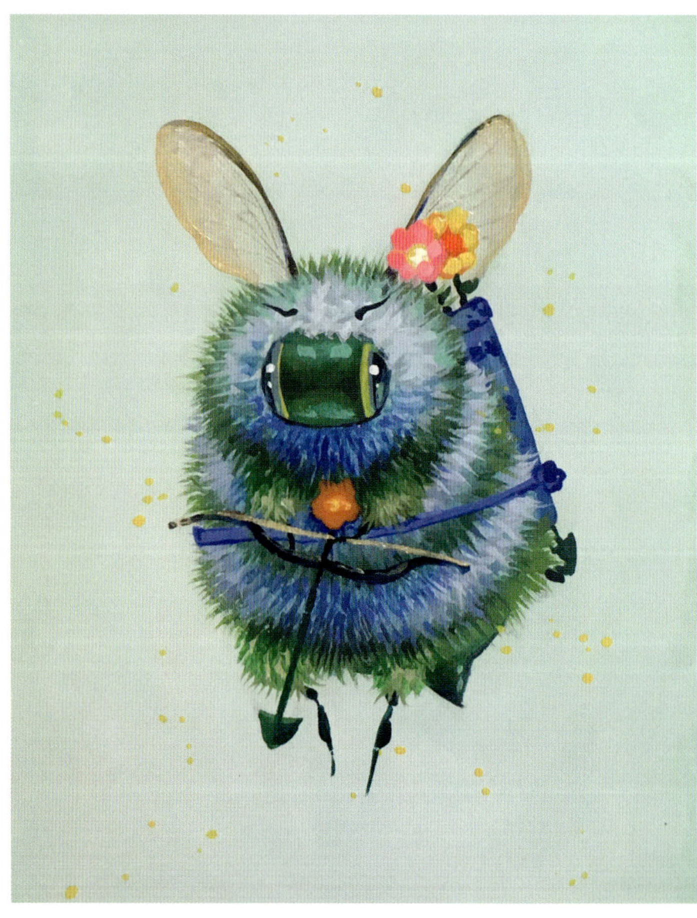

Buzzittarius | 5" X 7" | OIL and ACRYLIC | 2019

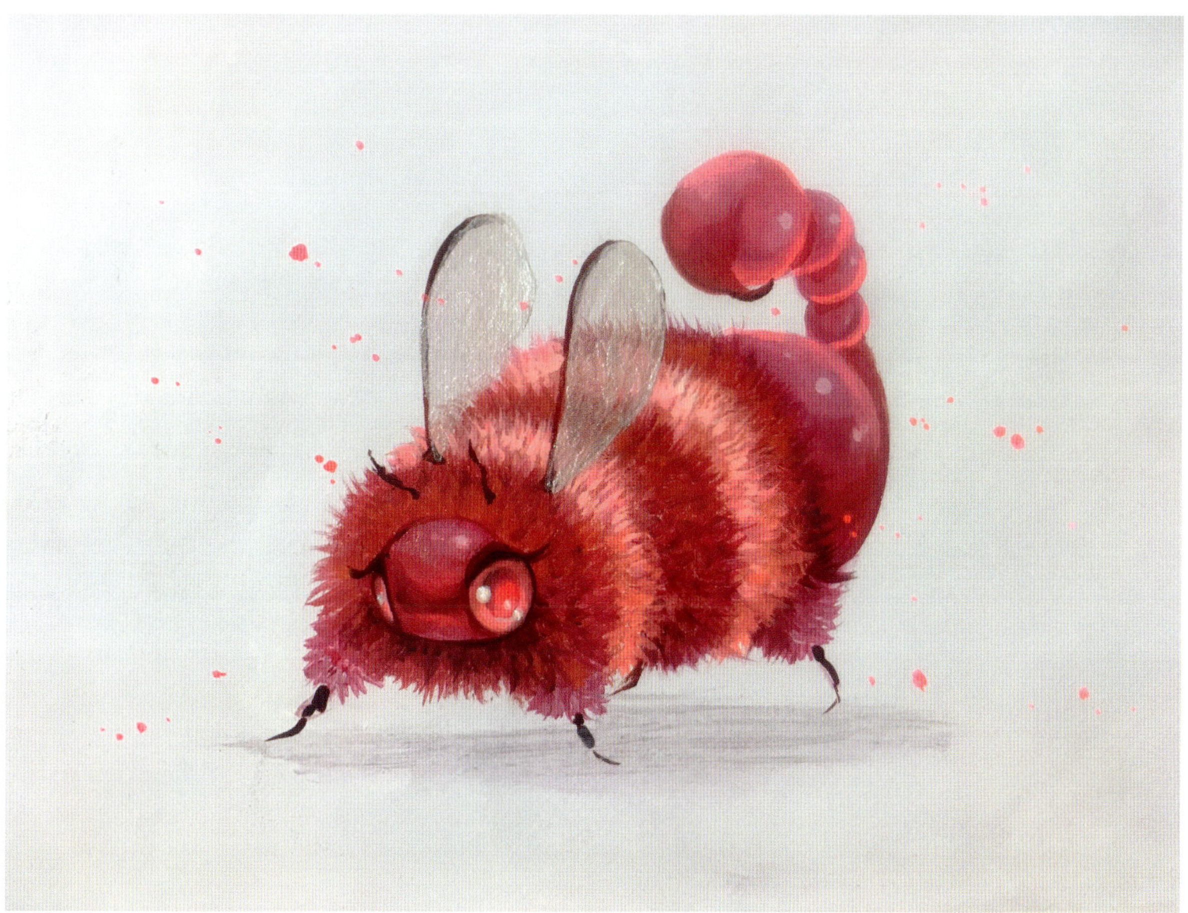

Buzzio | 5" X 7" | OIL and ACRYLIC | 2019

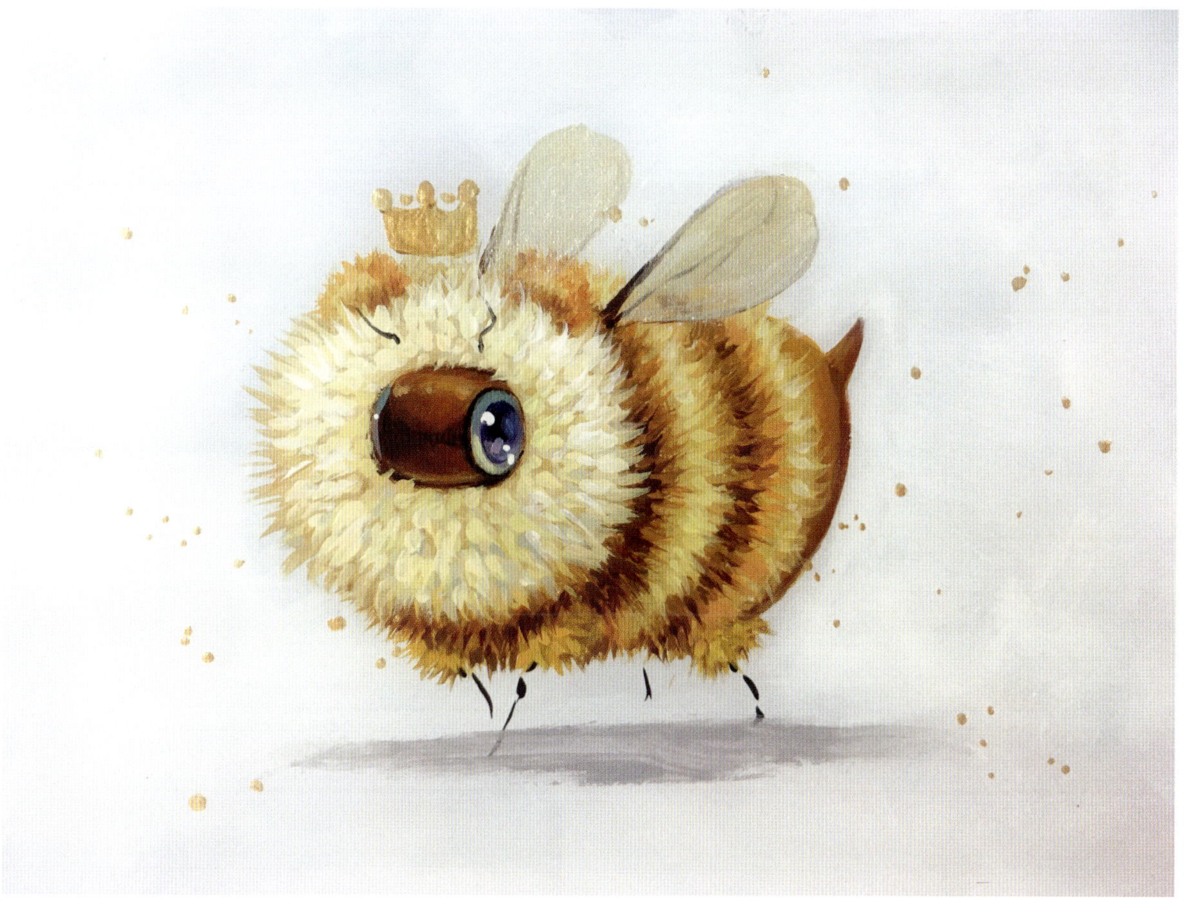

Beeo | 5" X 7" | OIL and ACRYLIC | 2019

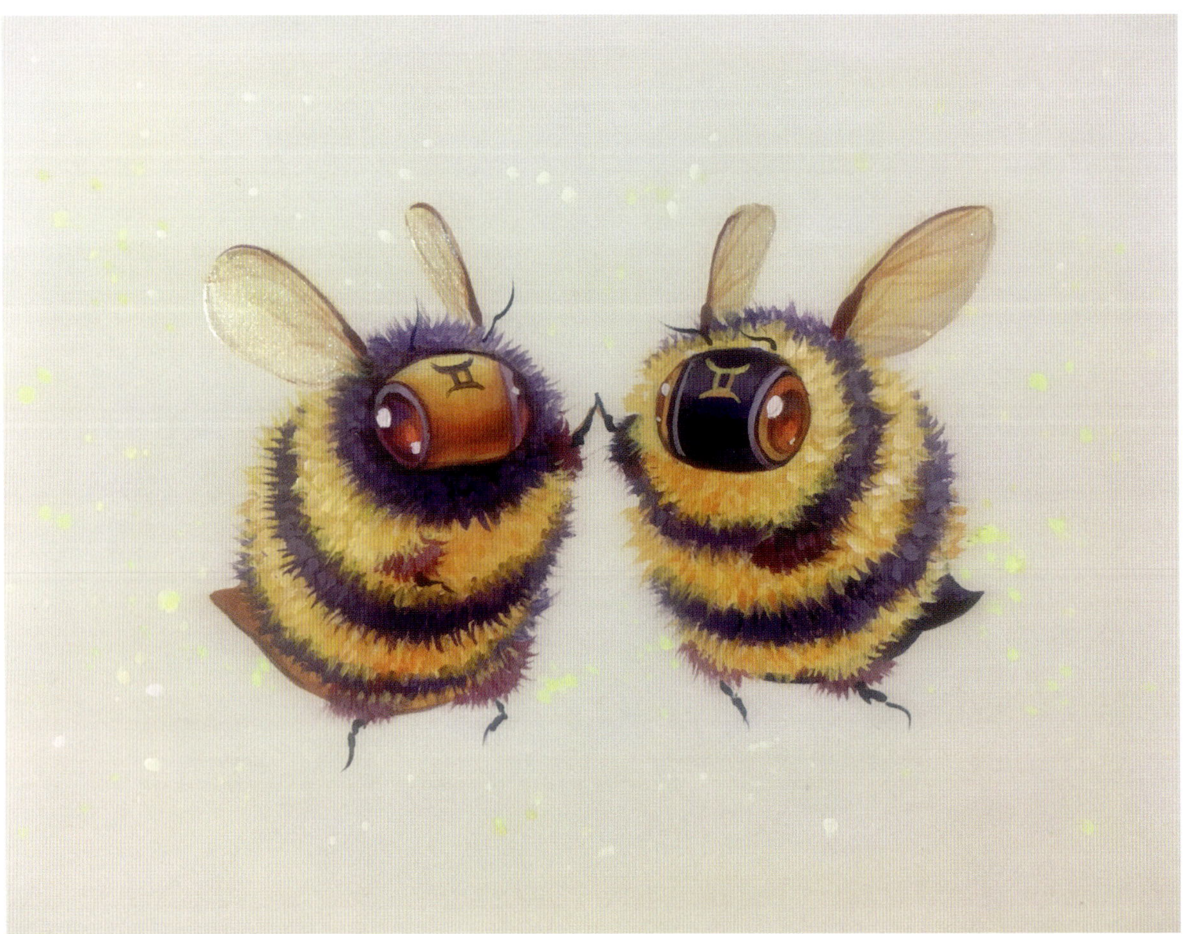

Gemihive | 5" X 7" | OIL and ACRYLIC | 2019

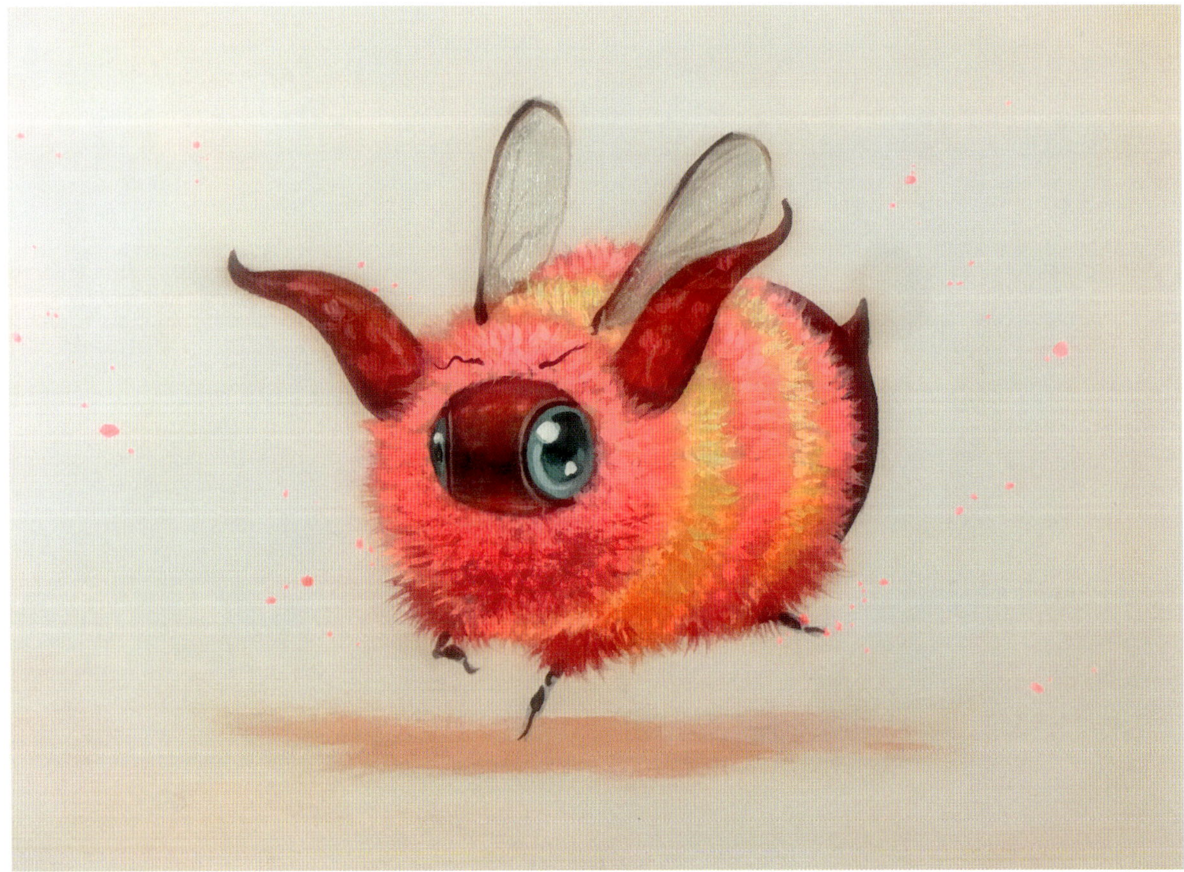

Taurbuzz | 5" X 7" | OIL and ACRYLIC | 2019

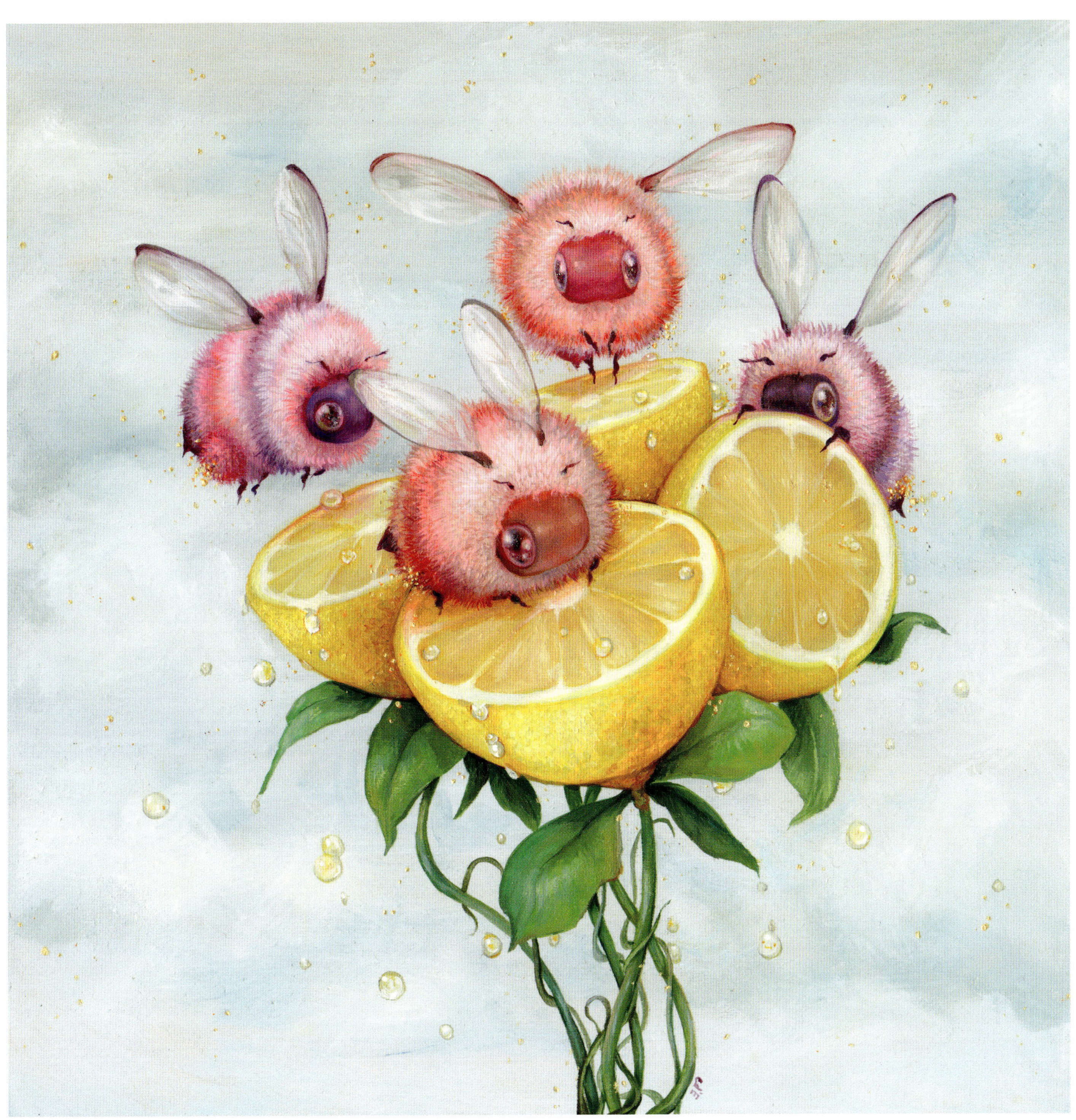

Pink Lemonade | 14" X 14" | OIL | 2017

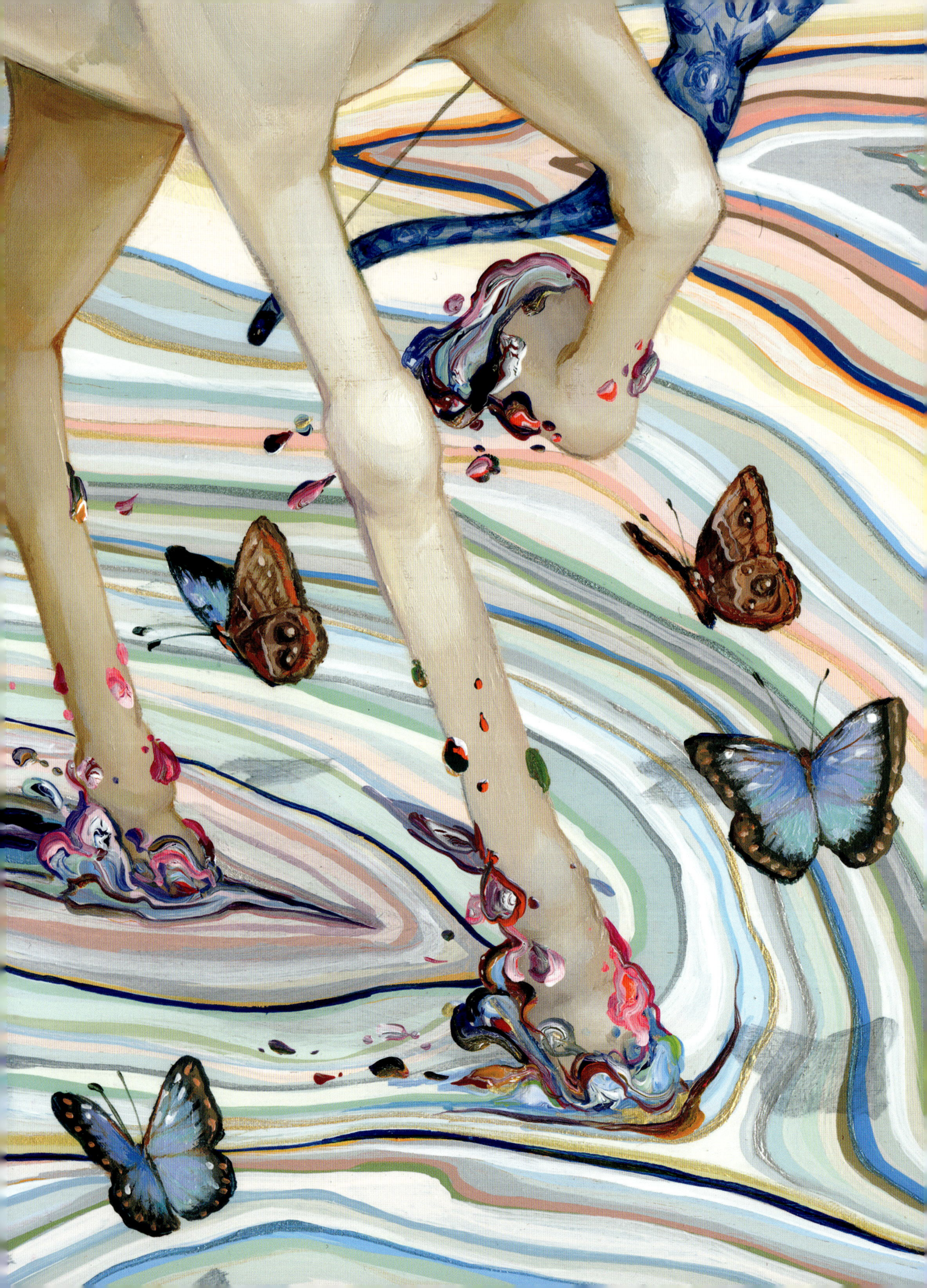

ZODIACAL ZENITH

Facing page:
Sagittarius | 14" X 18" | OIL | 2019

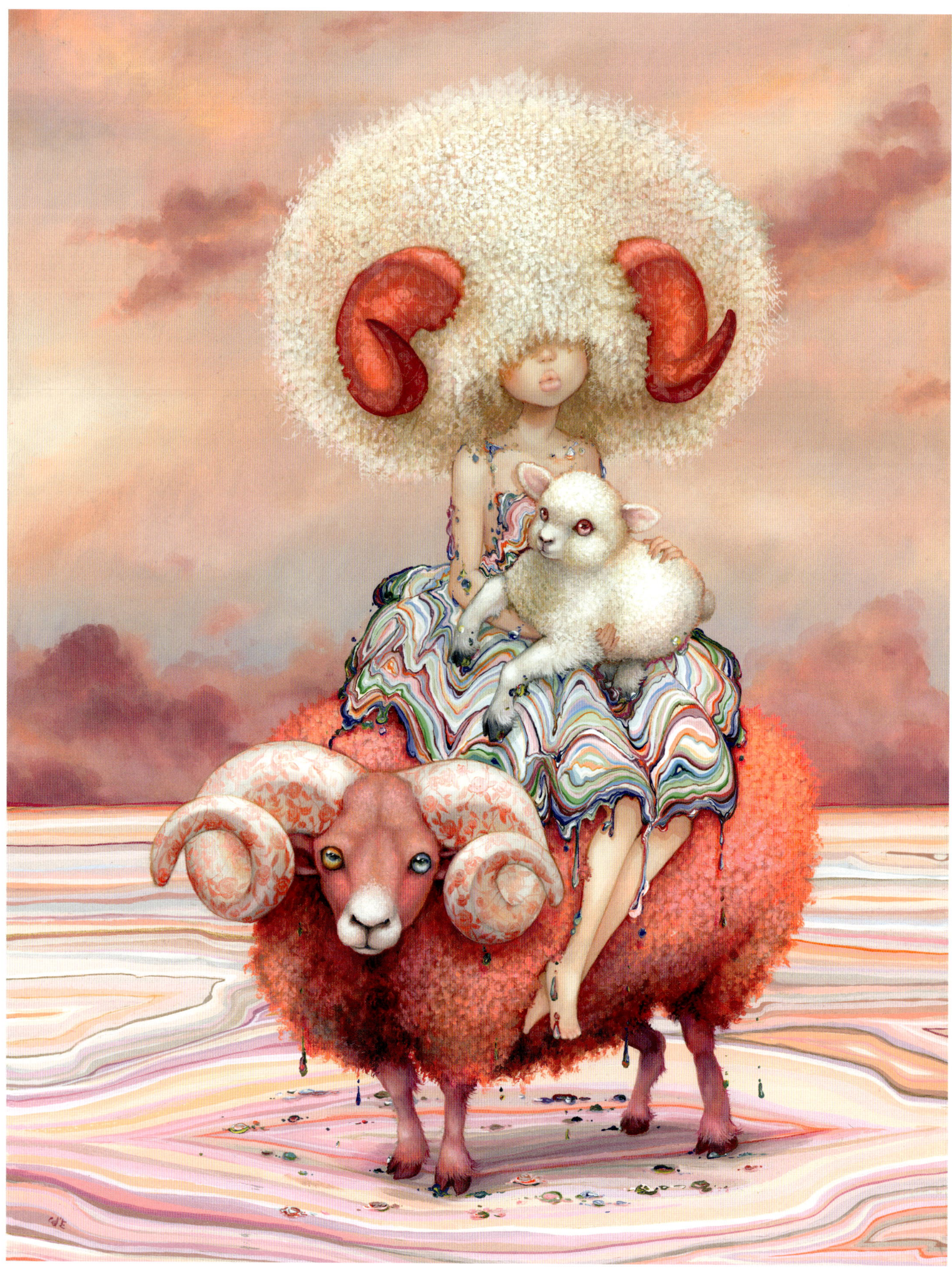

Aries | 18" X 24" | OIL | 2019

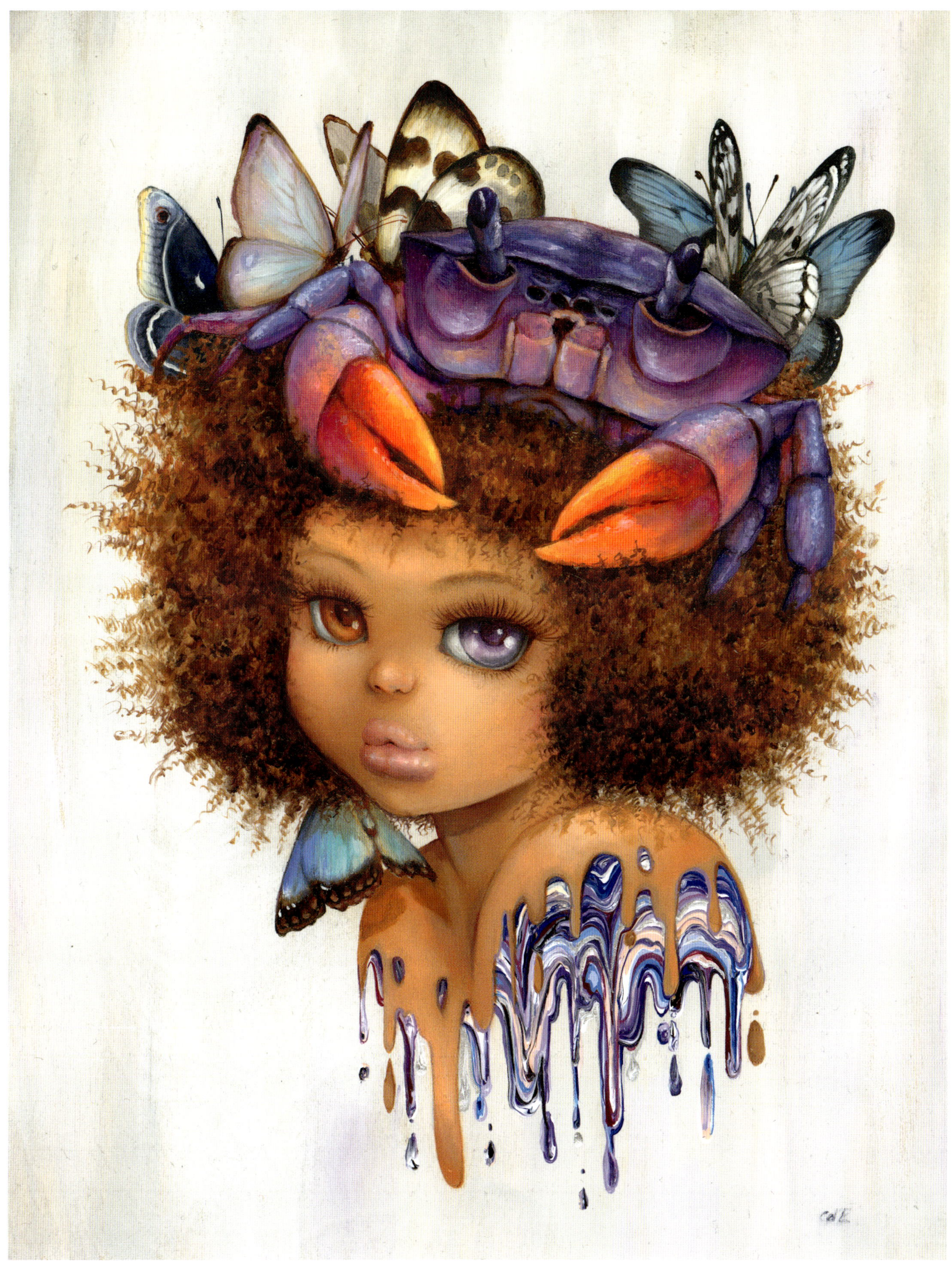

Cancer | 11" X 14" | OIL | 2019

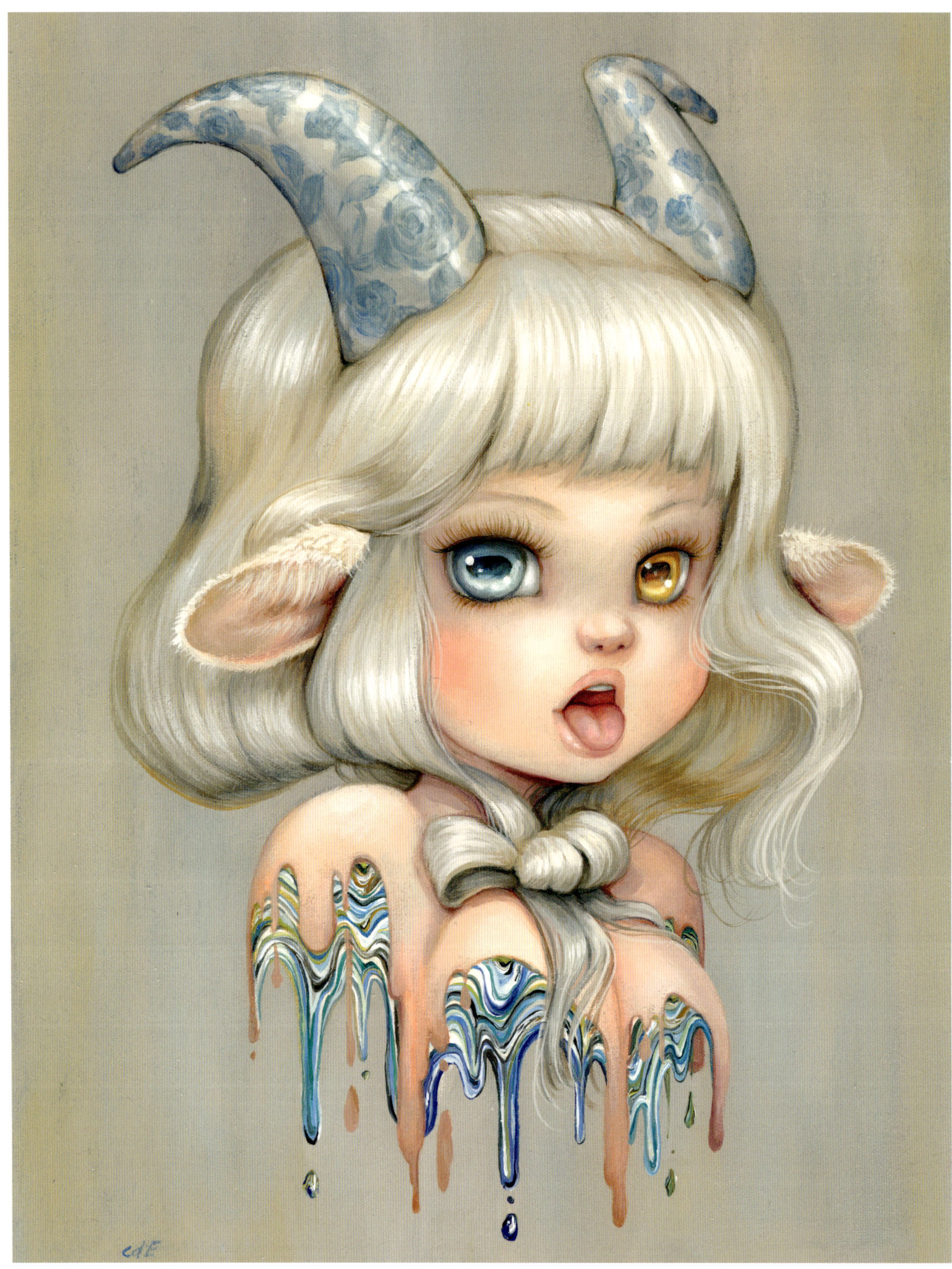

Capricorn | 10" X 14" | OIL | 2019

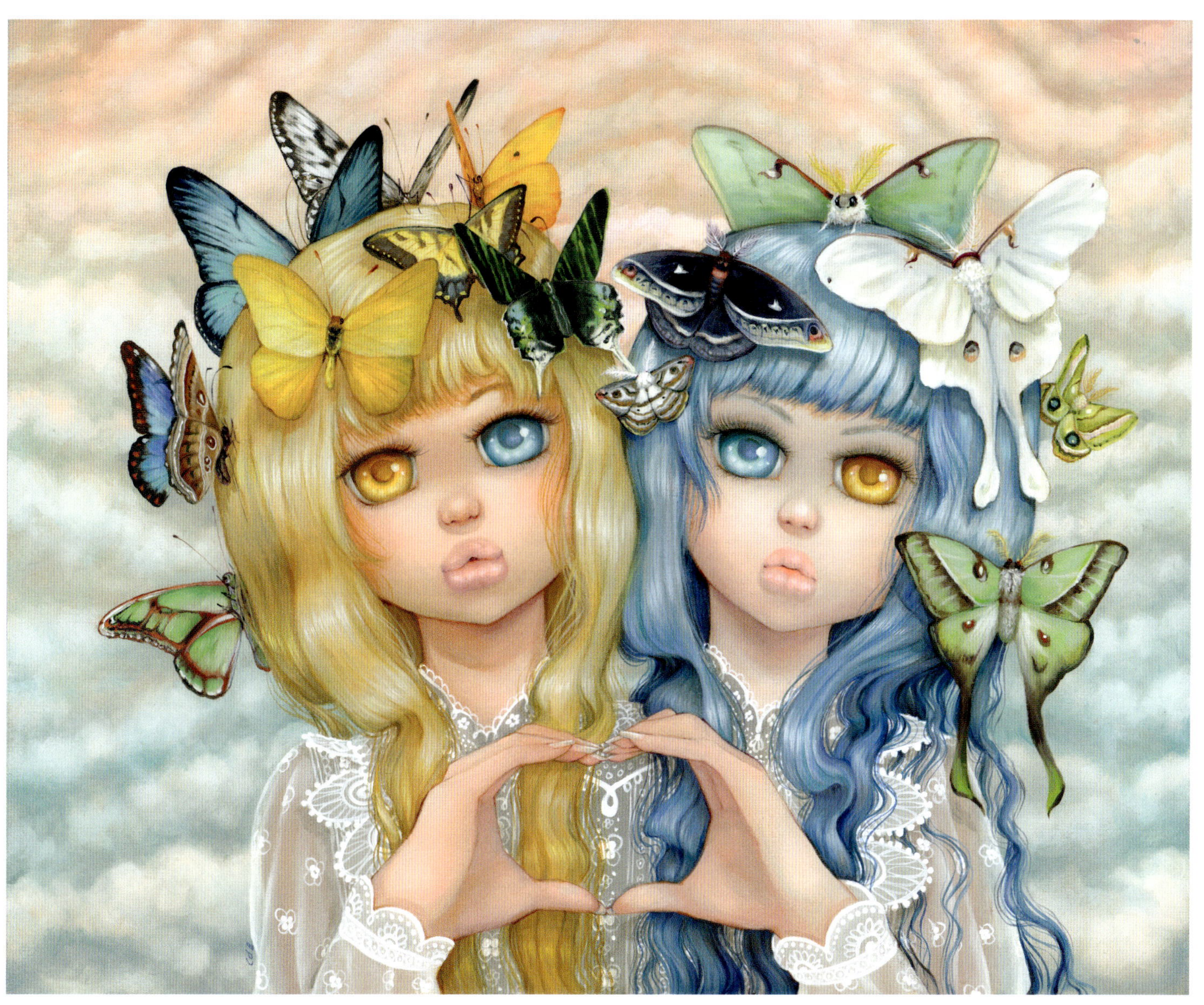

Gemini | 16" X 20" | OIL | 2019

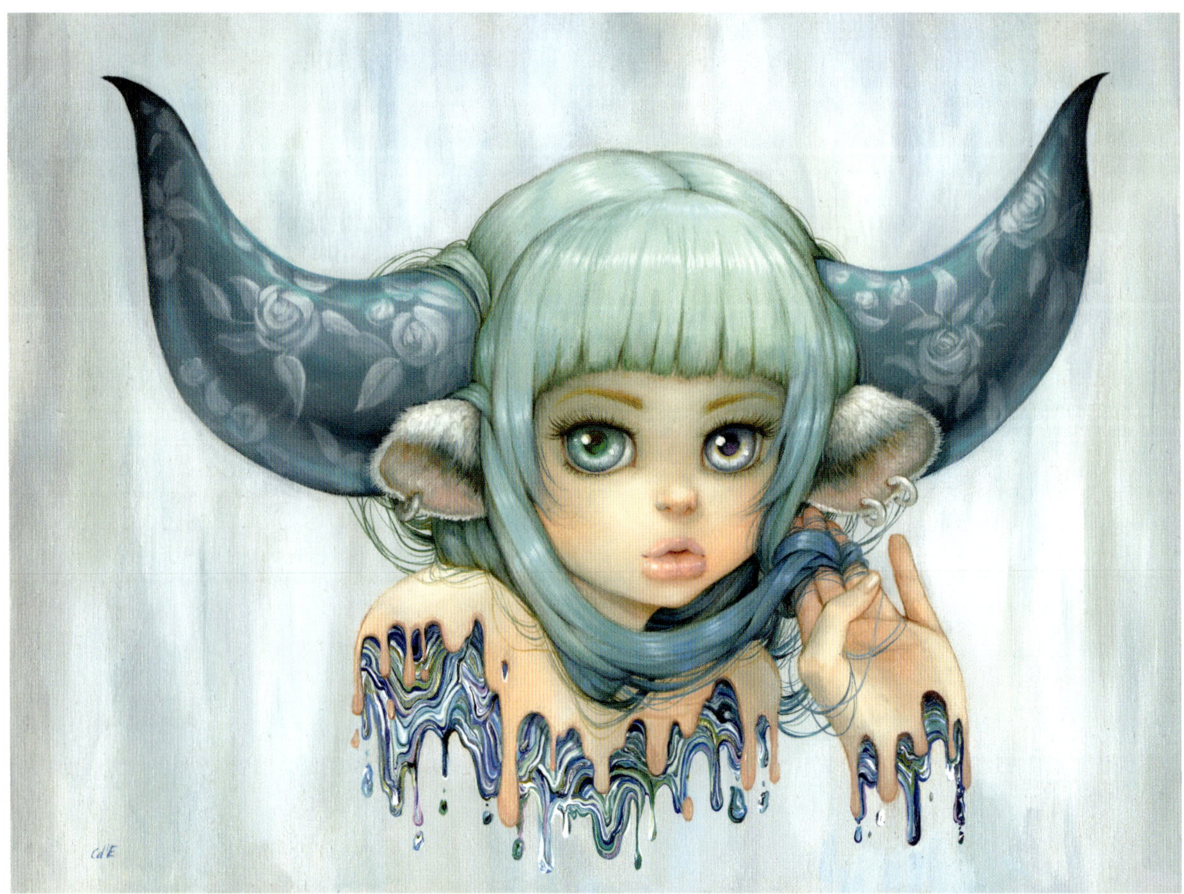

Taurus | 12" X 16" | OIL | 2019

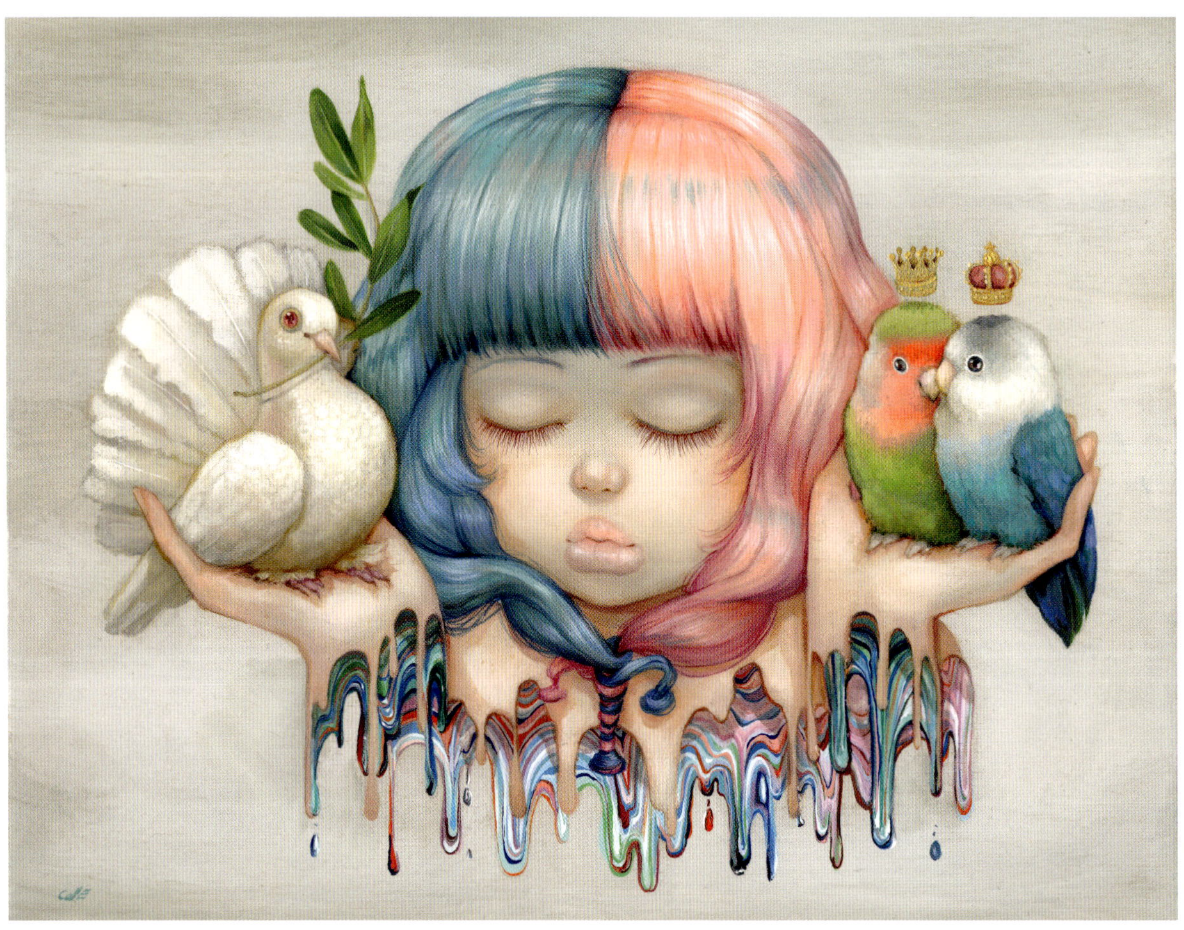

Libra | 11" X 14" | OIL | 2019

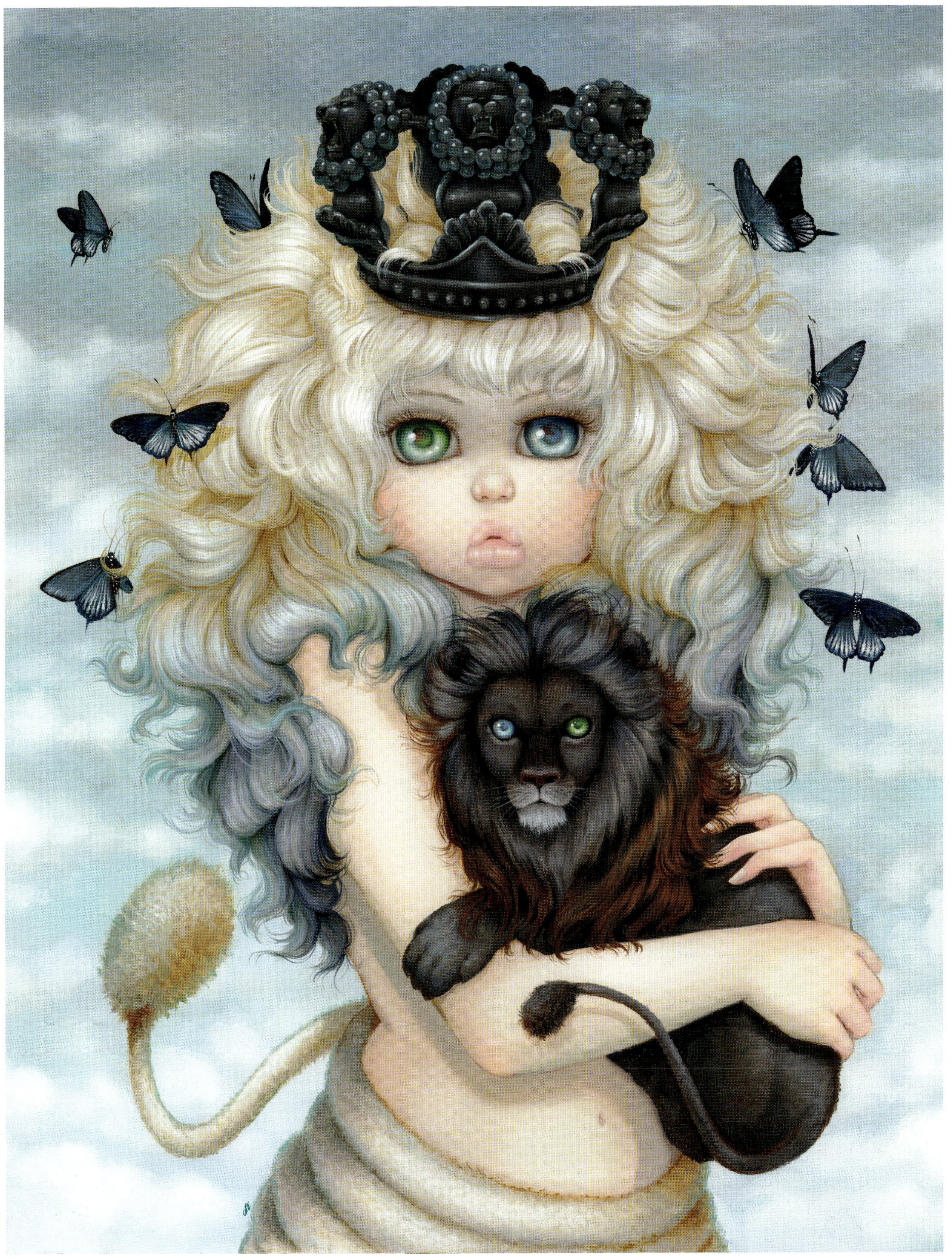

Leo | 20" X 24" | OIL | 2019

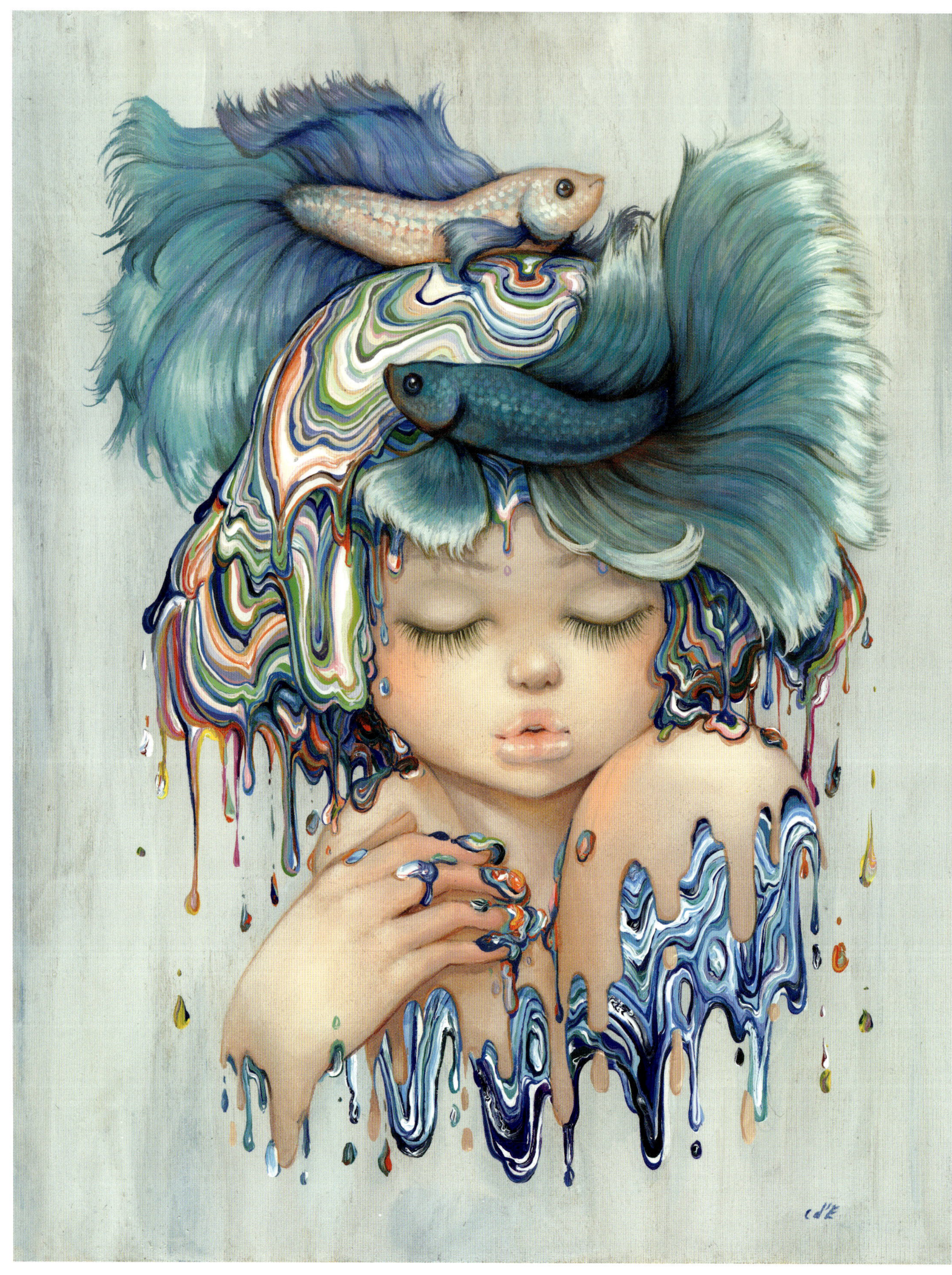

Pisces | 11" X 14" | OIL | 2019

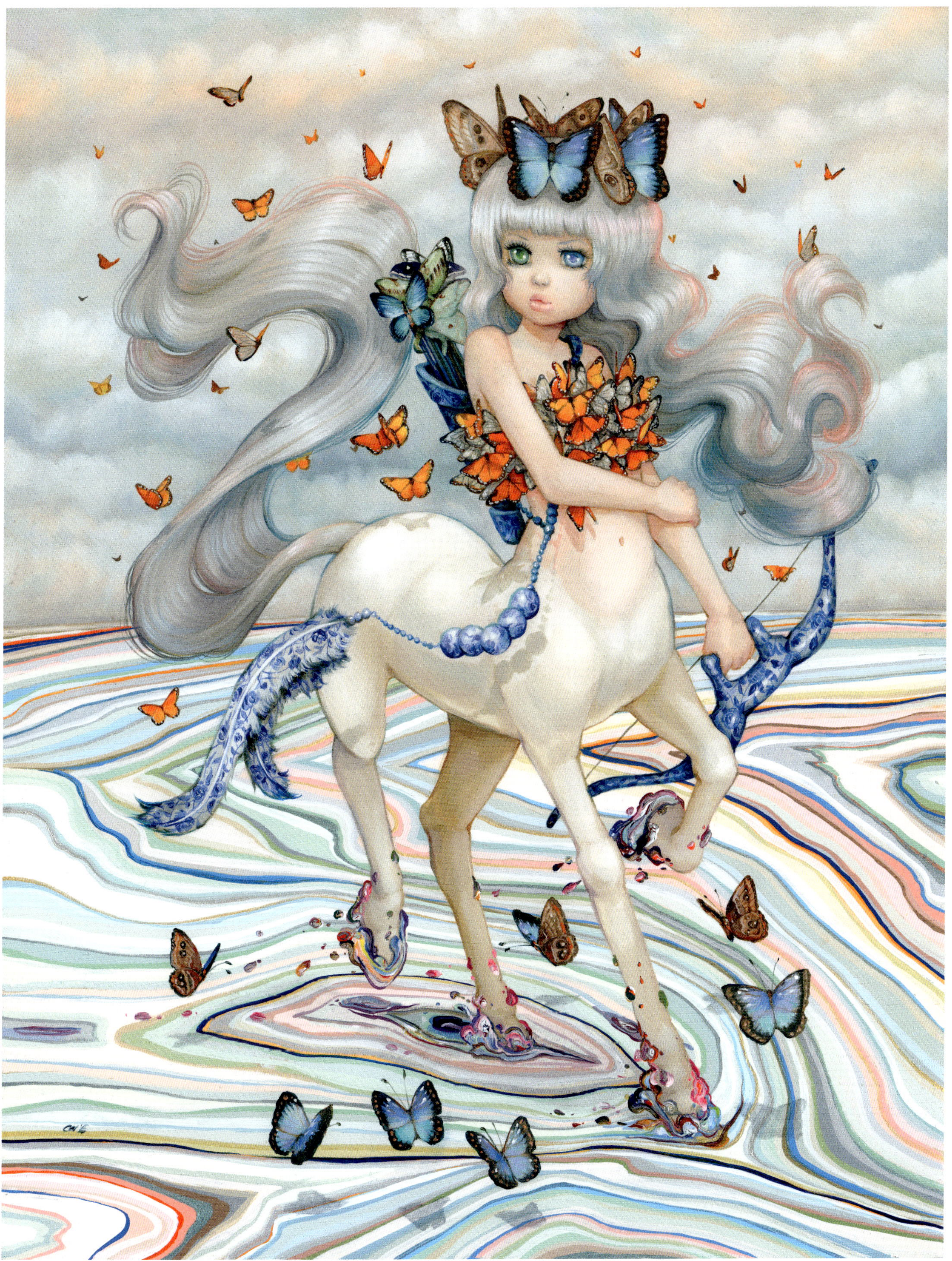

Sagittarius | 14" X 18" | OIL | 2019

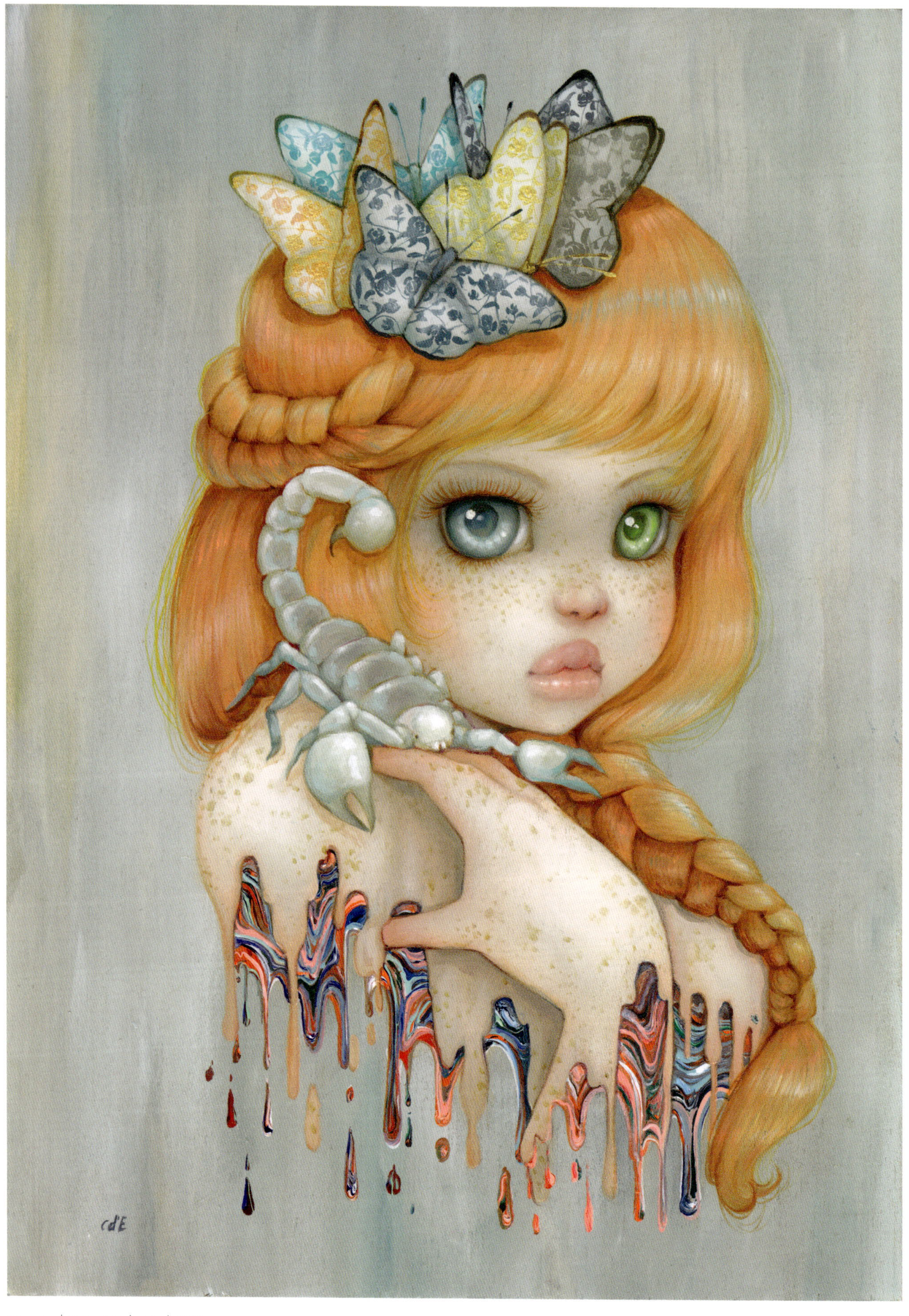

Scorpio | 10" X 14" | OIL | 2019

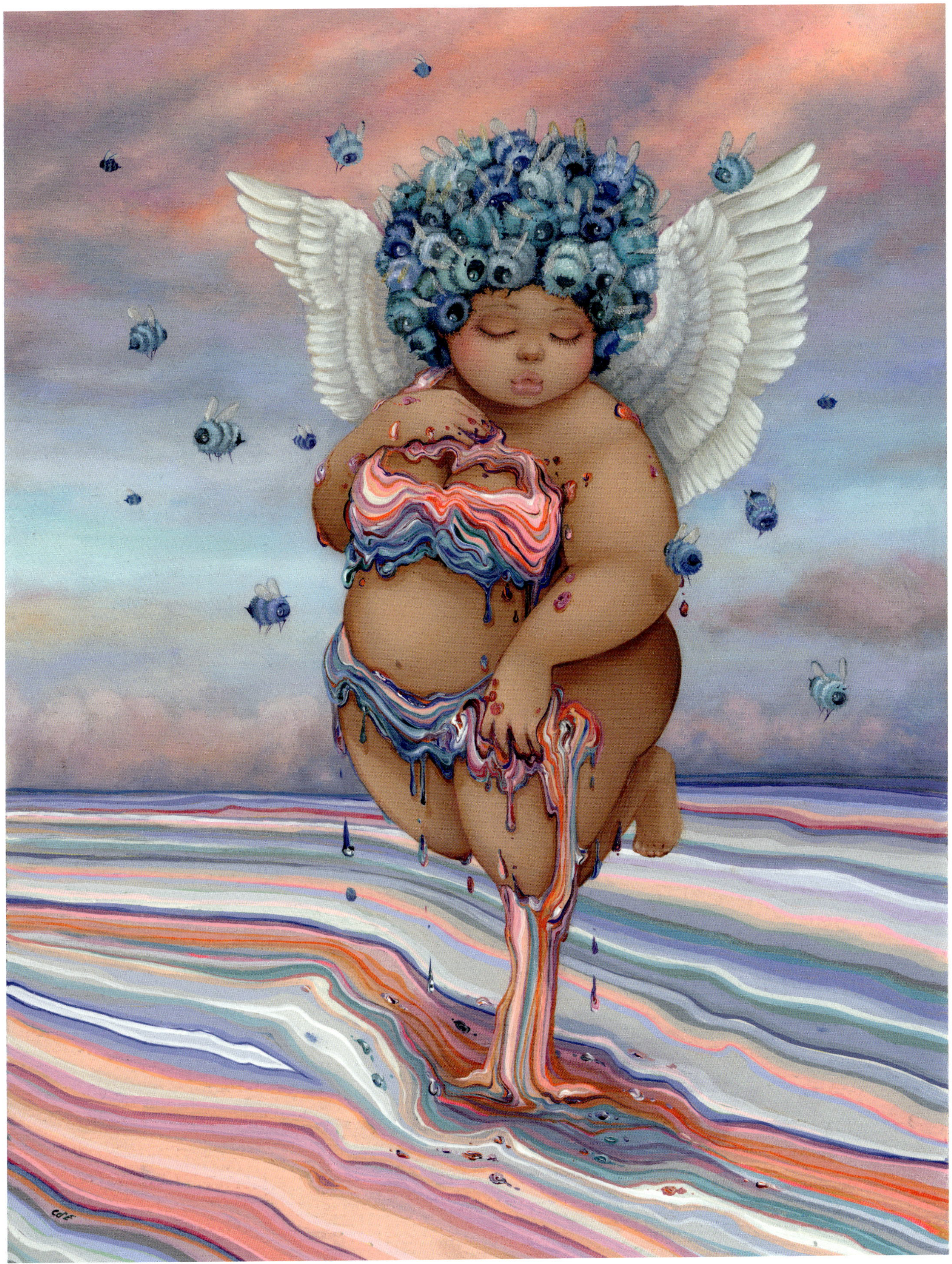

Virgo | 12" X 16" | OIL | 2019

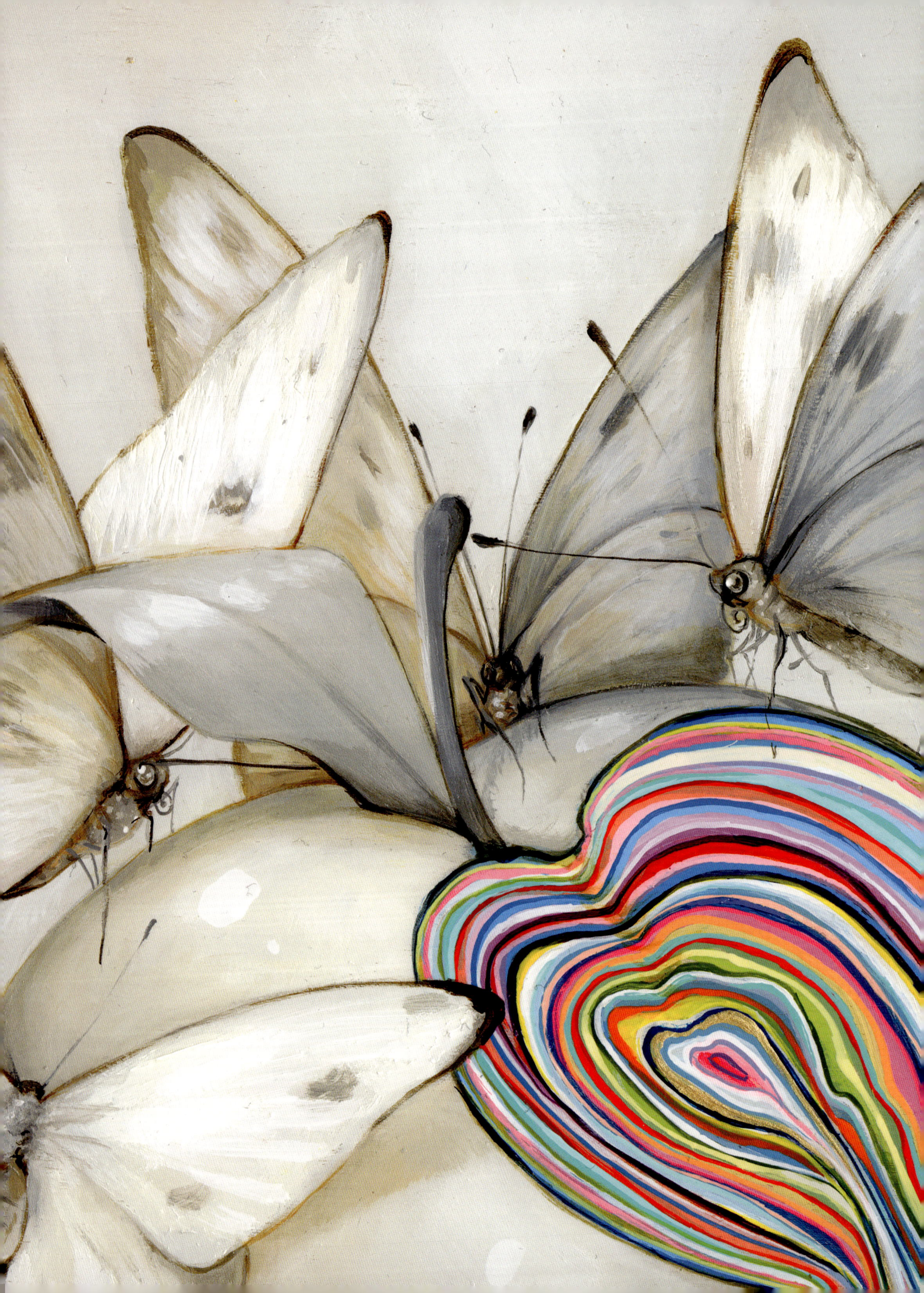

CAPTIVATING CHROMA

Facing page:
Centrum | 16" X 20" | OIL | 2020

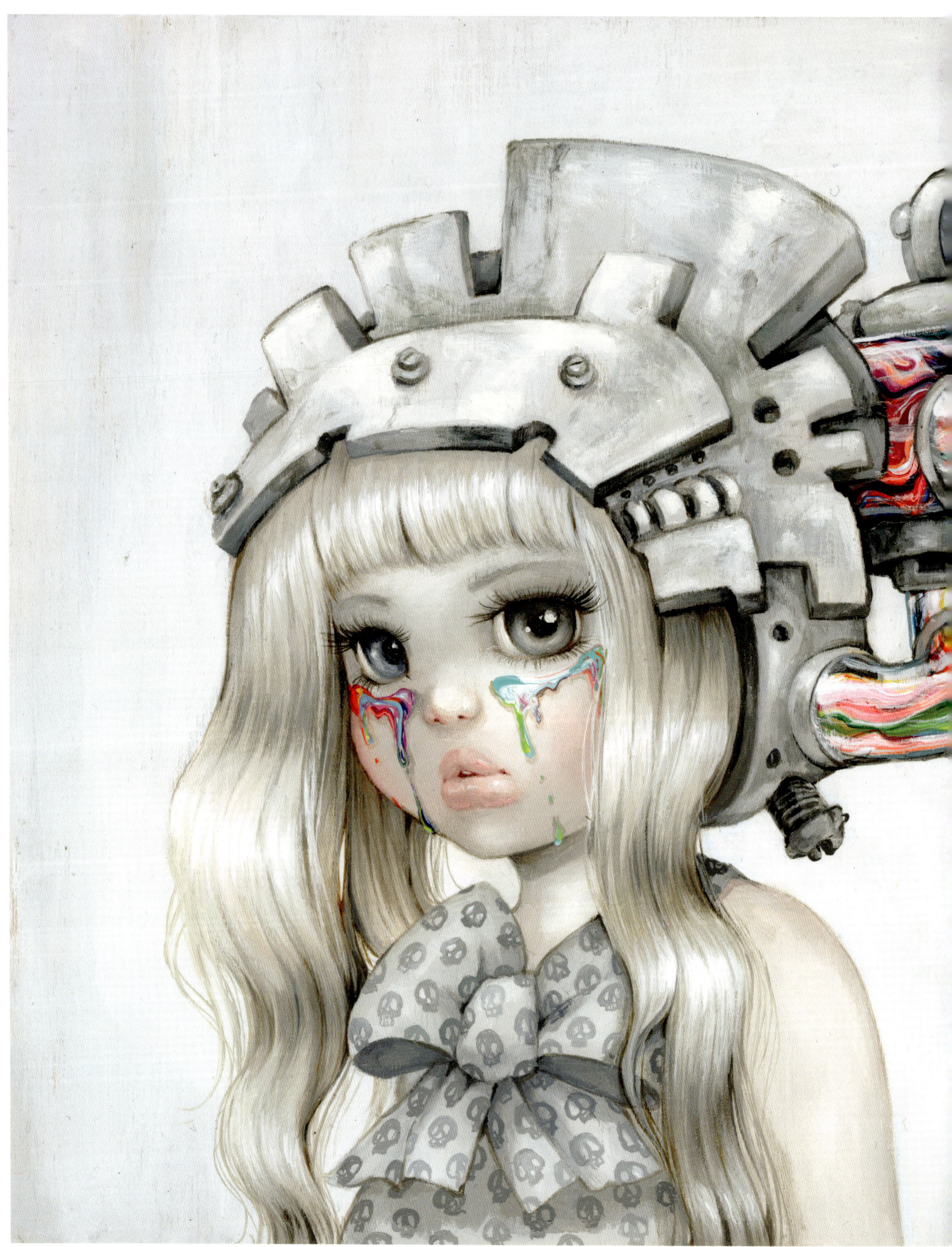

Bellator | 11" X 14" | OIL | 2020

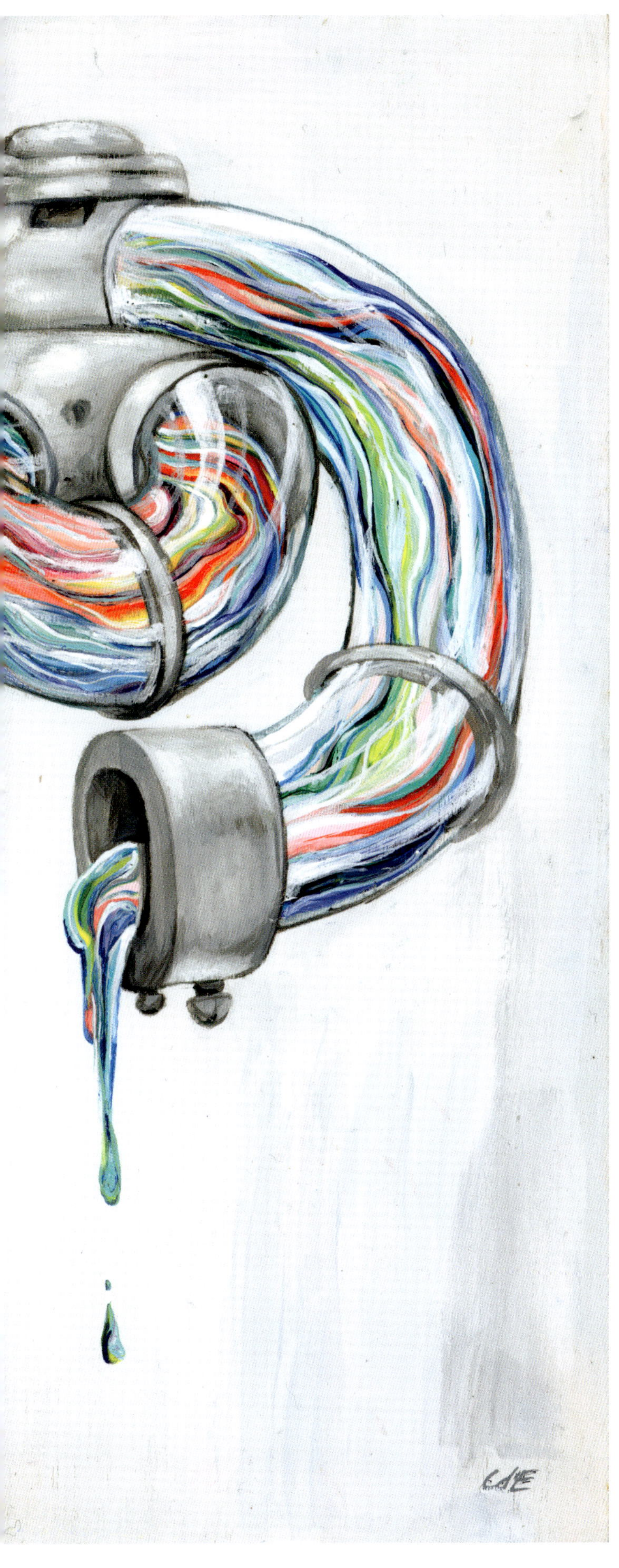

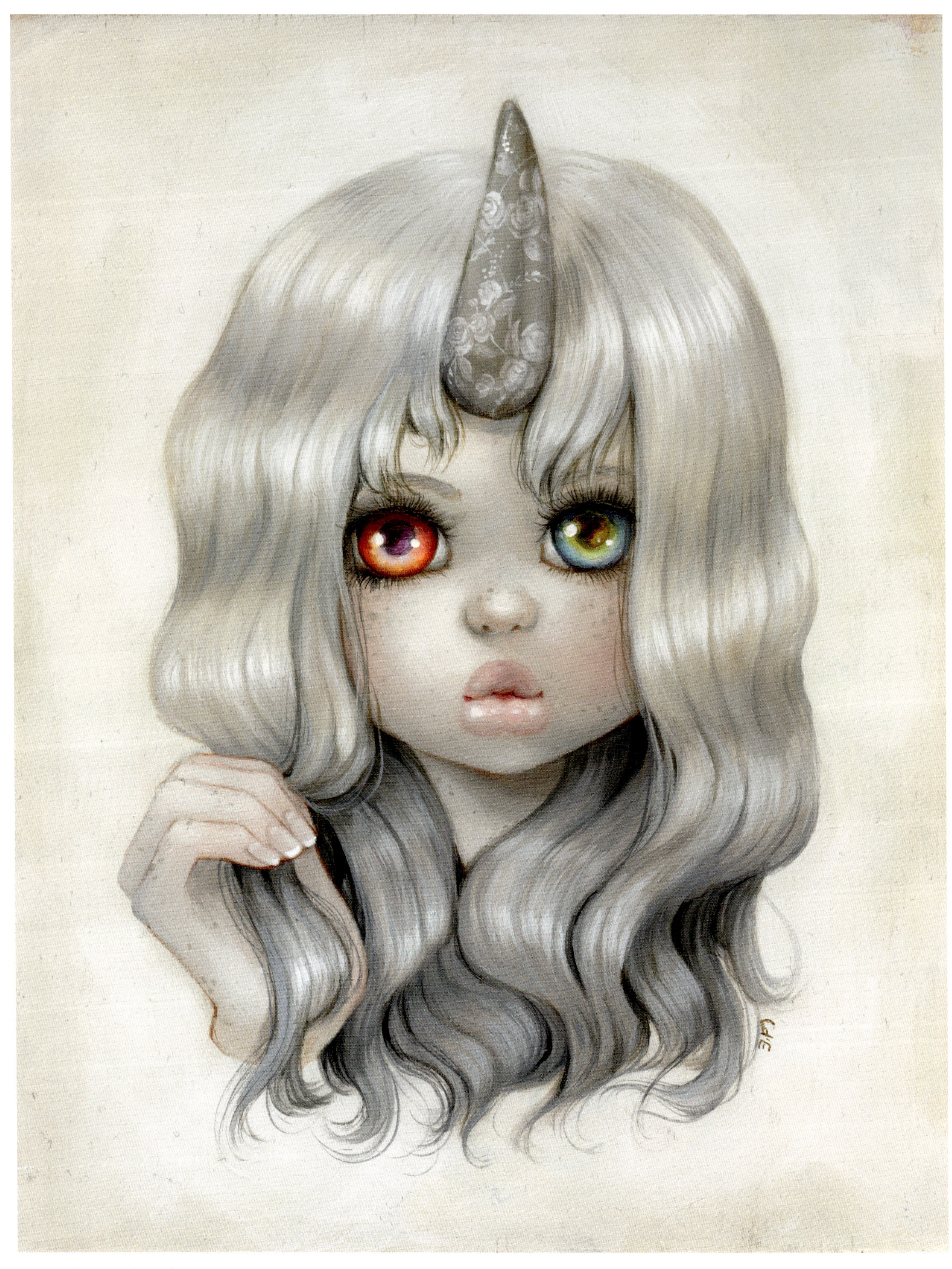

Chromia | 8" X 10" | OIL | 2020

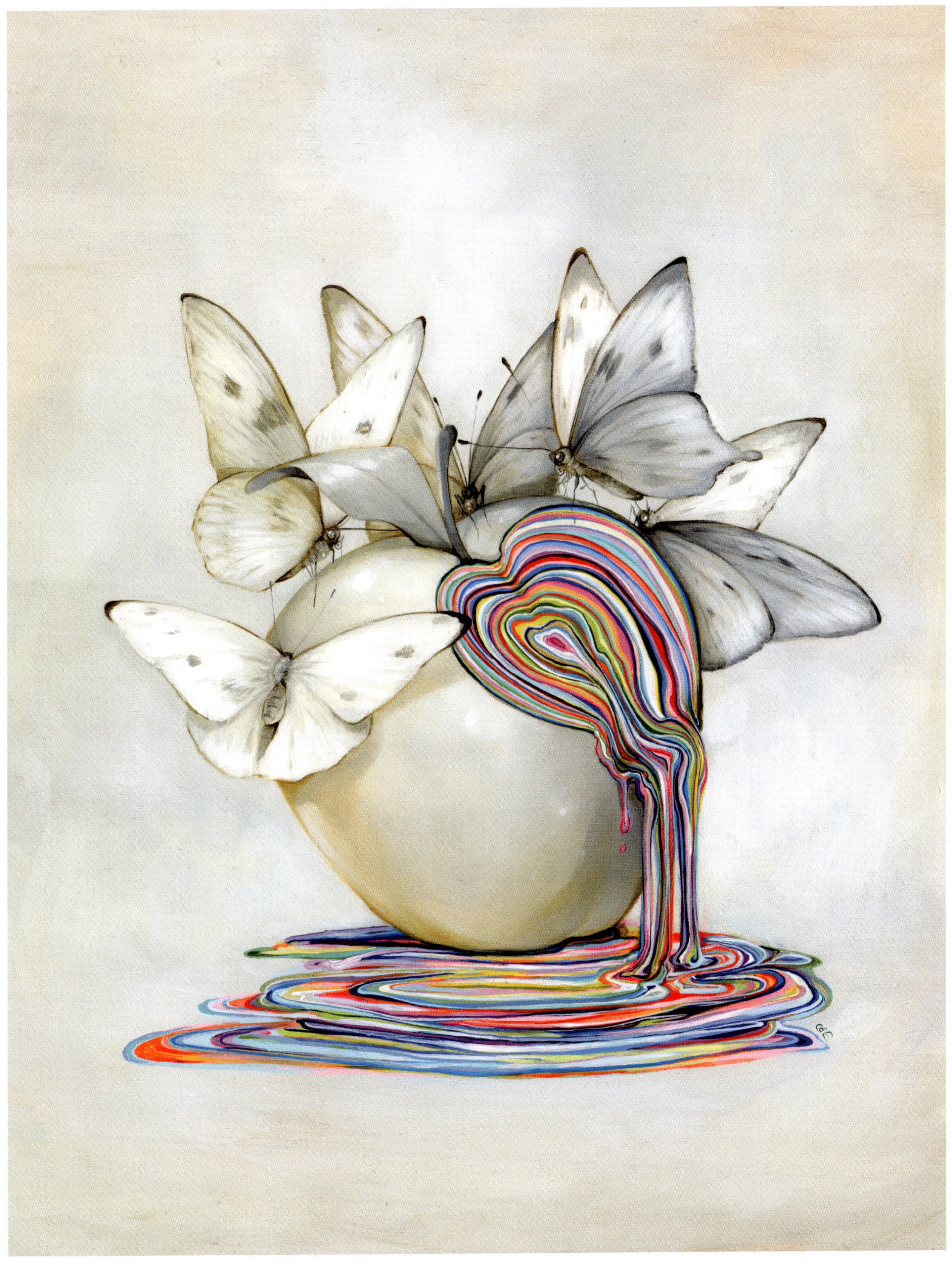

Centrum | 16" X 20" | OIL | 2020

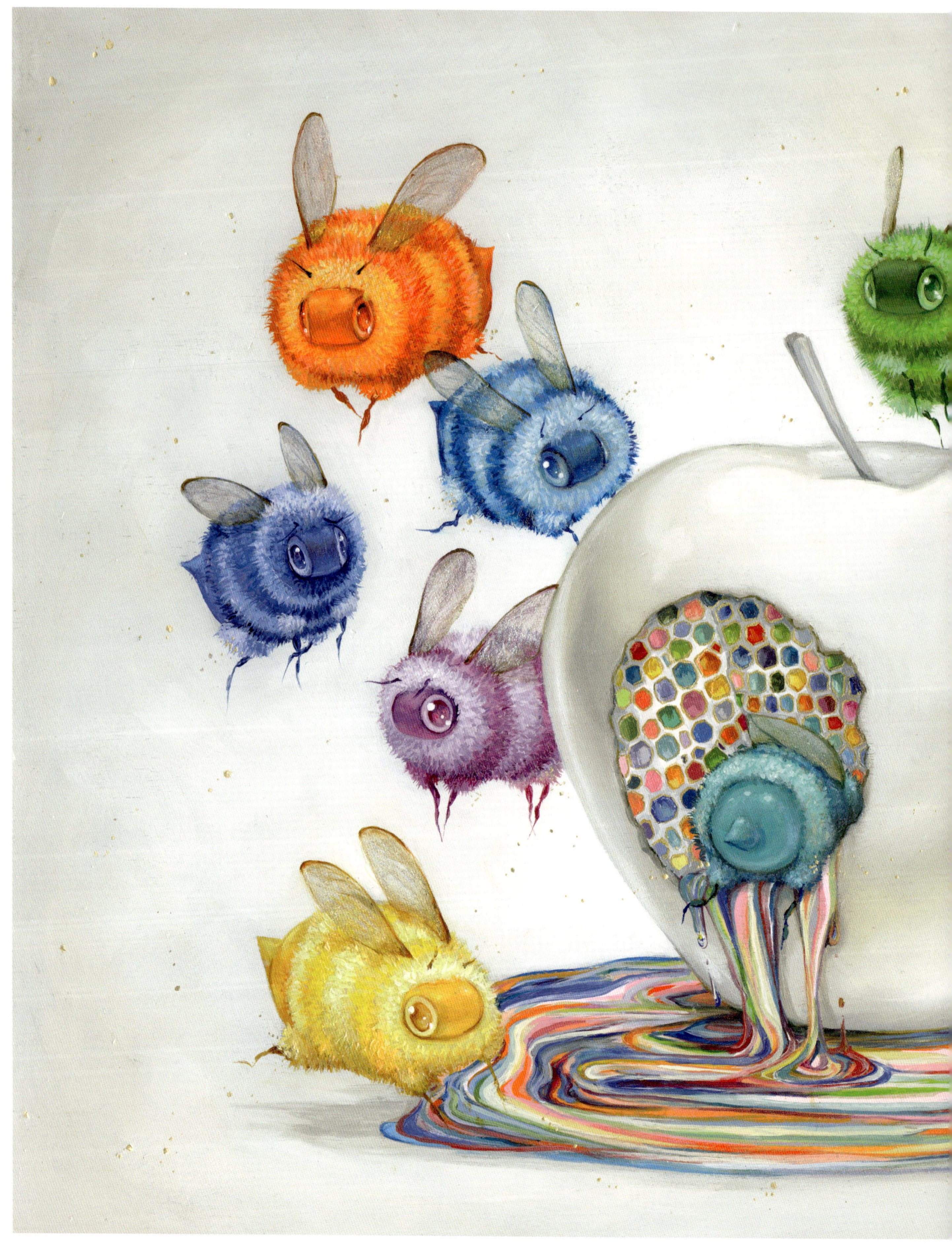

Fuzz Mellis | 16" X 20" | OIL | 2020

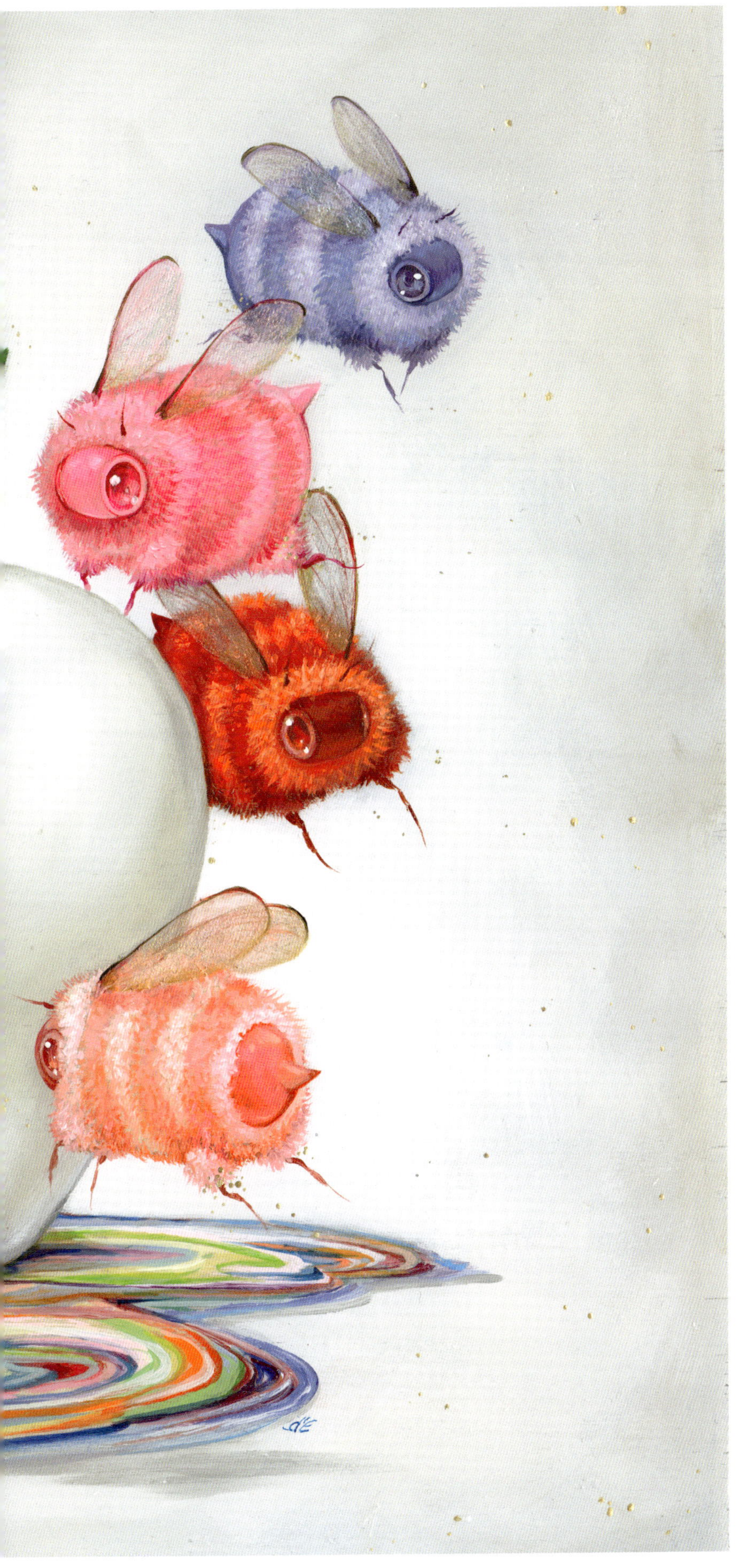

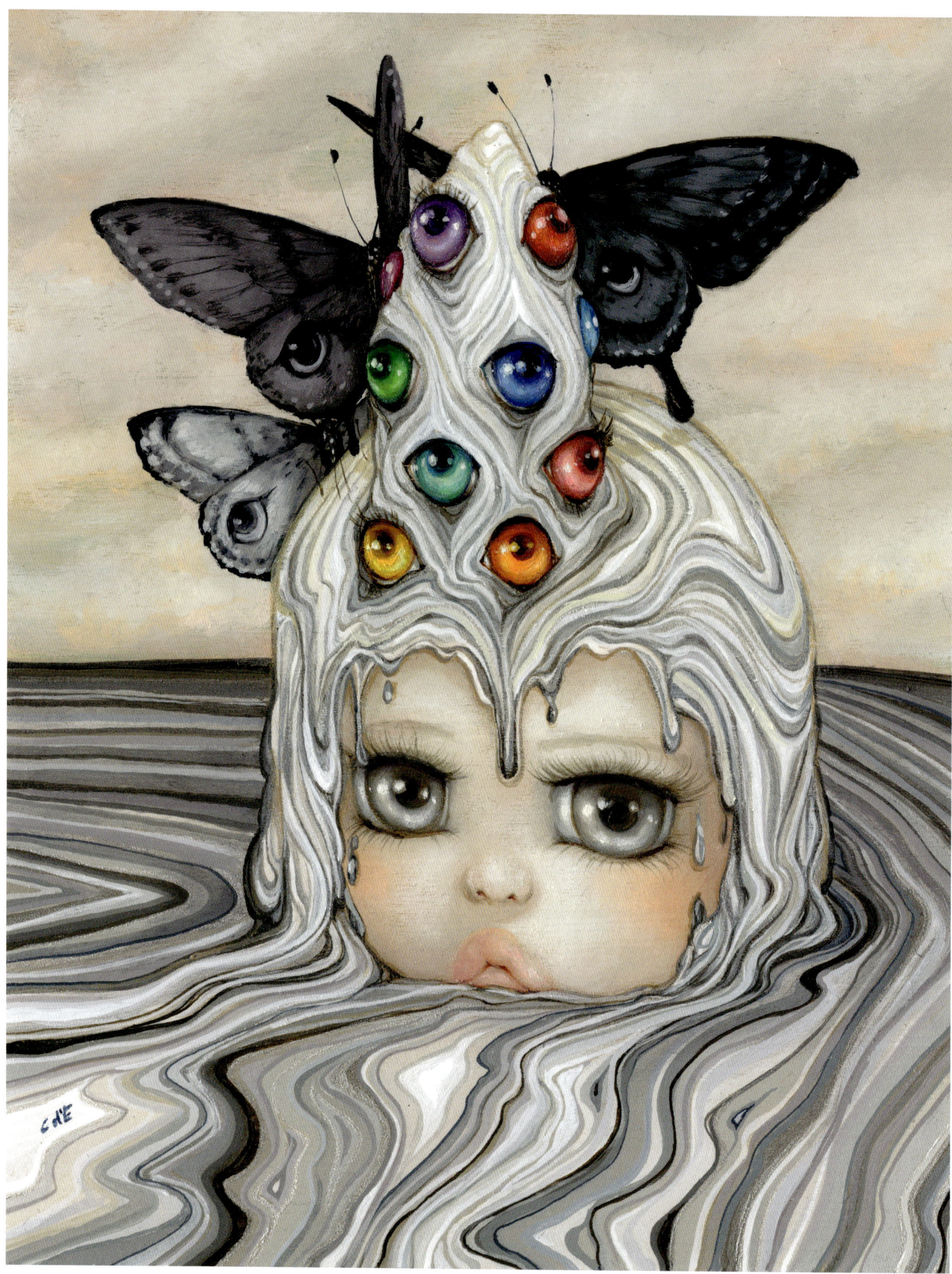

Joella | 8" X 10" | OIL | 2017

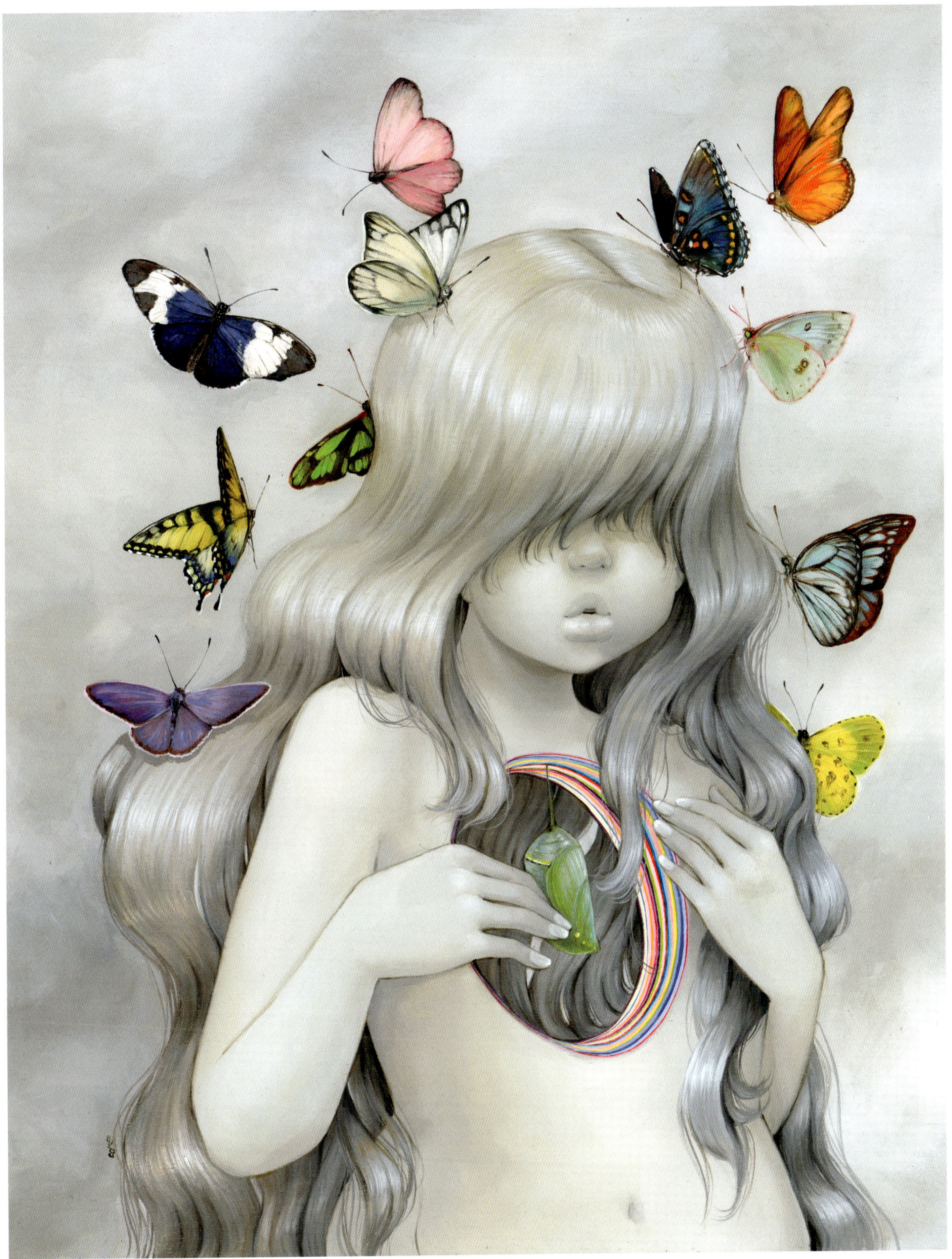

Eros | 20" X 24" | OIL | 2020

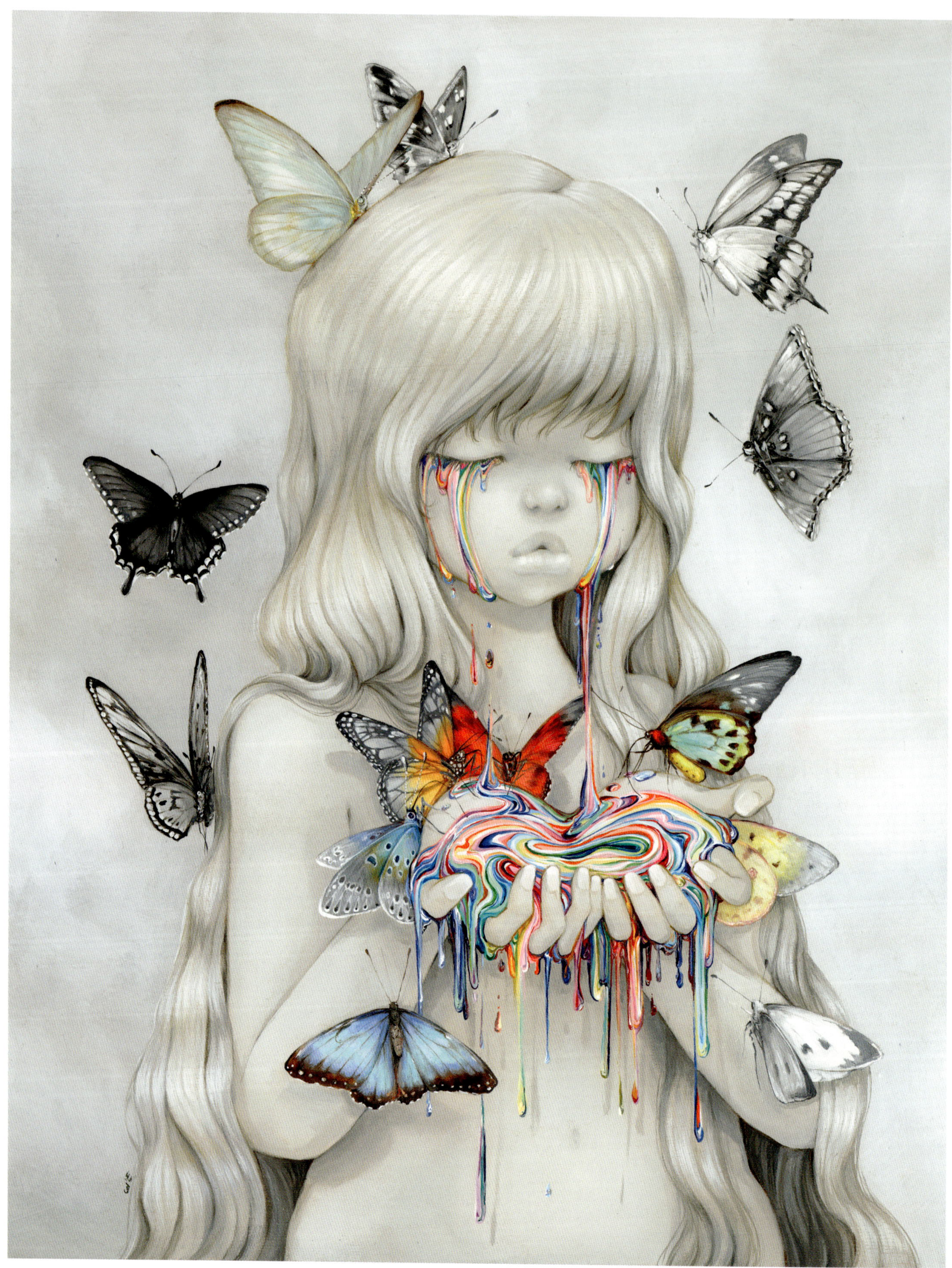

Vitae Arcu | 20" X 24" | OIL | 2020

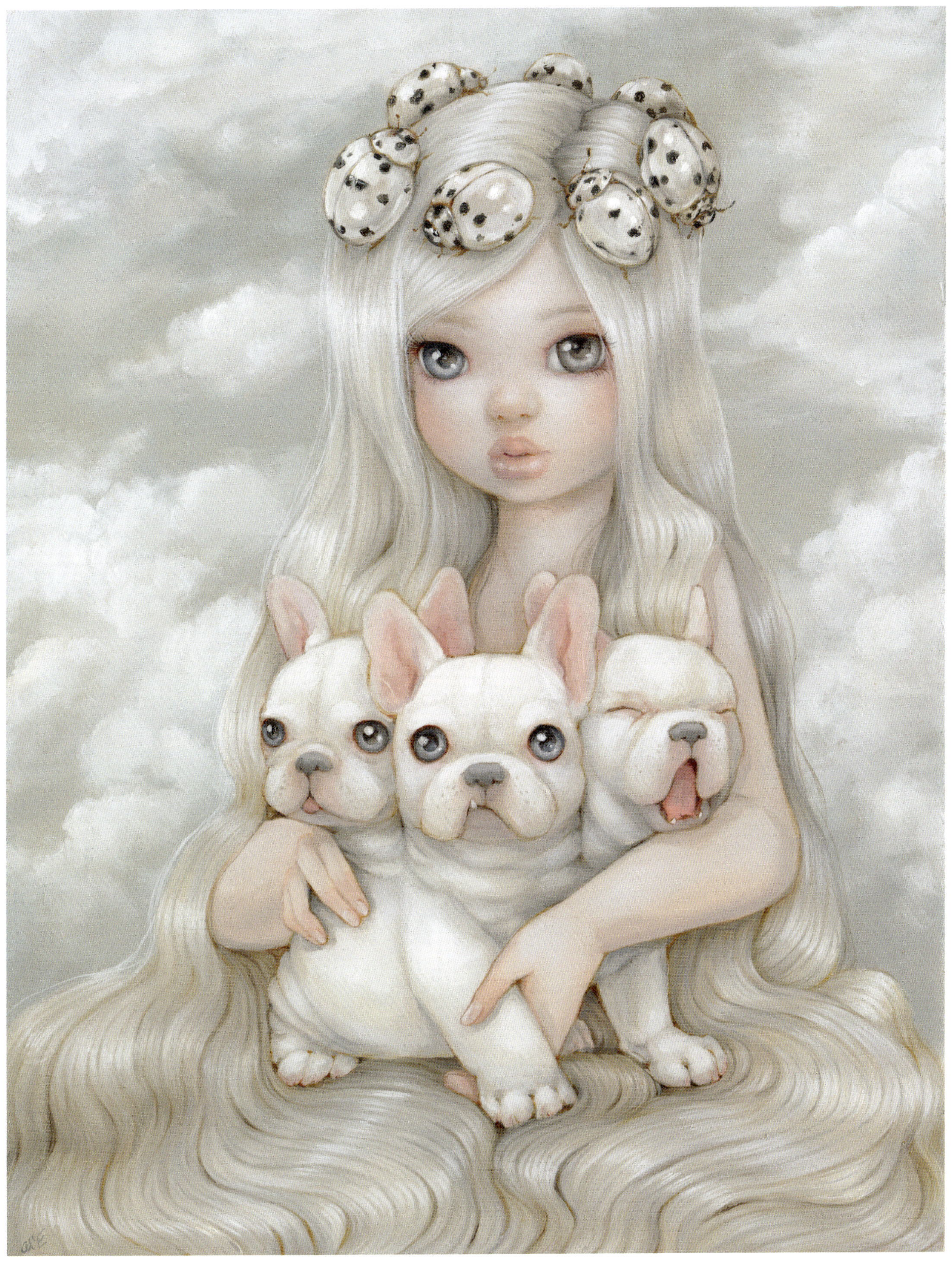

The Overworld and the Underbite | 12" X 16" | OIL | 2021

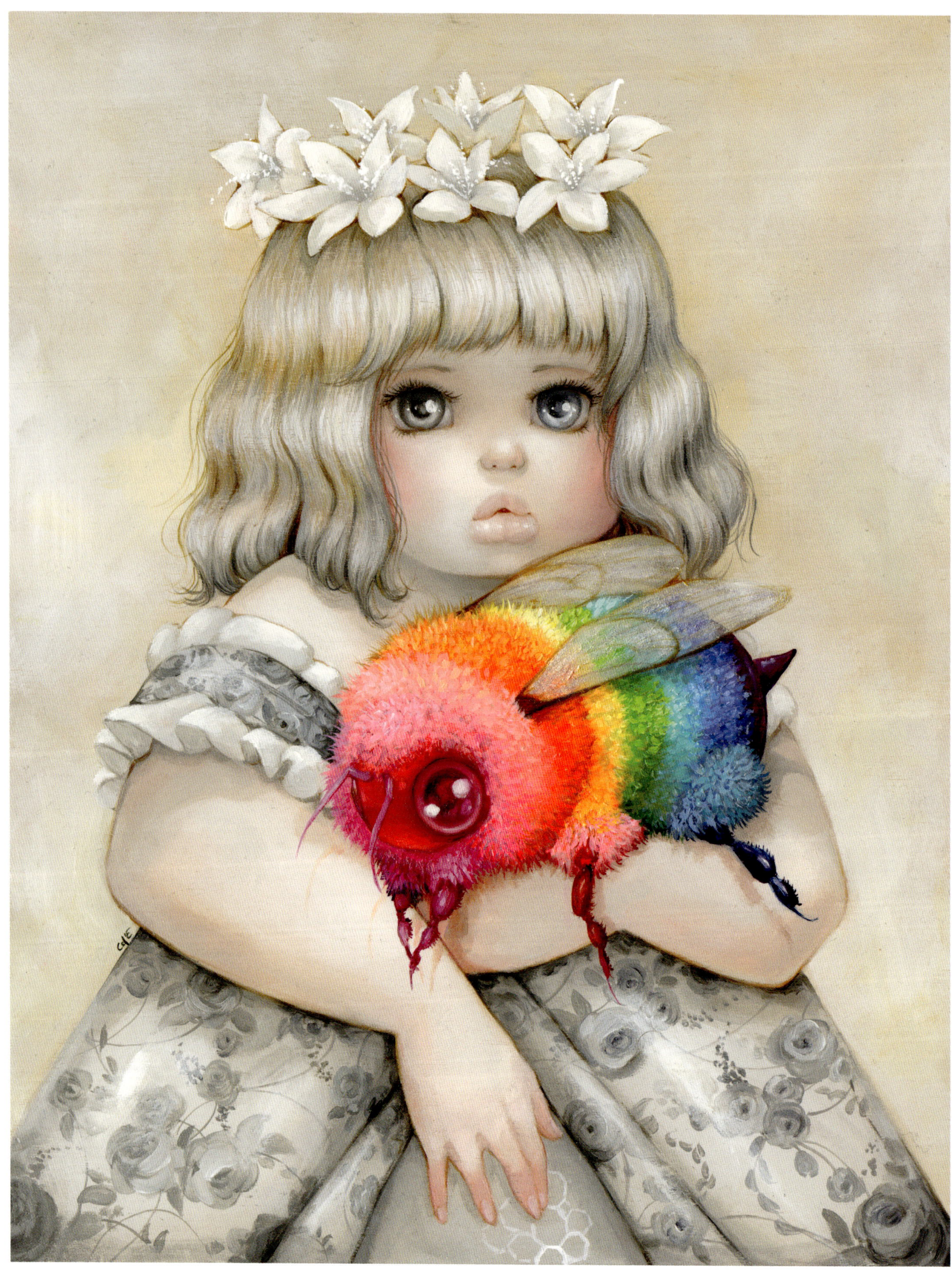

Bombus | 11" X 14" | OIL | 2020

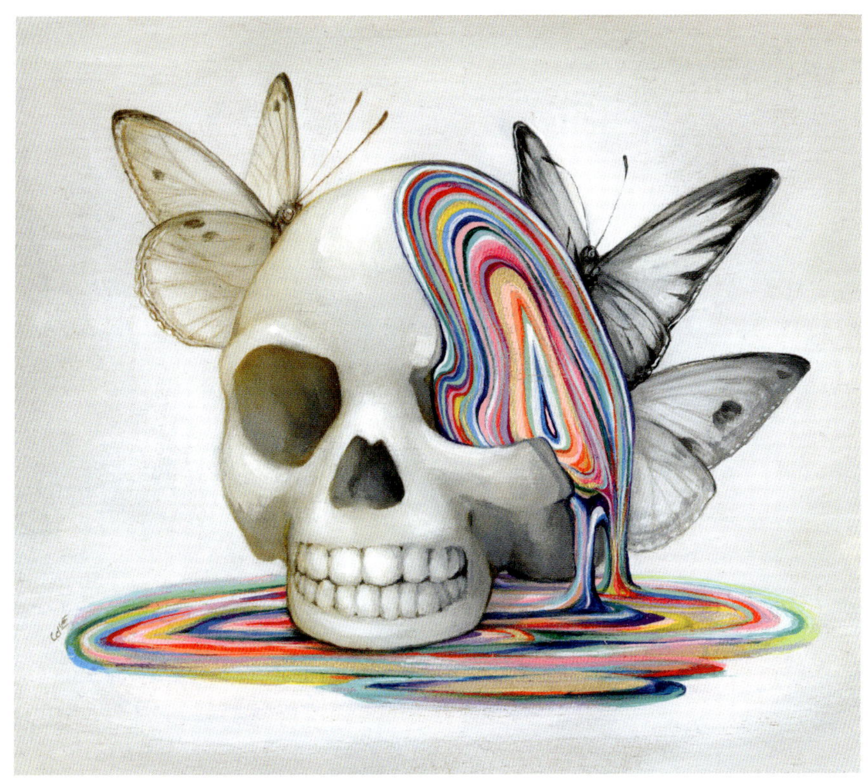

Thanatos | 8" X 10" | OIL | 2020

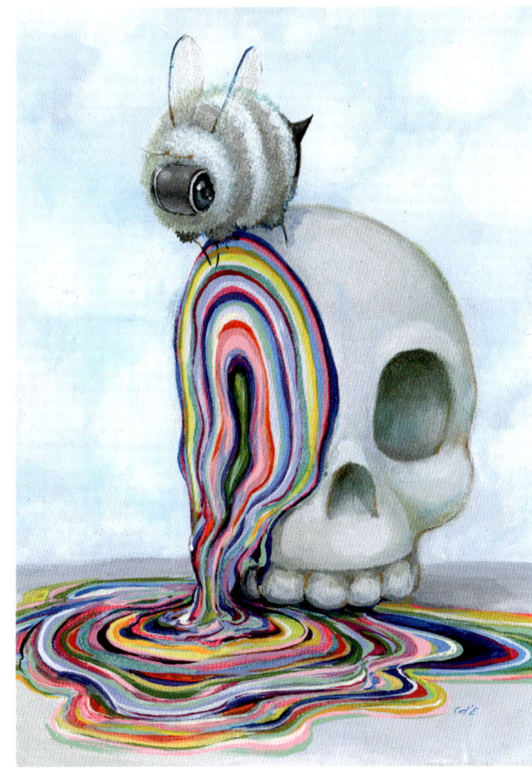

Mortum | 5" X 7" | OIL and ACRYLIC | 2020

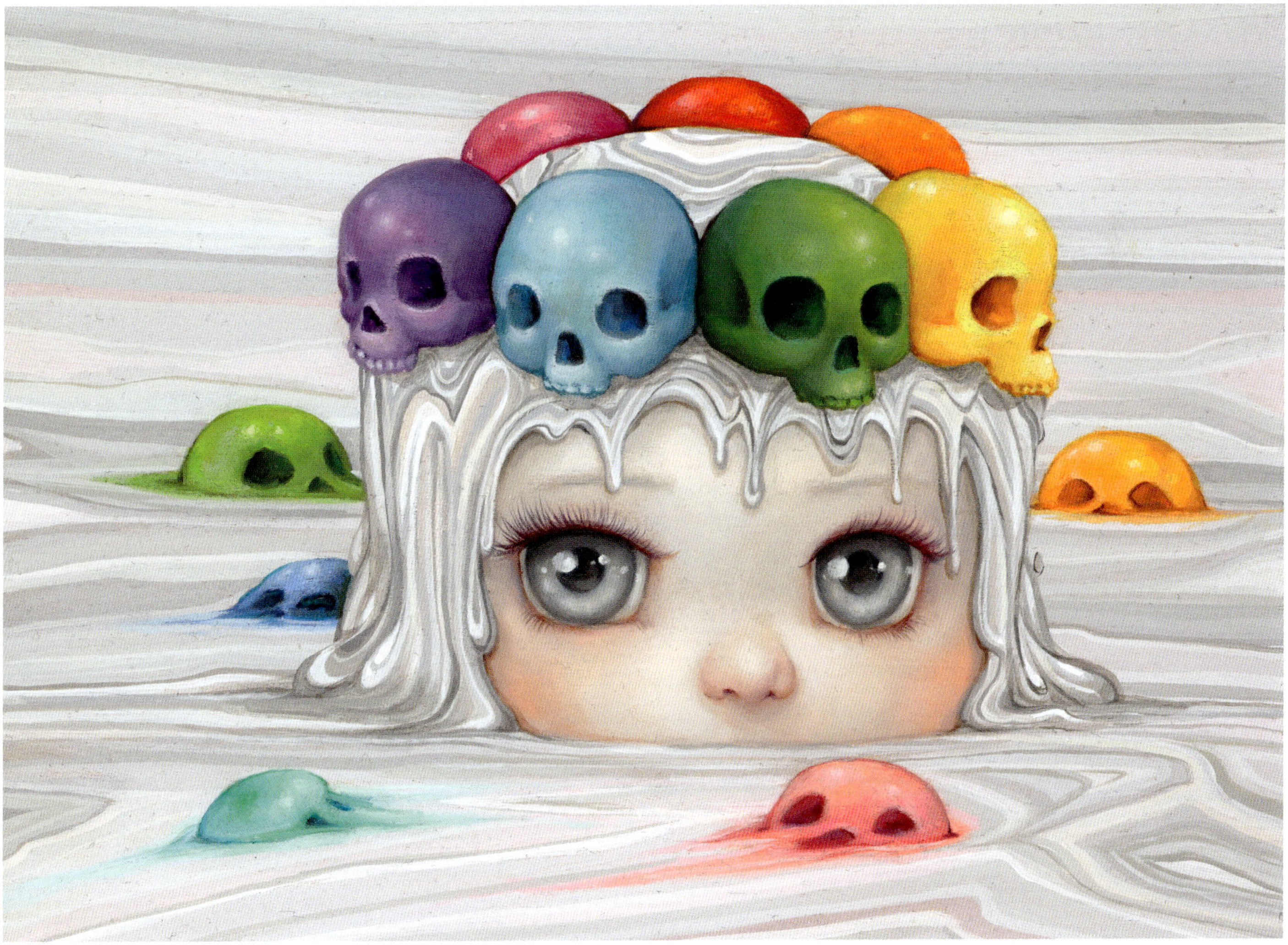

Capuchina | 8" X 10" | OIL | 2017

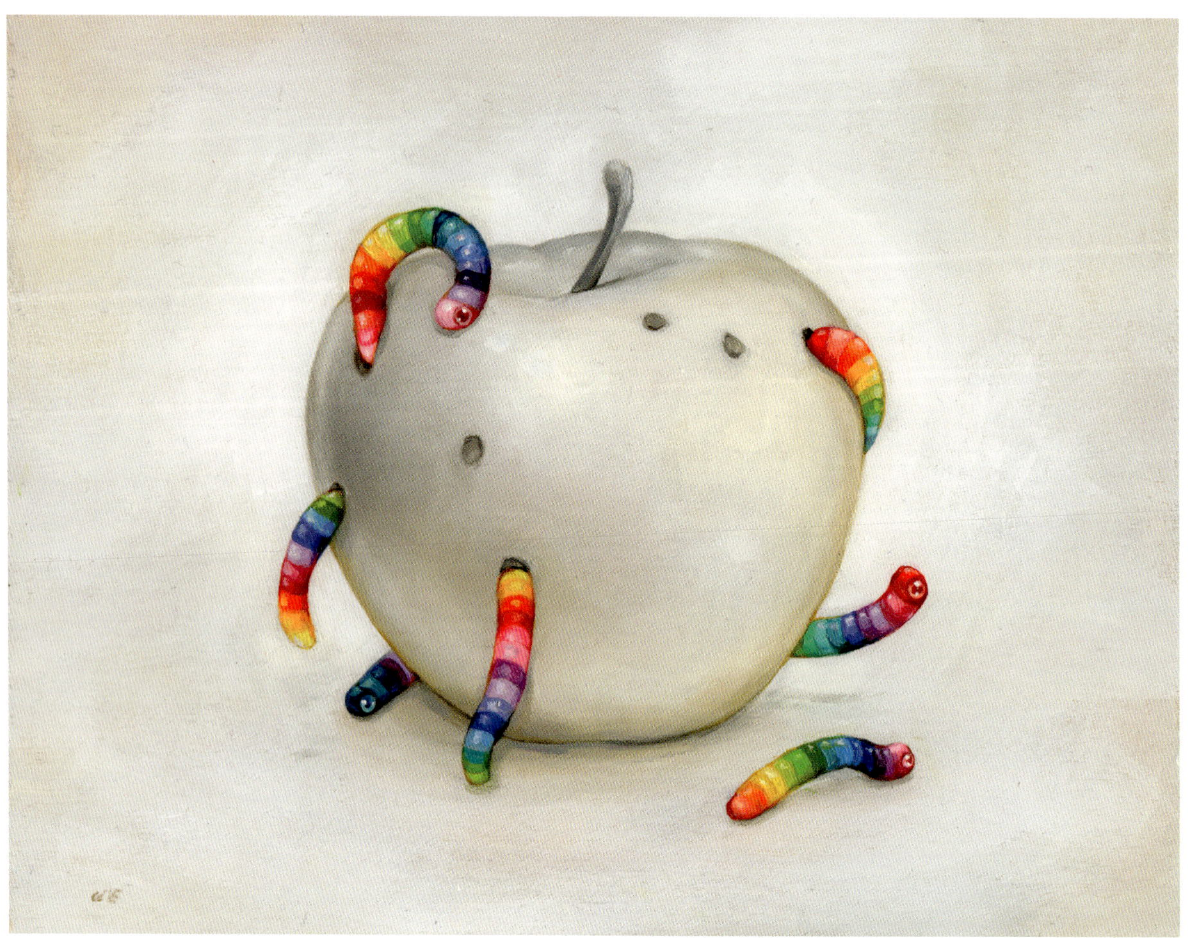

Vermis | 8" X 10" | OIL | 2020

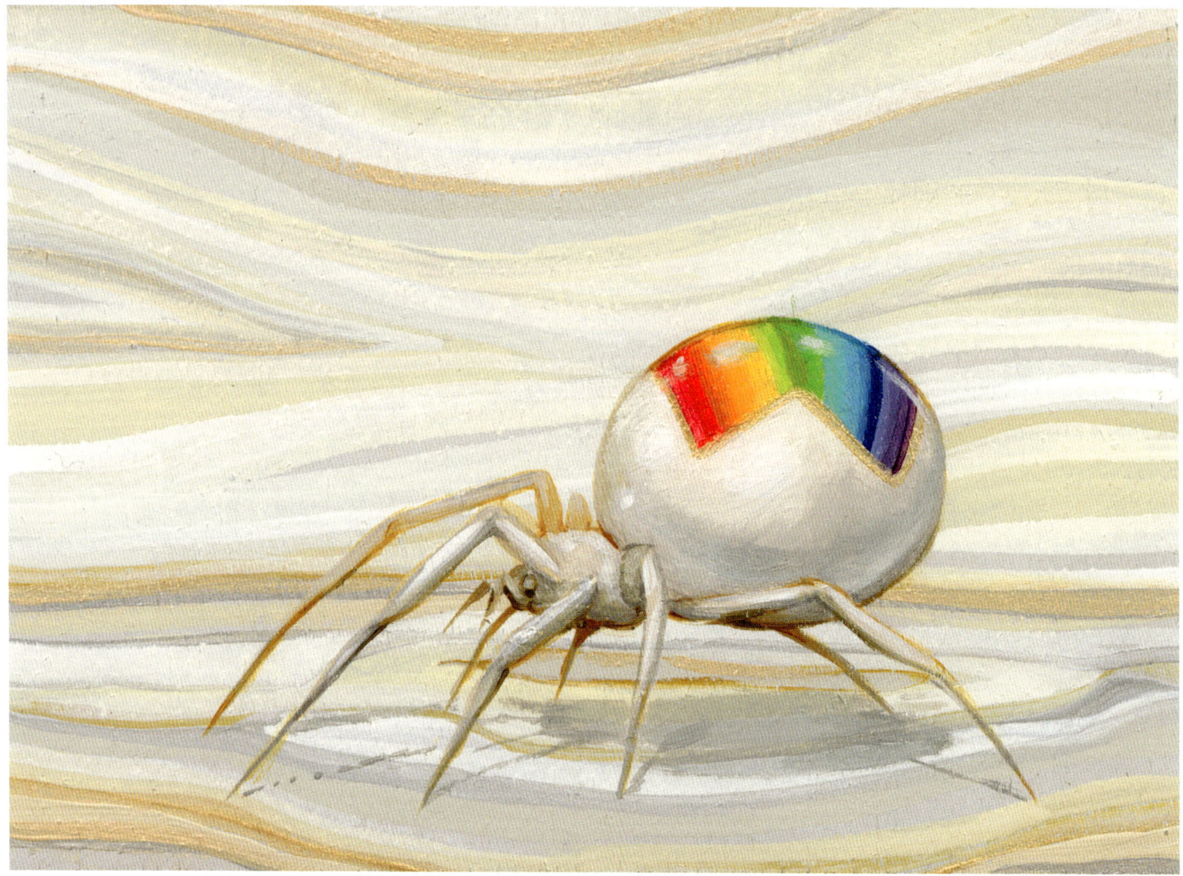

Aranea | 5" X 7" | OIL and ACRYLIC | 2020

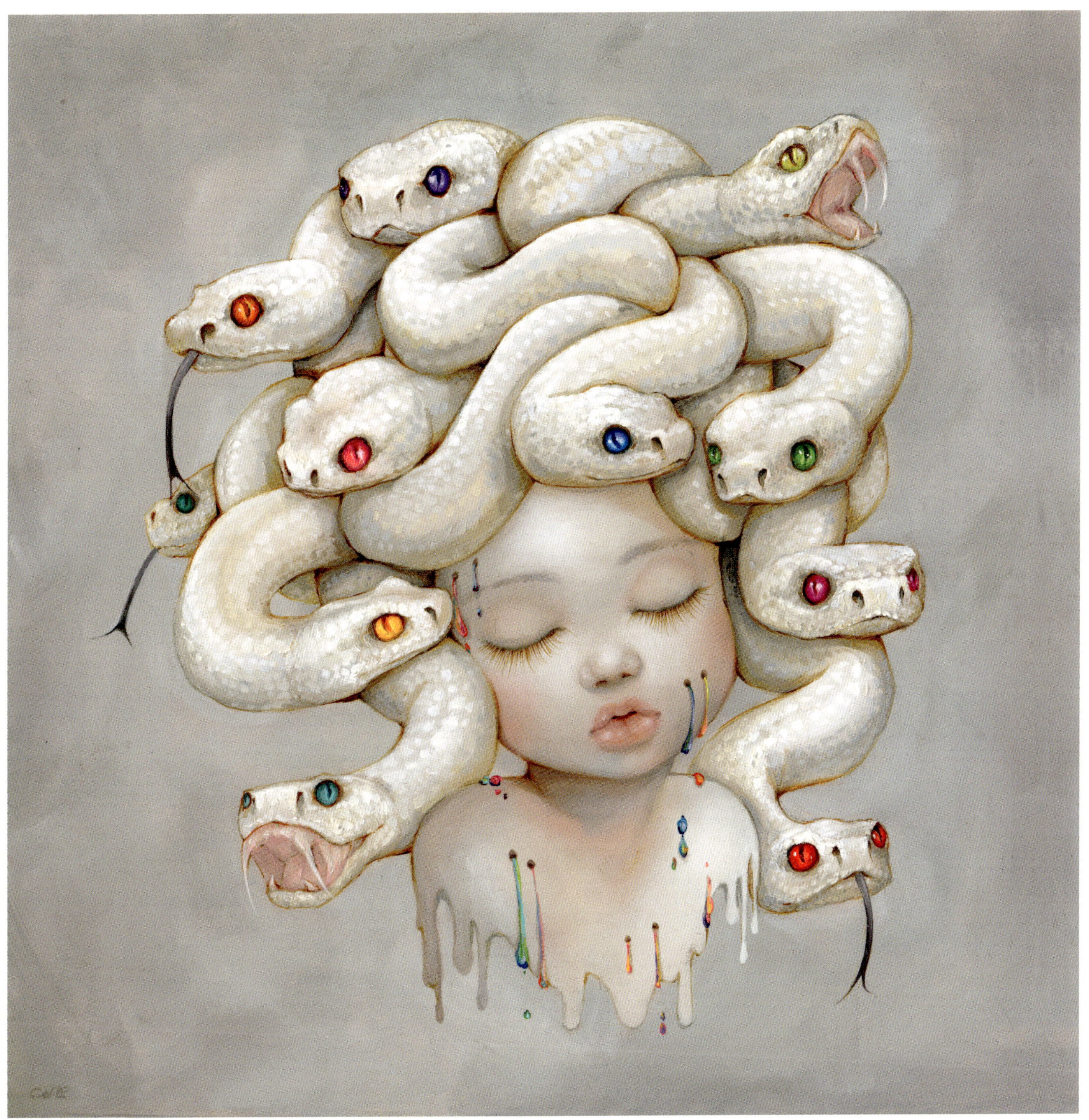

A Reflection of the Fates | 12" X 12" | OIL | 2021

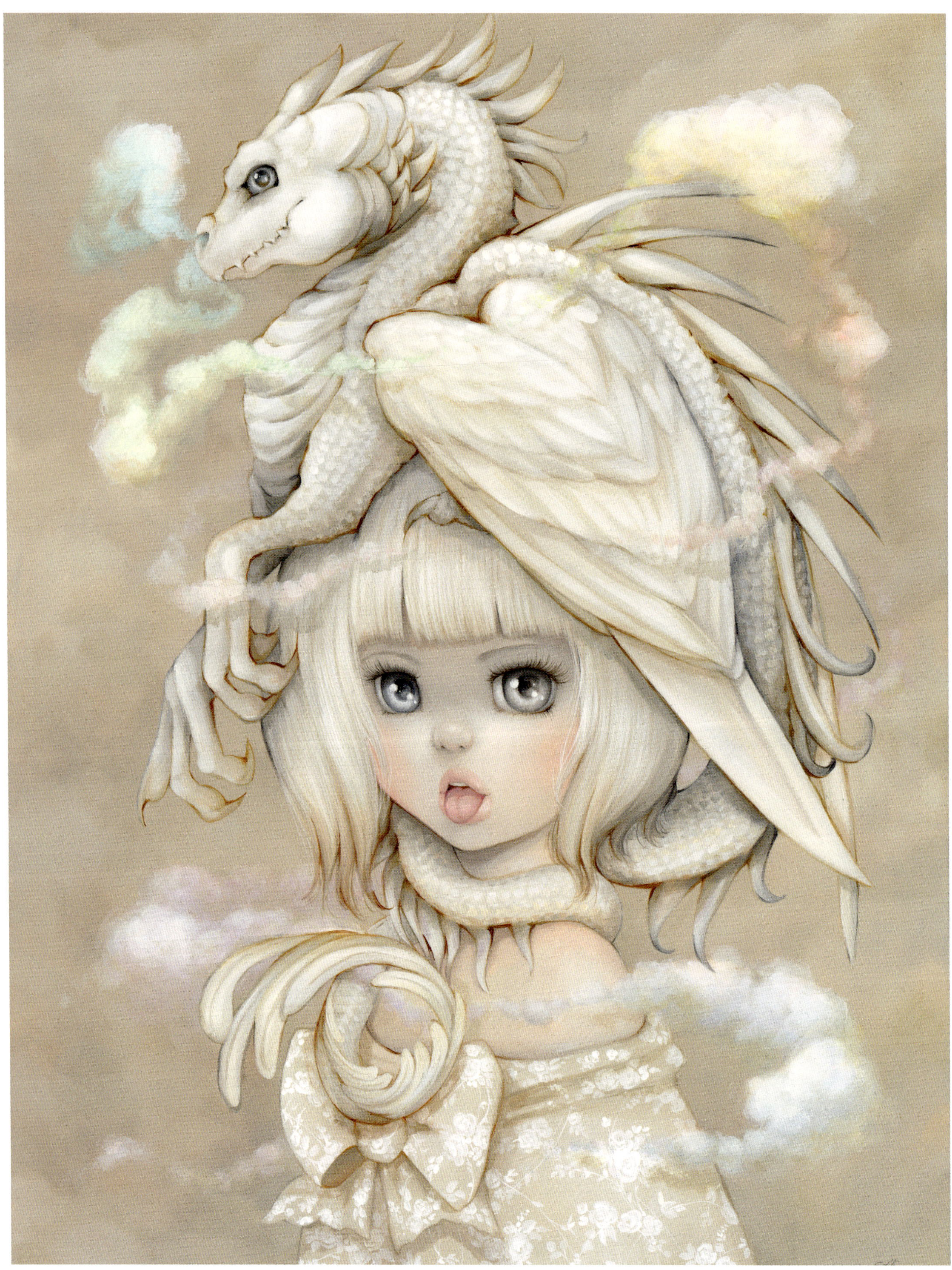

Viseria | 18" X 24" | OIL | 2020

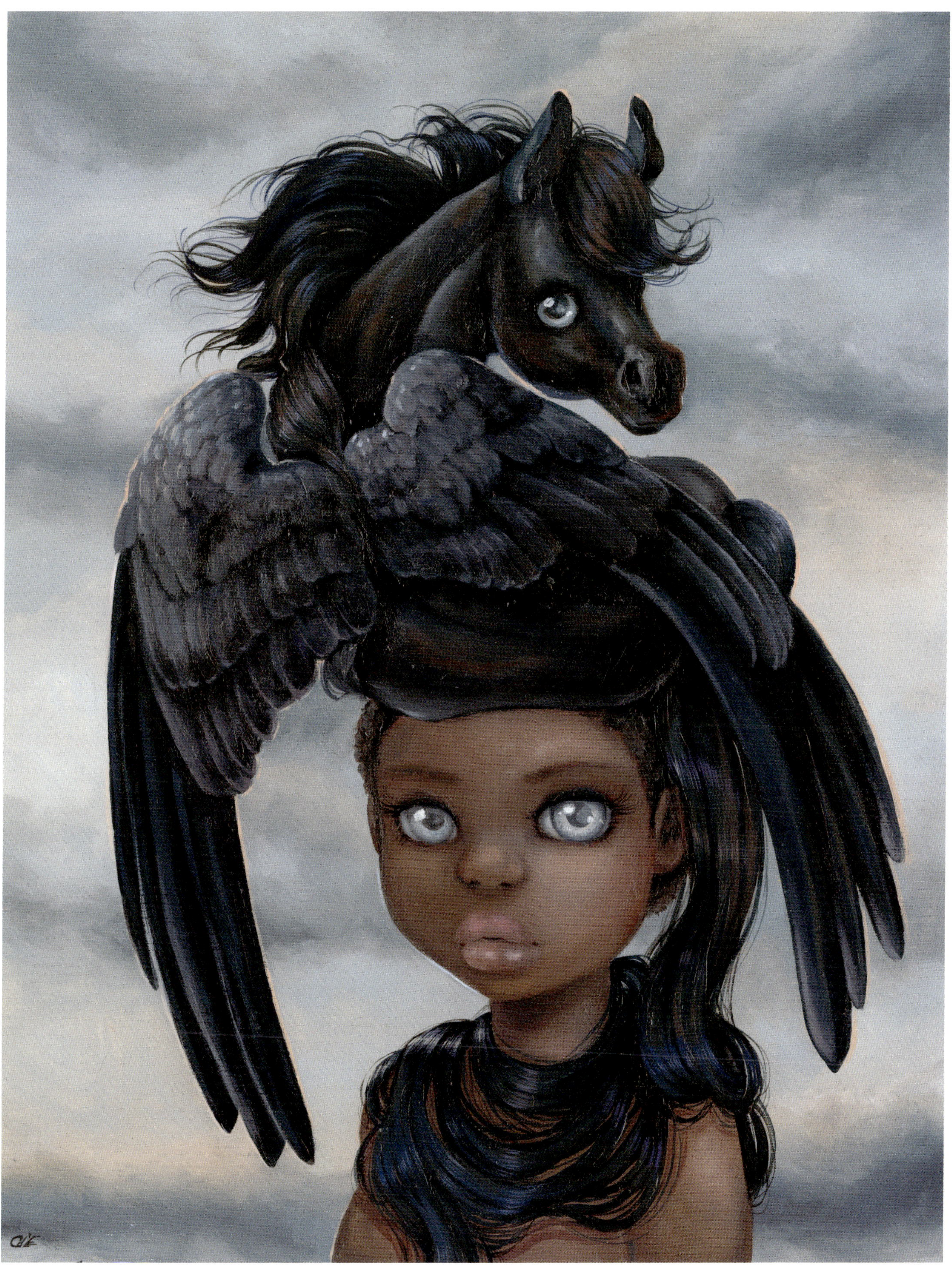

Light as a Feather Strong as a Stone | 11" X 14" | OIL | 2021

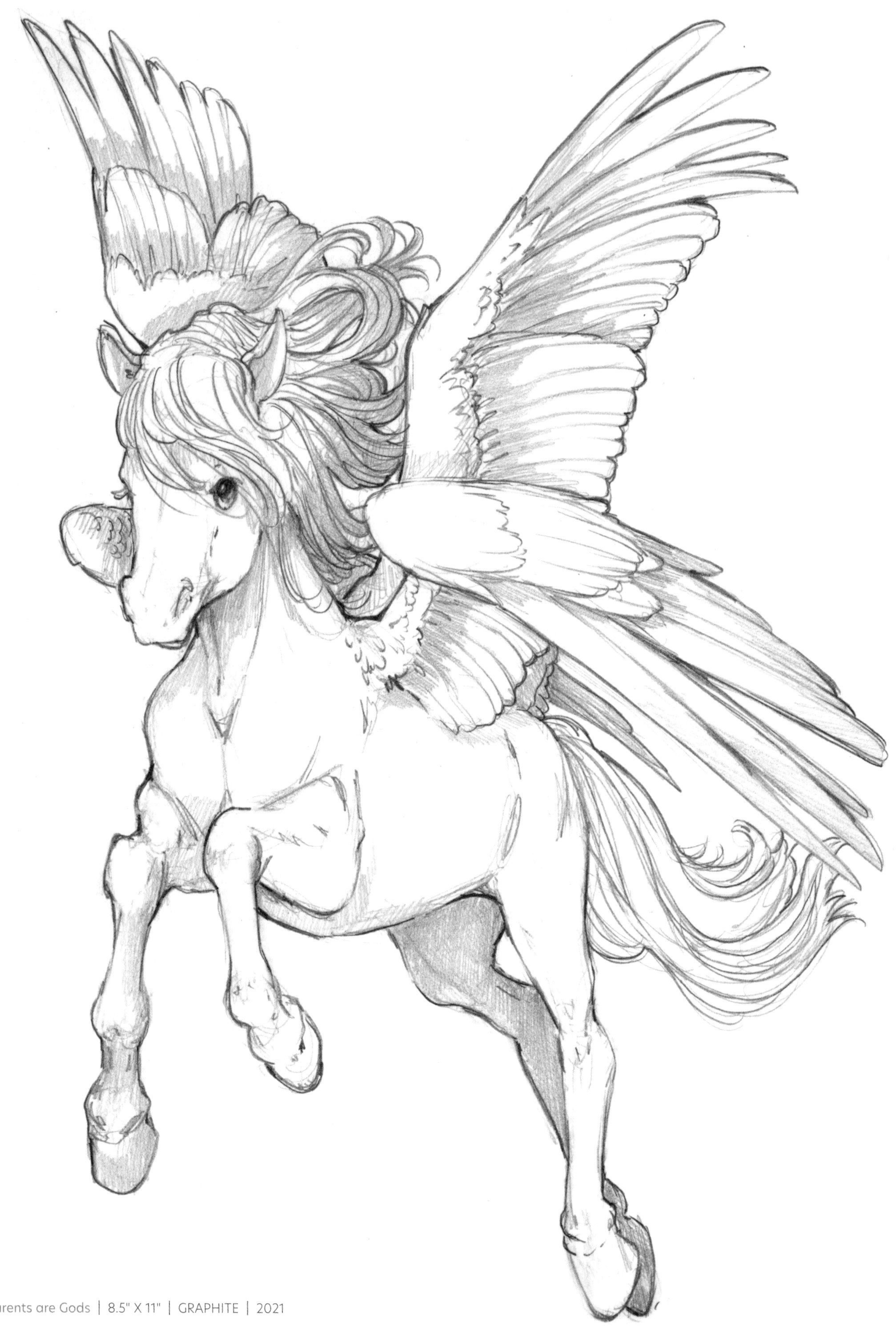

My Parents are Gods | 8.5" X 11" | GRAPHITE | 2021

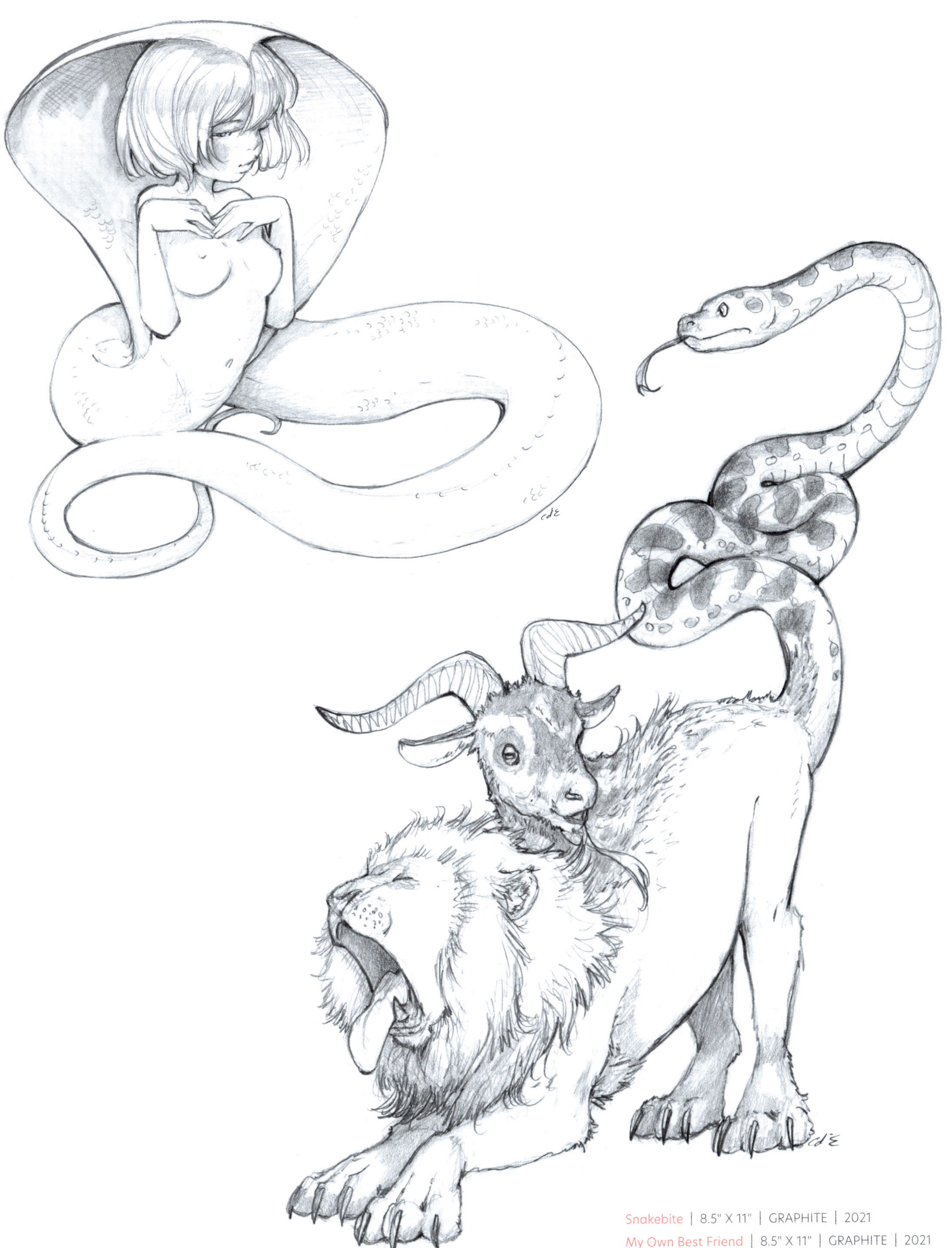

Snakebite | 8.5" X 11" | GRAPHITE | 2021

My Own Best Friend | 8.5" X 11" | GRAPHITE | 2021

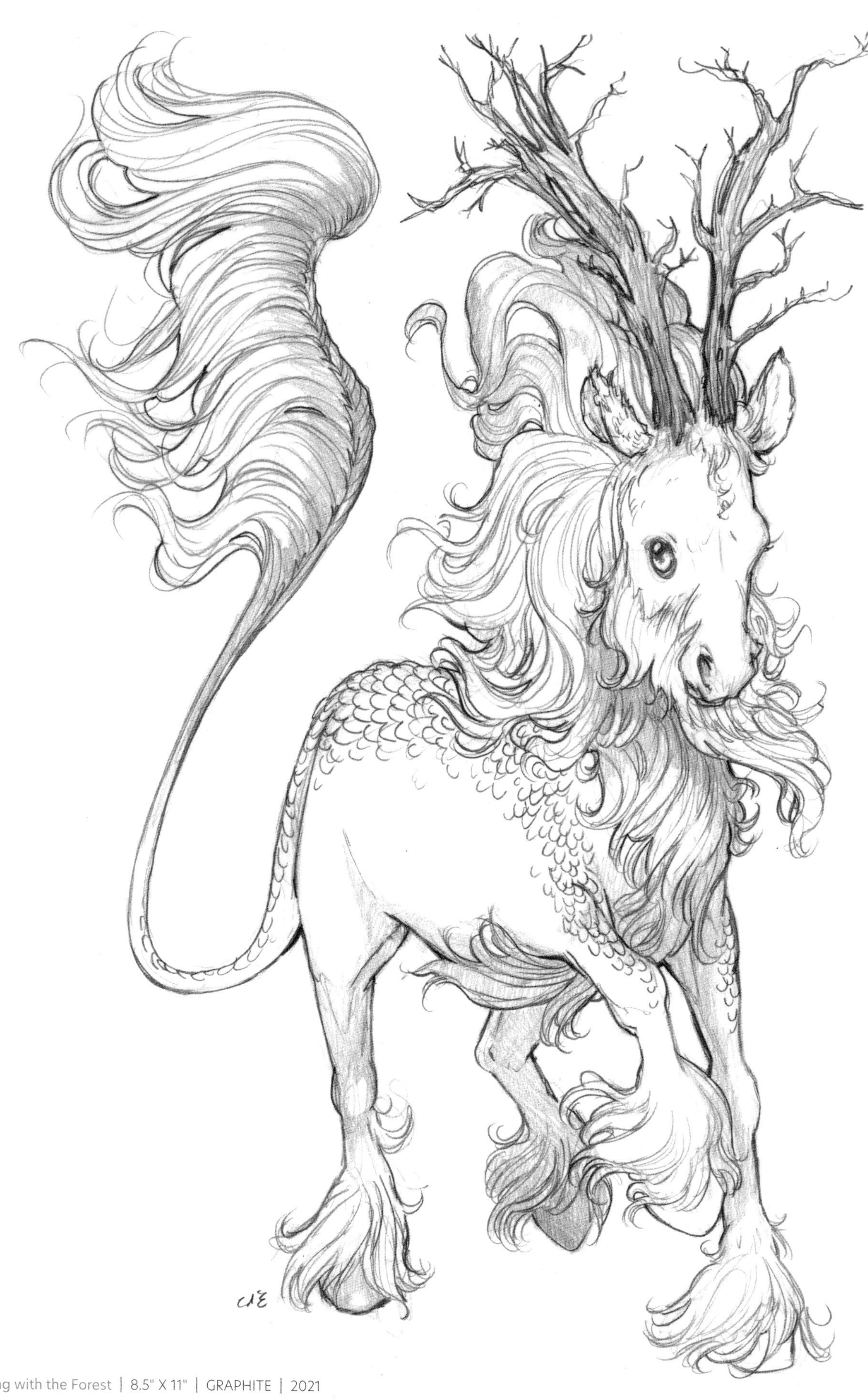

Dancing with the Forest | 8.5" X 11" | GRAPHITE | 2021

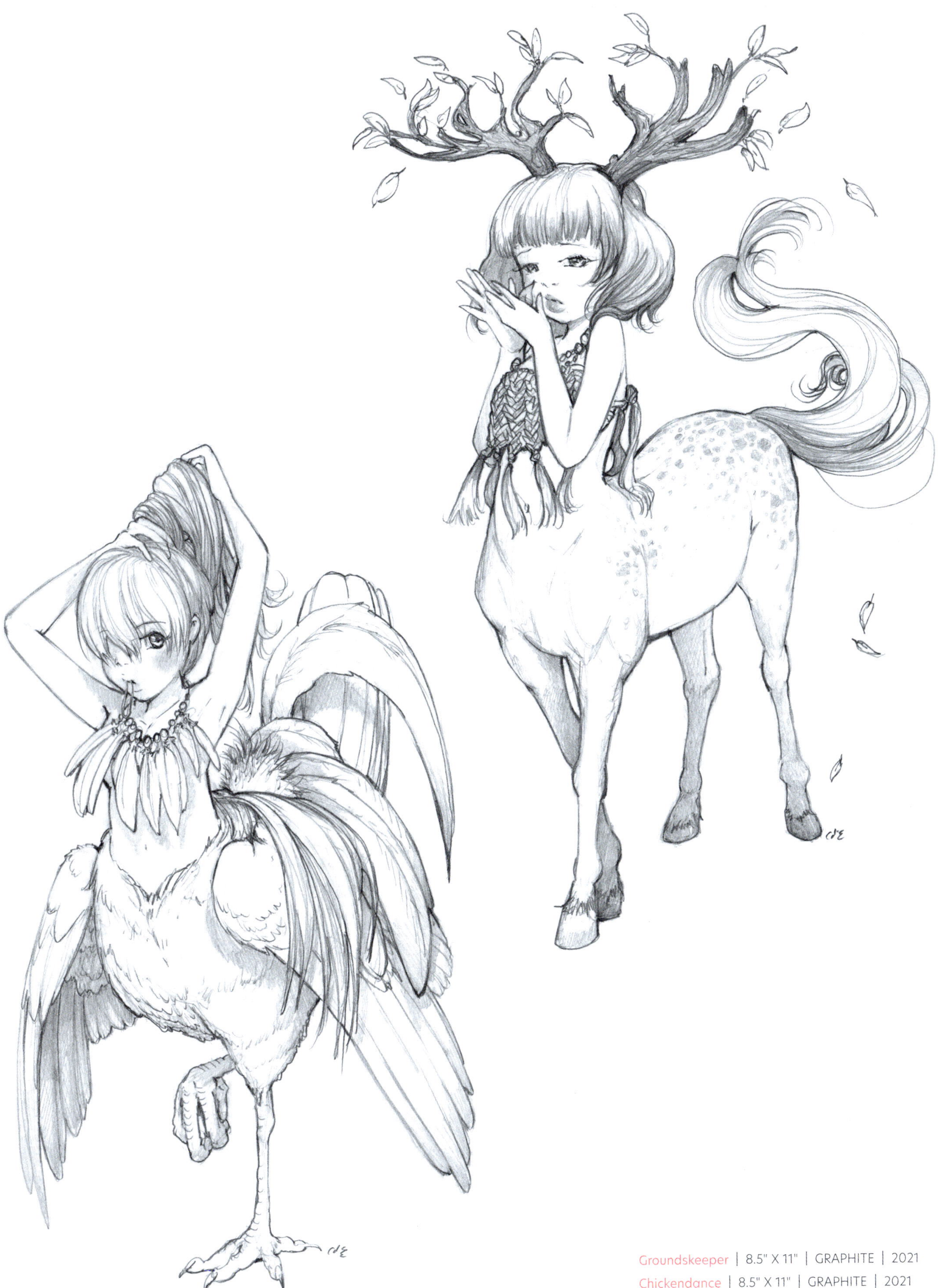

Groundskeeper | 8.5" X 11" | GRAPHITE | 2021
Chickendance | 8.5" X 11" | GRAPHITE | 2021

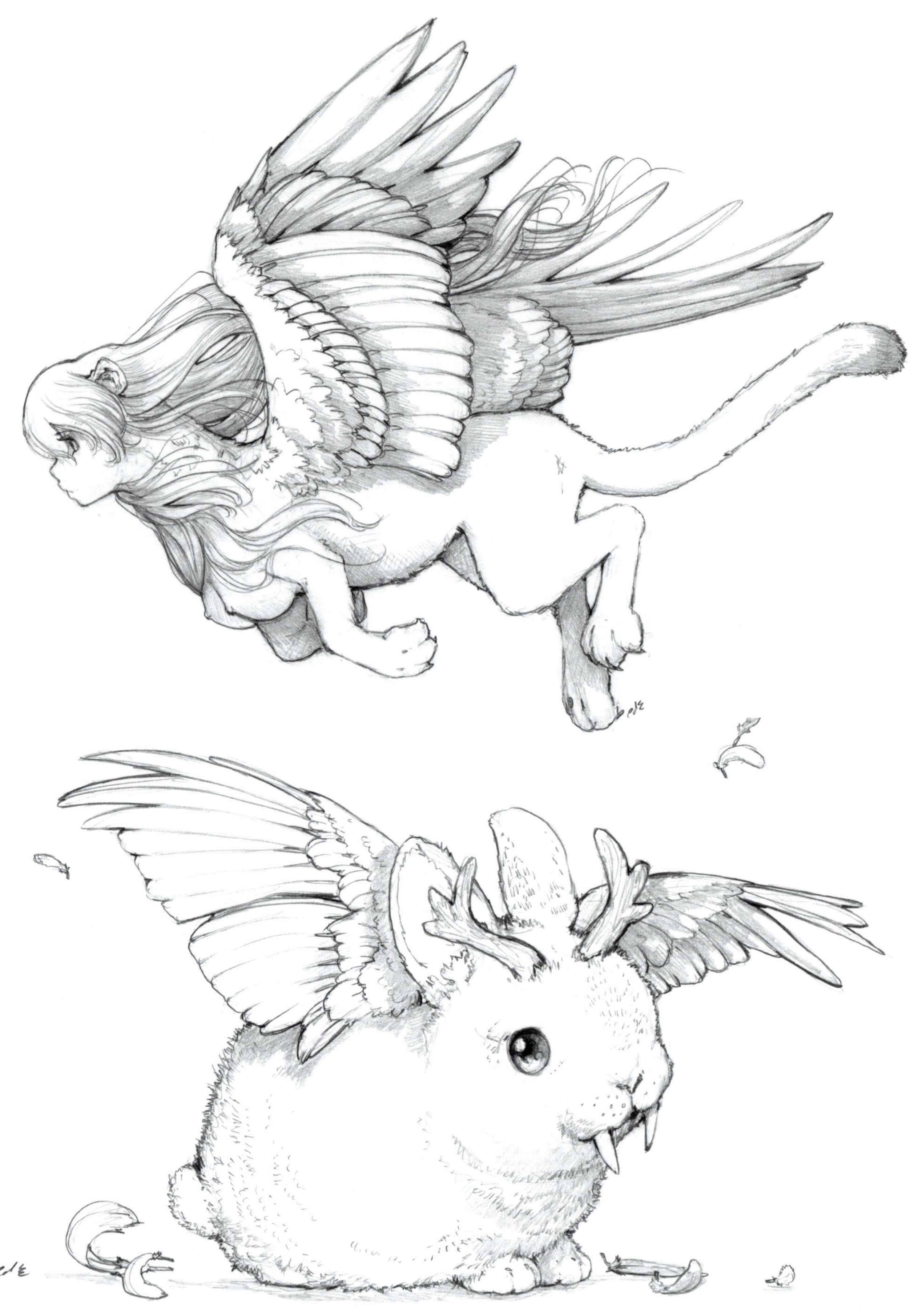

Riddle Me This | 8.5" X 11" | GRAPHITE | 2021
Ich Bin ein Jackolope | 8.5" X 11" | GRAPHITE | 2021

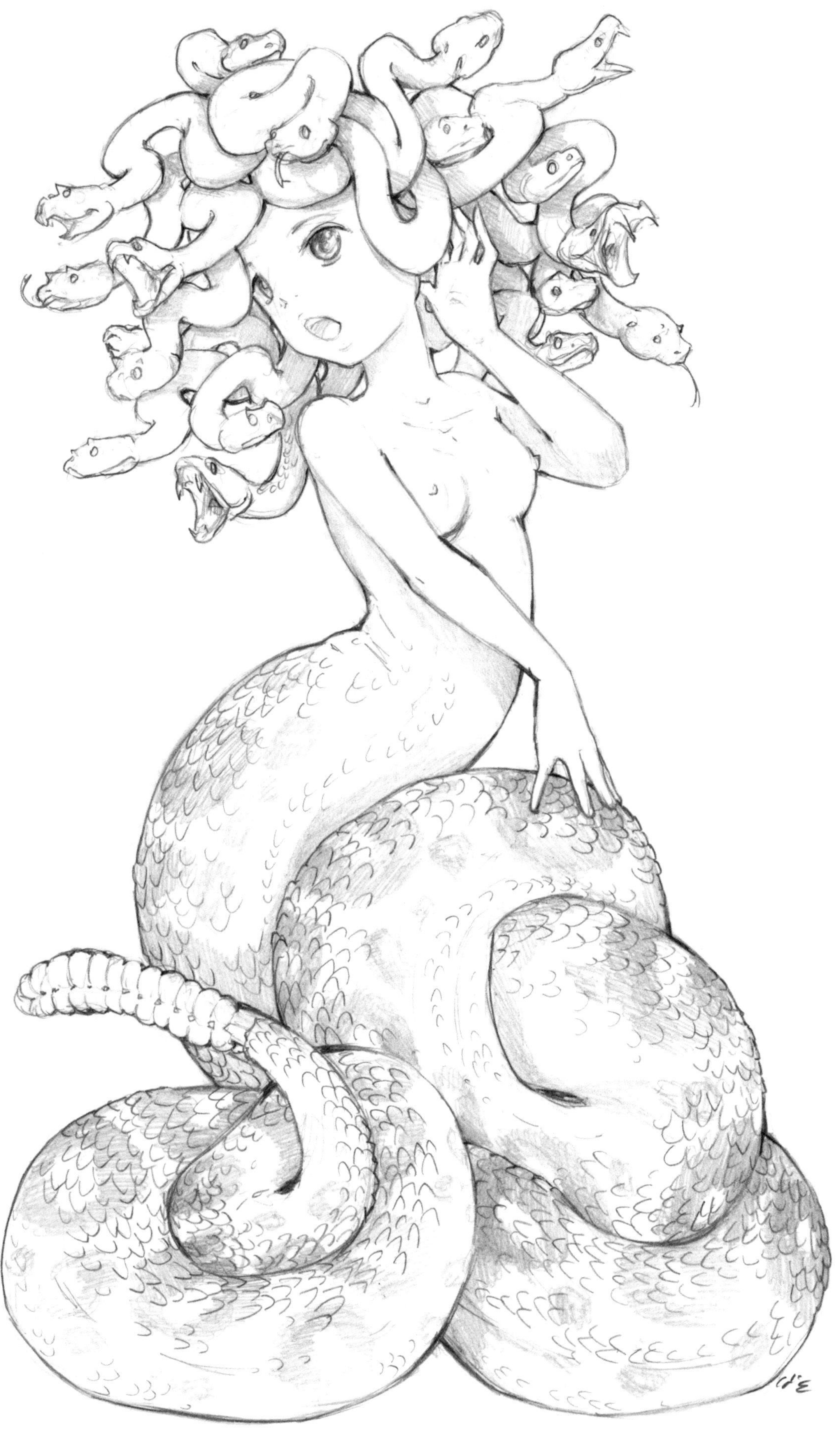

A Date with a Gorgon | 8.5" X 11" | GRAPHITE | 2021

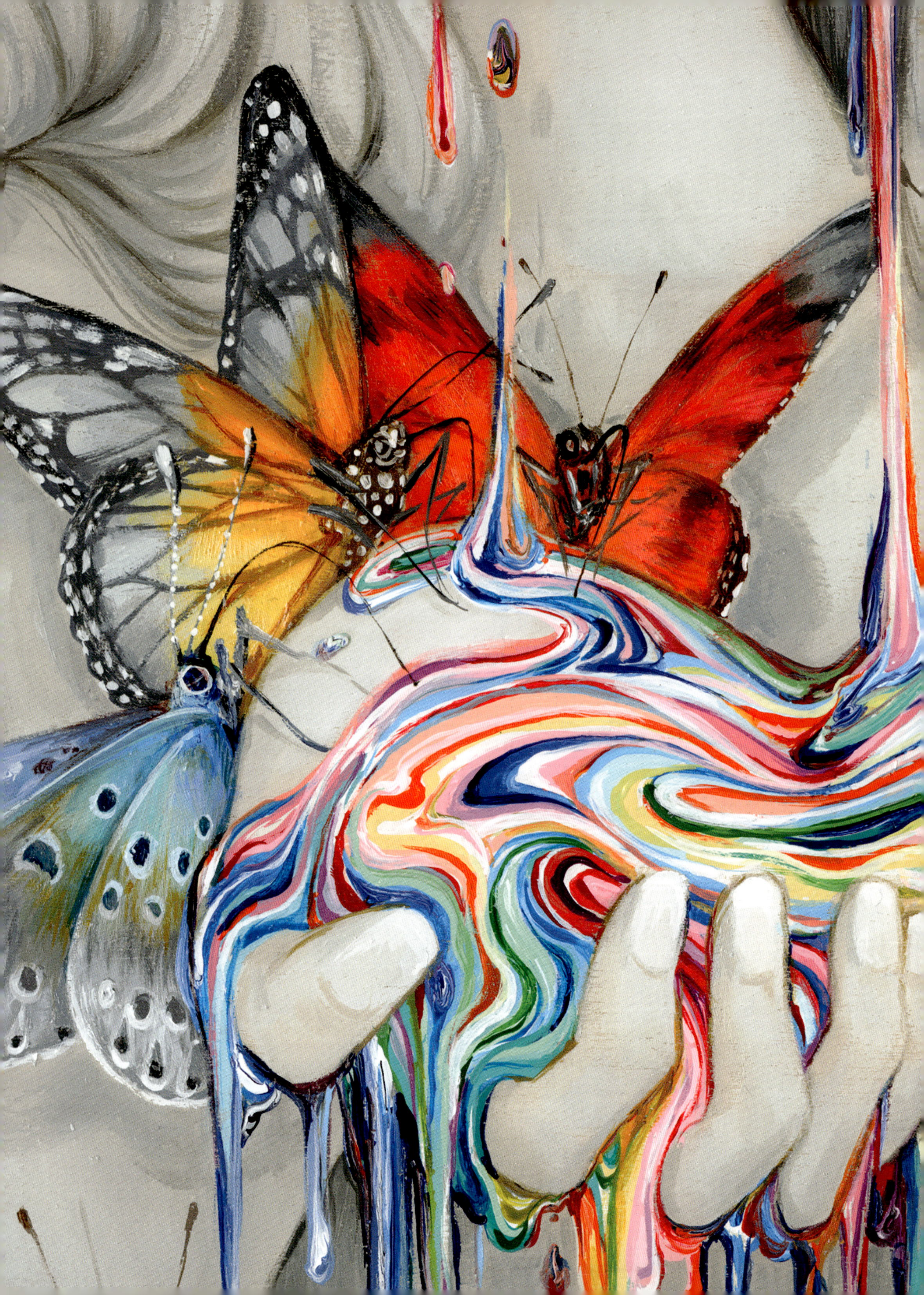

SUBLIME SPECTRUM

Facing page:
Vitae Arcu | 20" X 24" | OIL | 2020

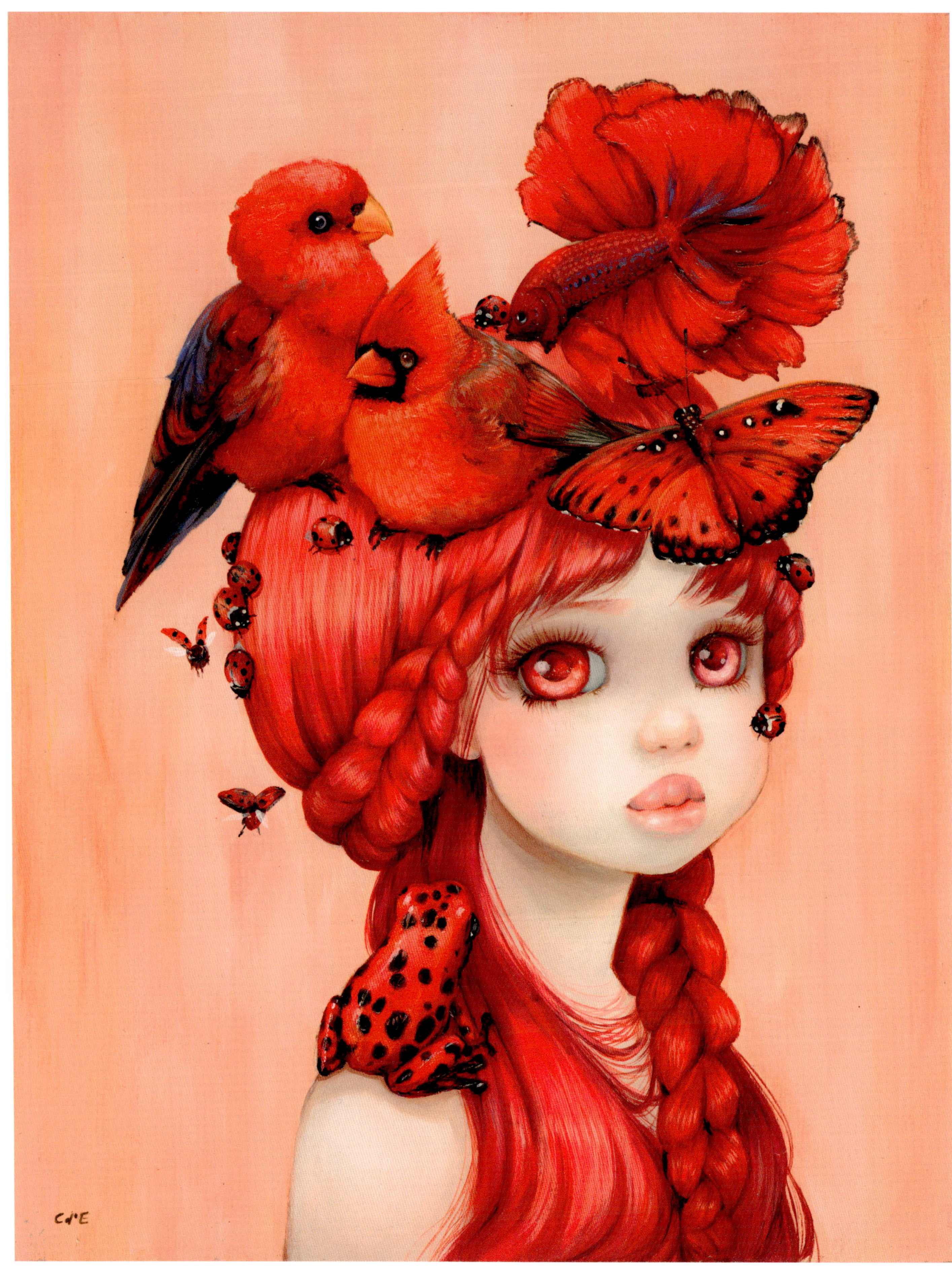

Senora Rubrum | 11" X 14" | OIL | 2020

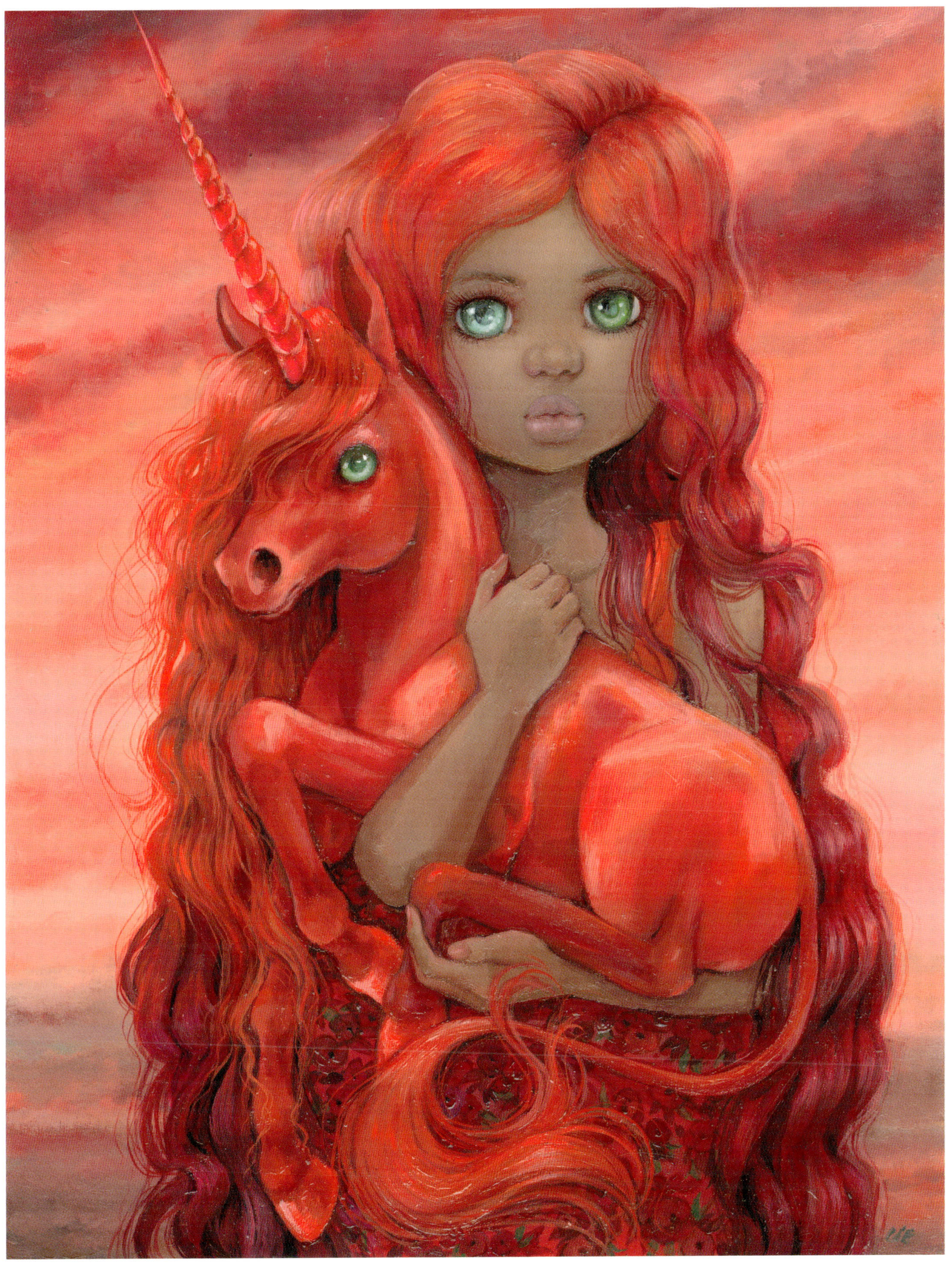

She Who Greets with Fire | 9" X 12" | OIL | 2021

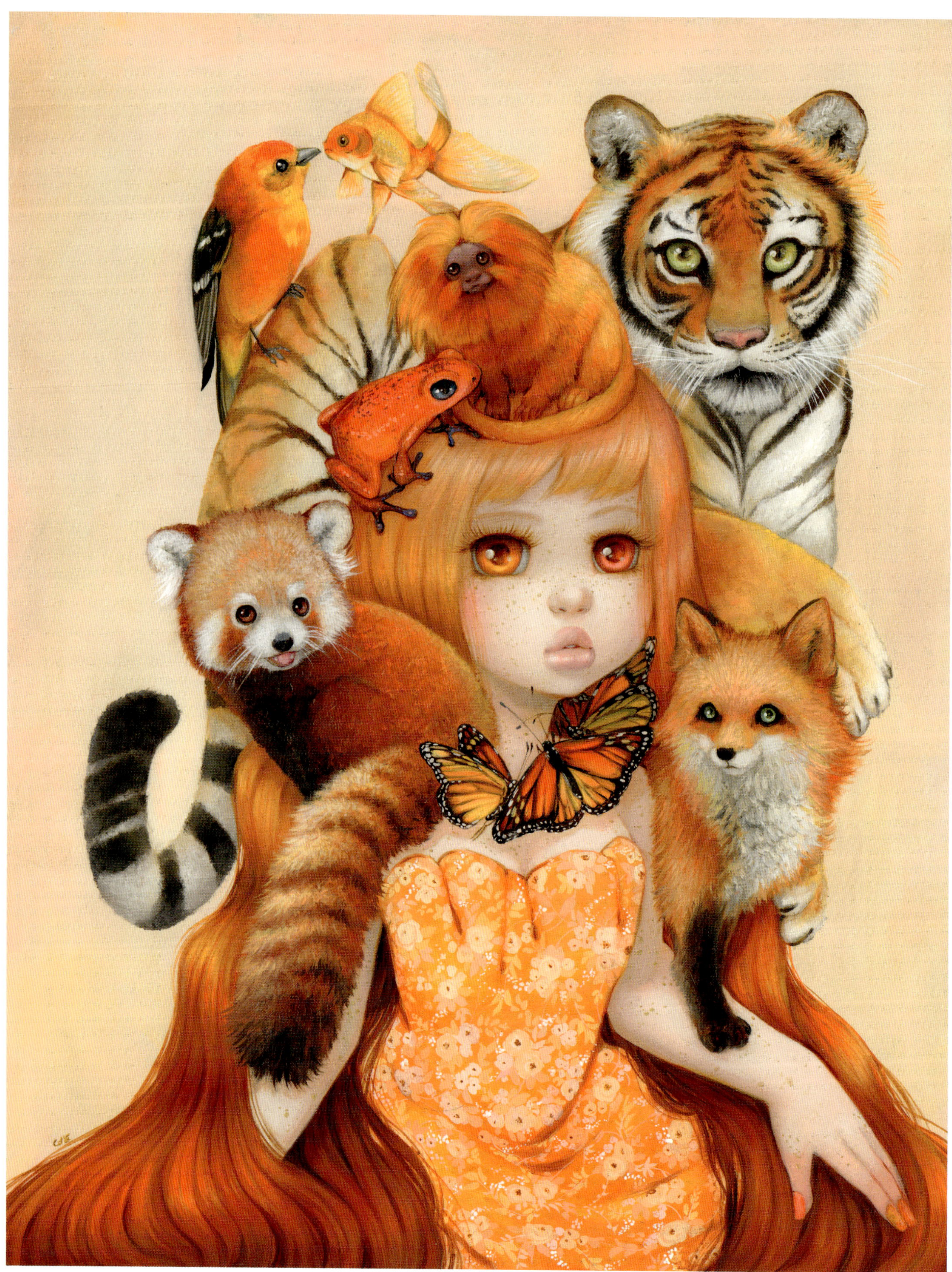

Donna Aurantiaco | 16" X 20" | OIL | 2020

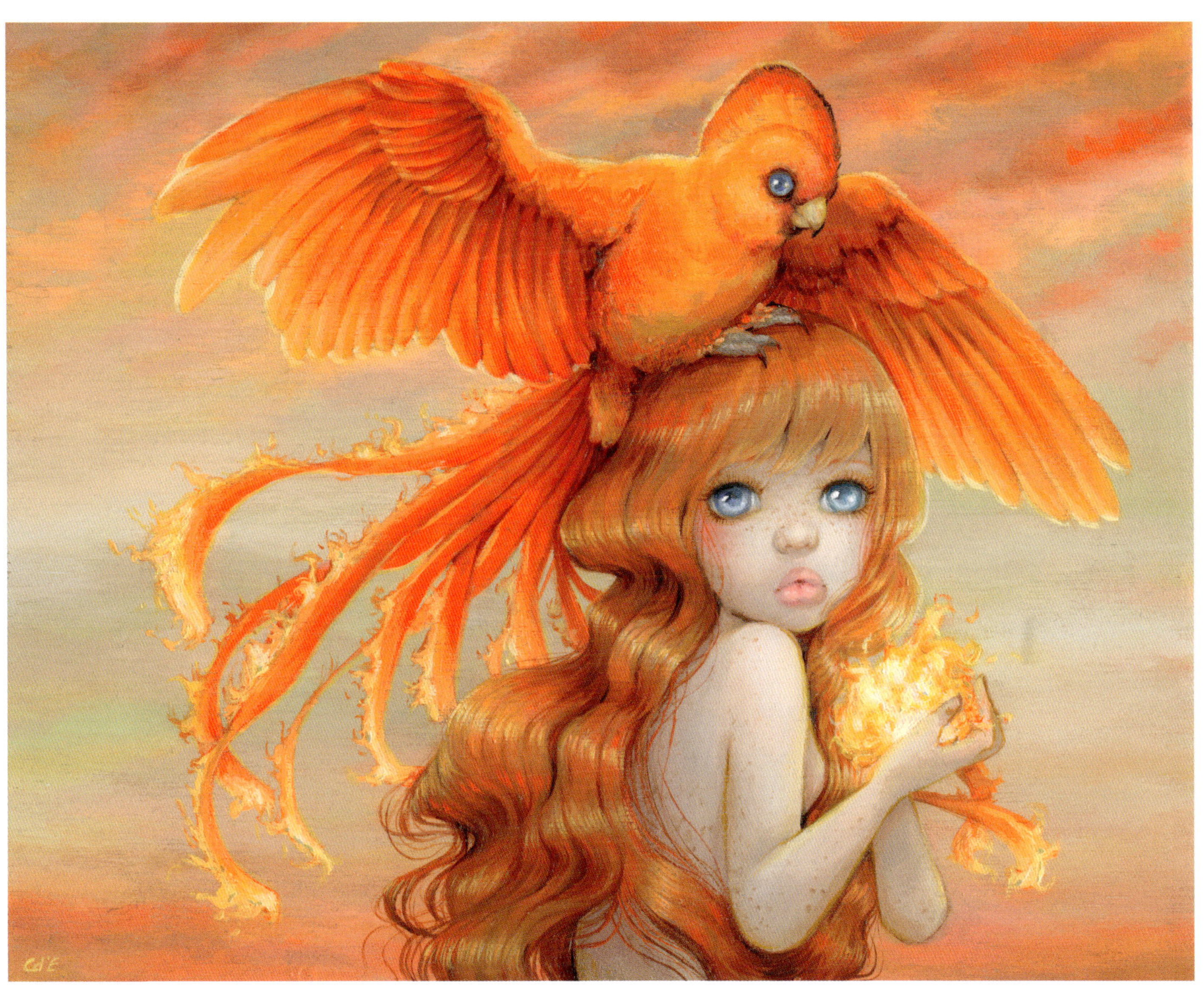

This Little Light of Mine | 8" X 10" | OIL | 2021

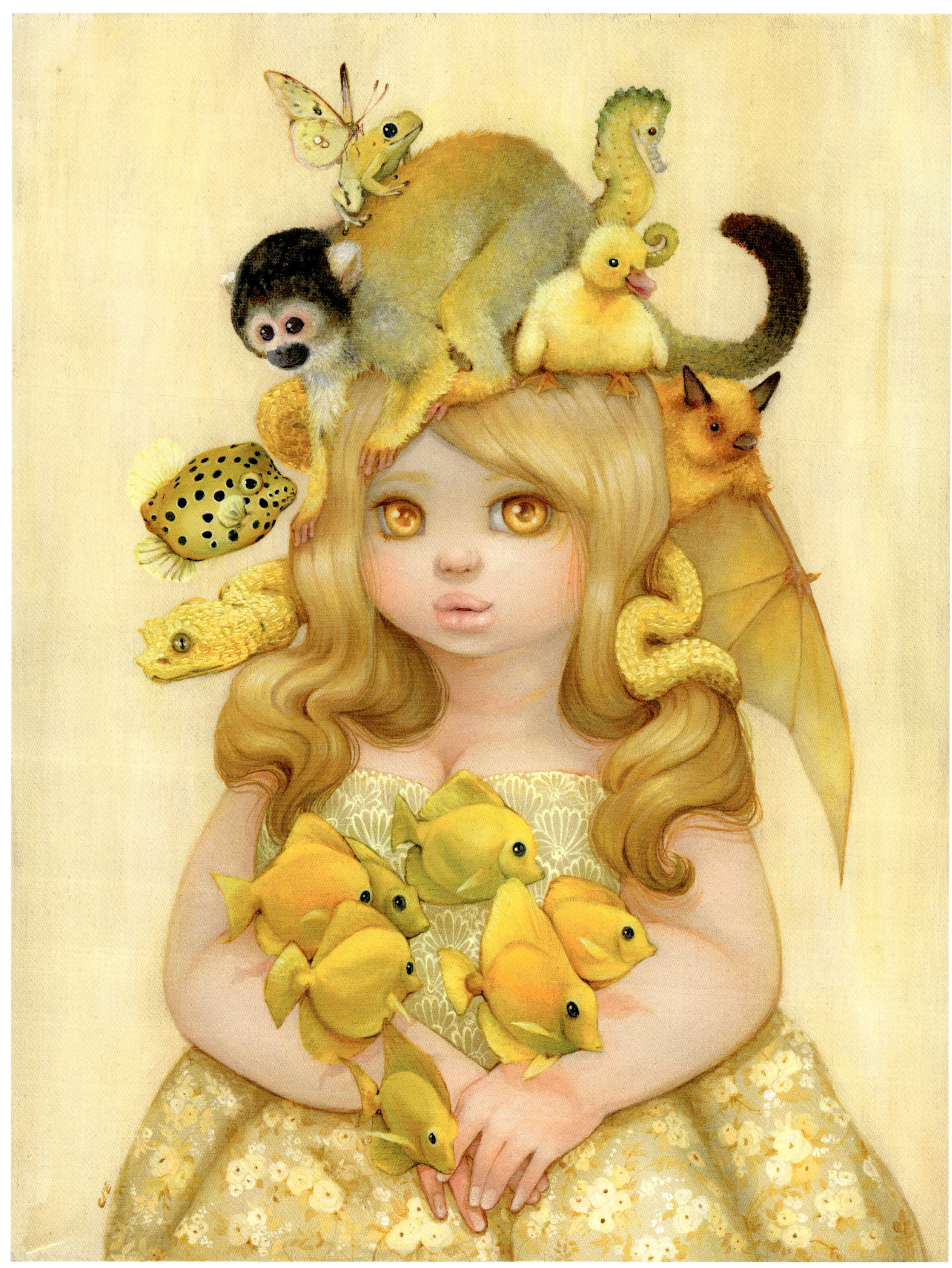

Dear Flavo | 14" X 18" | OIL | 2020

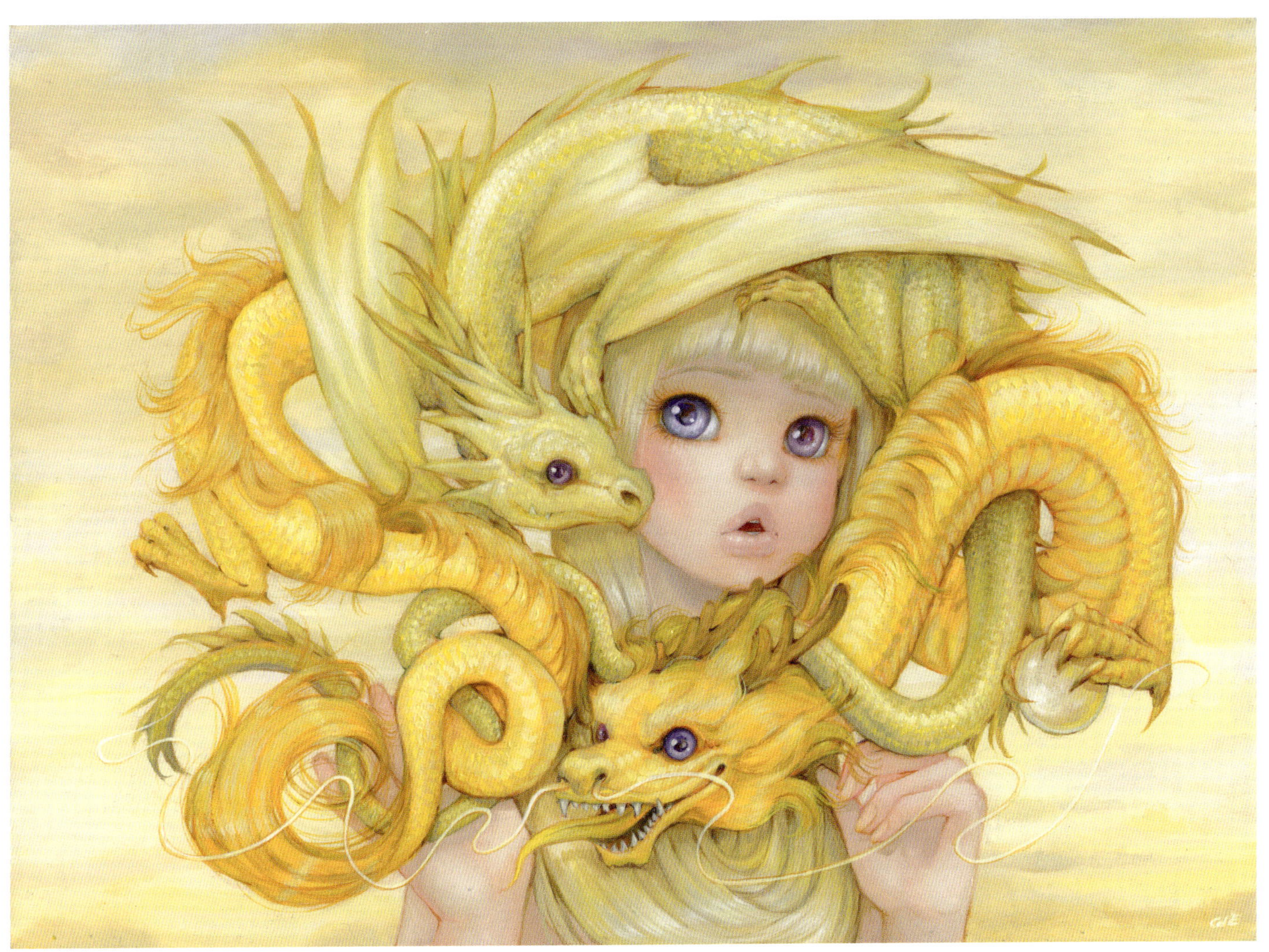

Of Fate and Fortune | 10" X 14" | OIL | 2021

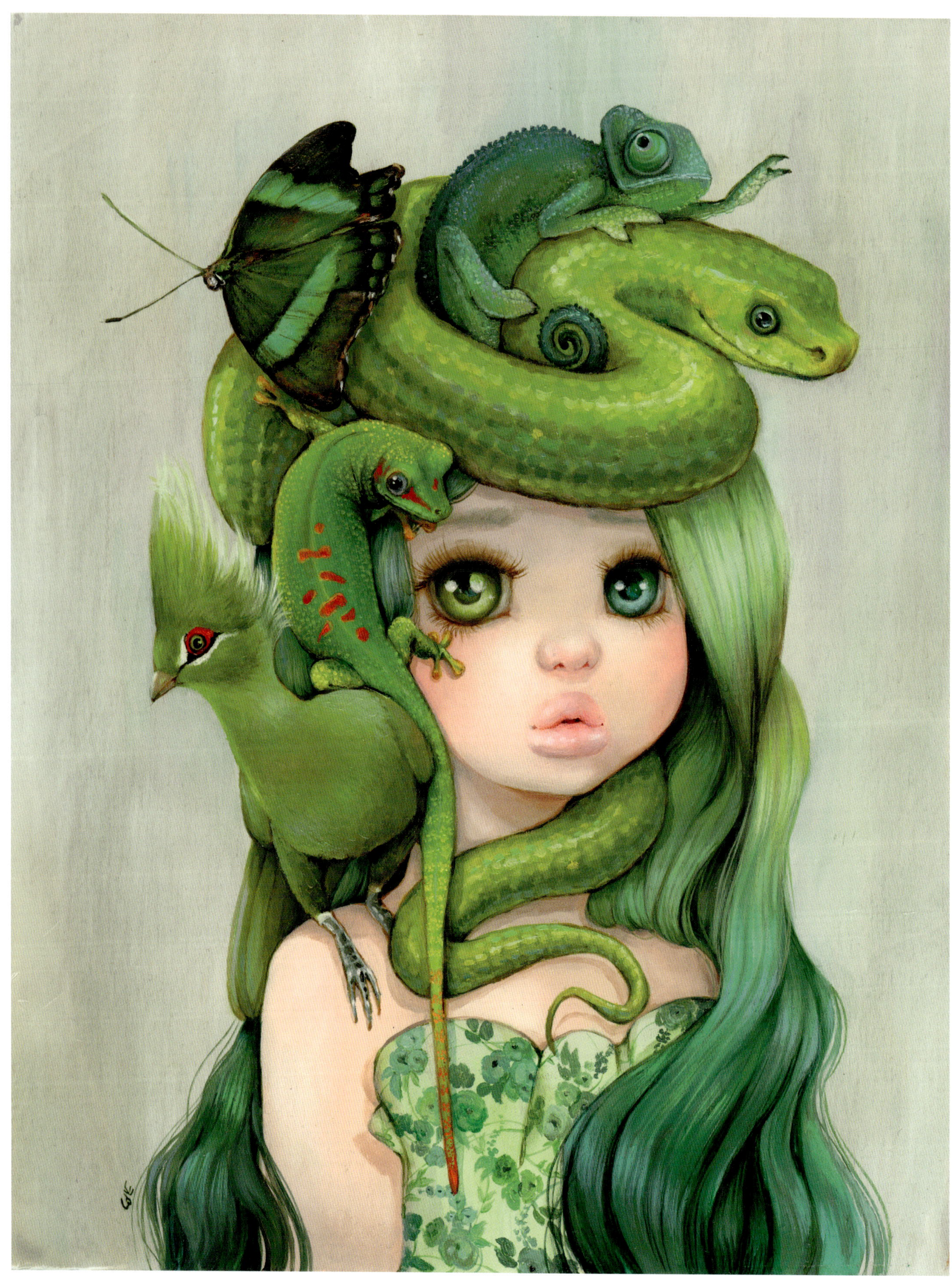

Viridi | 11" X 14" | OIL | 2020

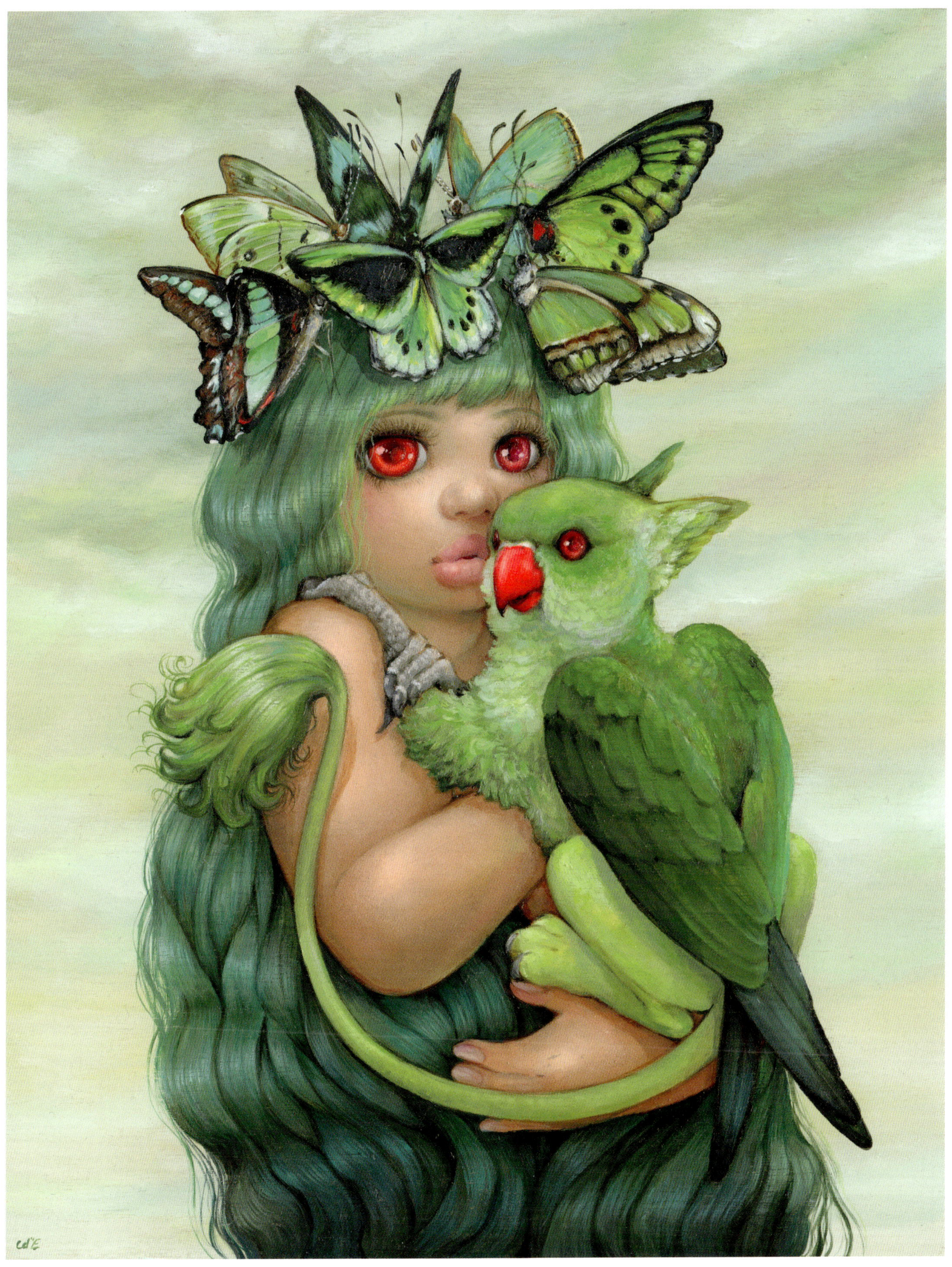

A Nurturing Touch with a Deadly Kiss | 11" X 14" | OIL | 2021

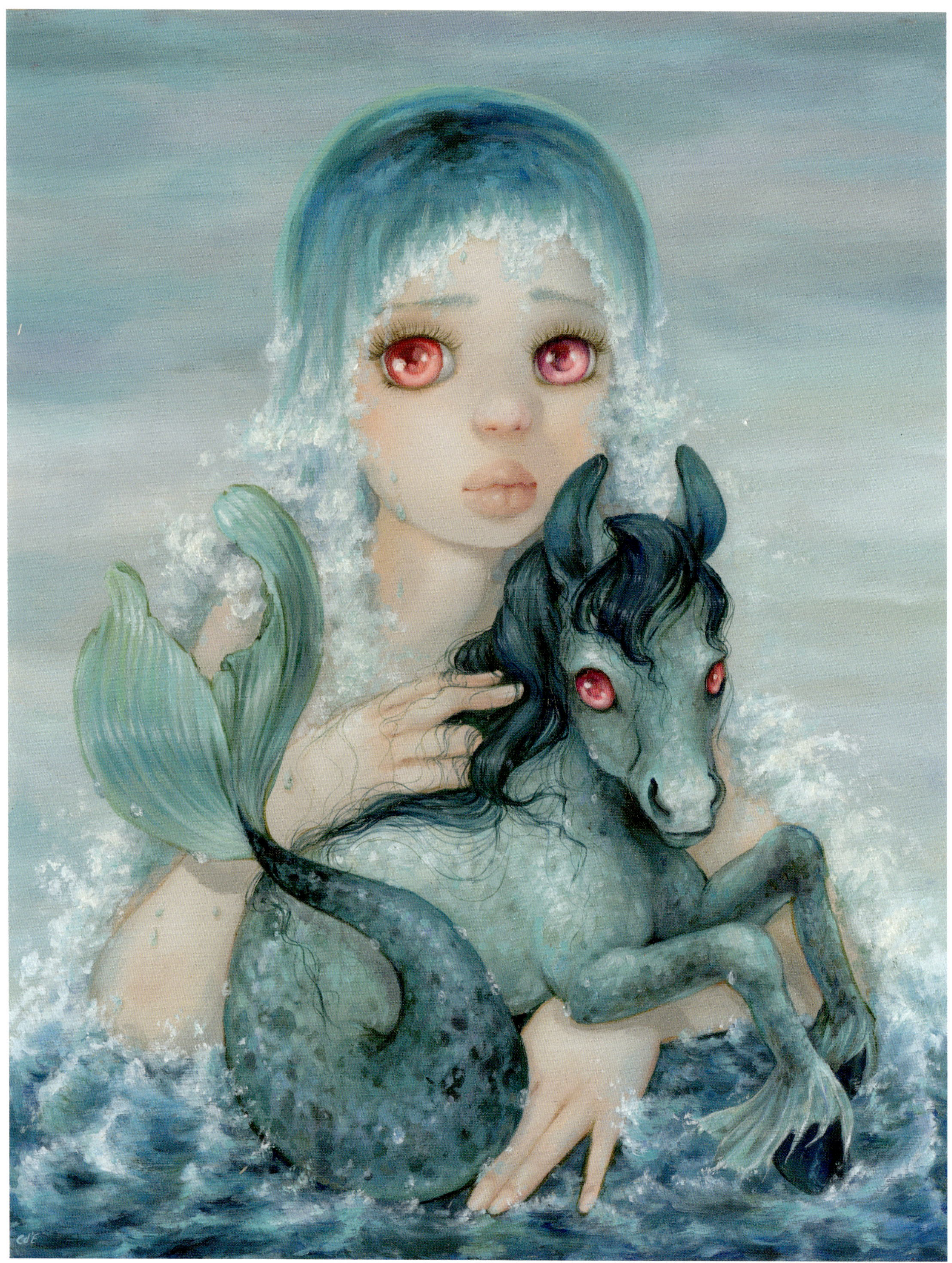

My Little Maneater | 11" X 14" | OIL | 2021

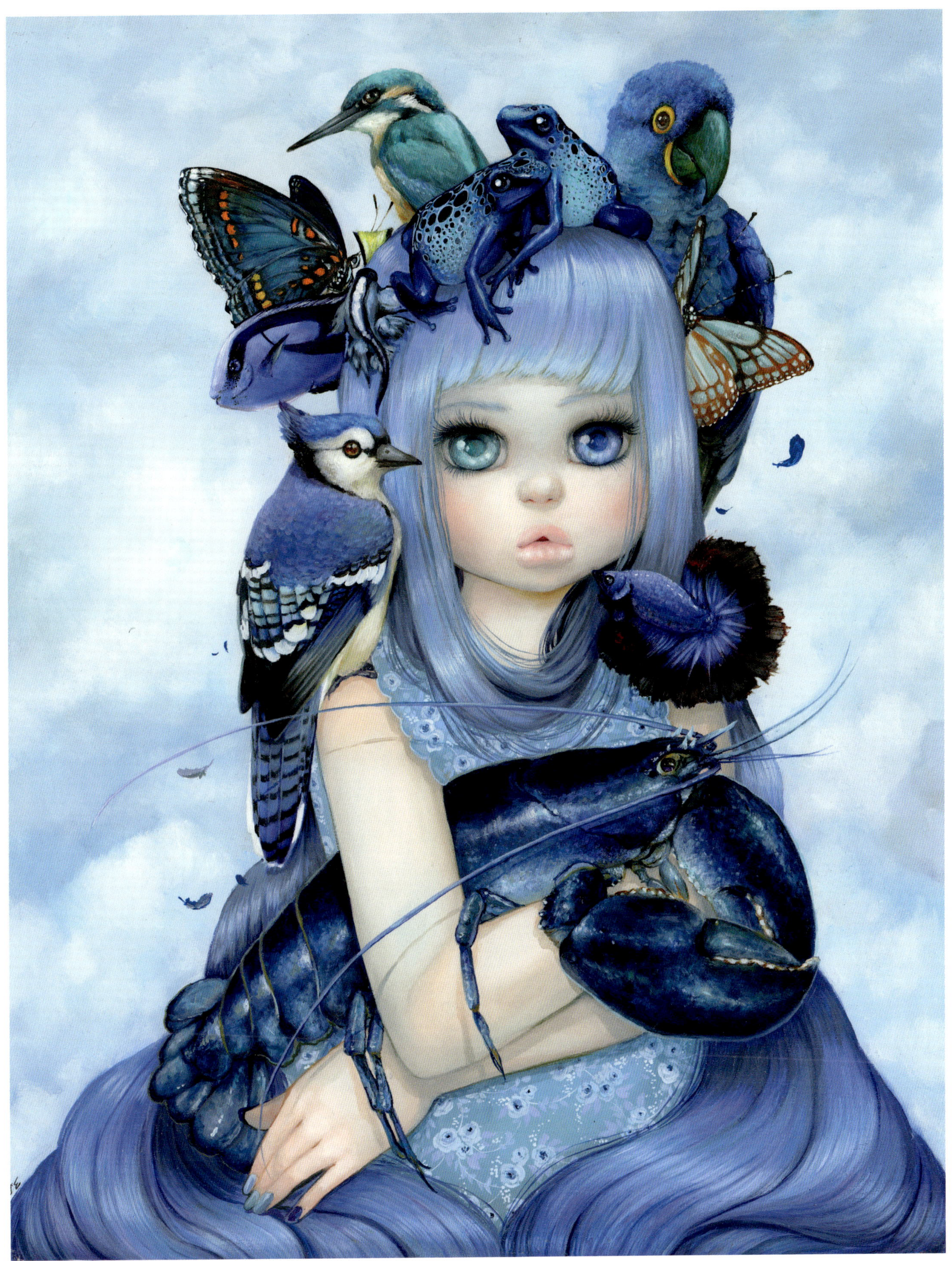

Sister Cearuleum | 16" X 20" | OIL | 2020

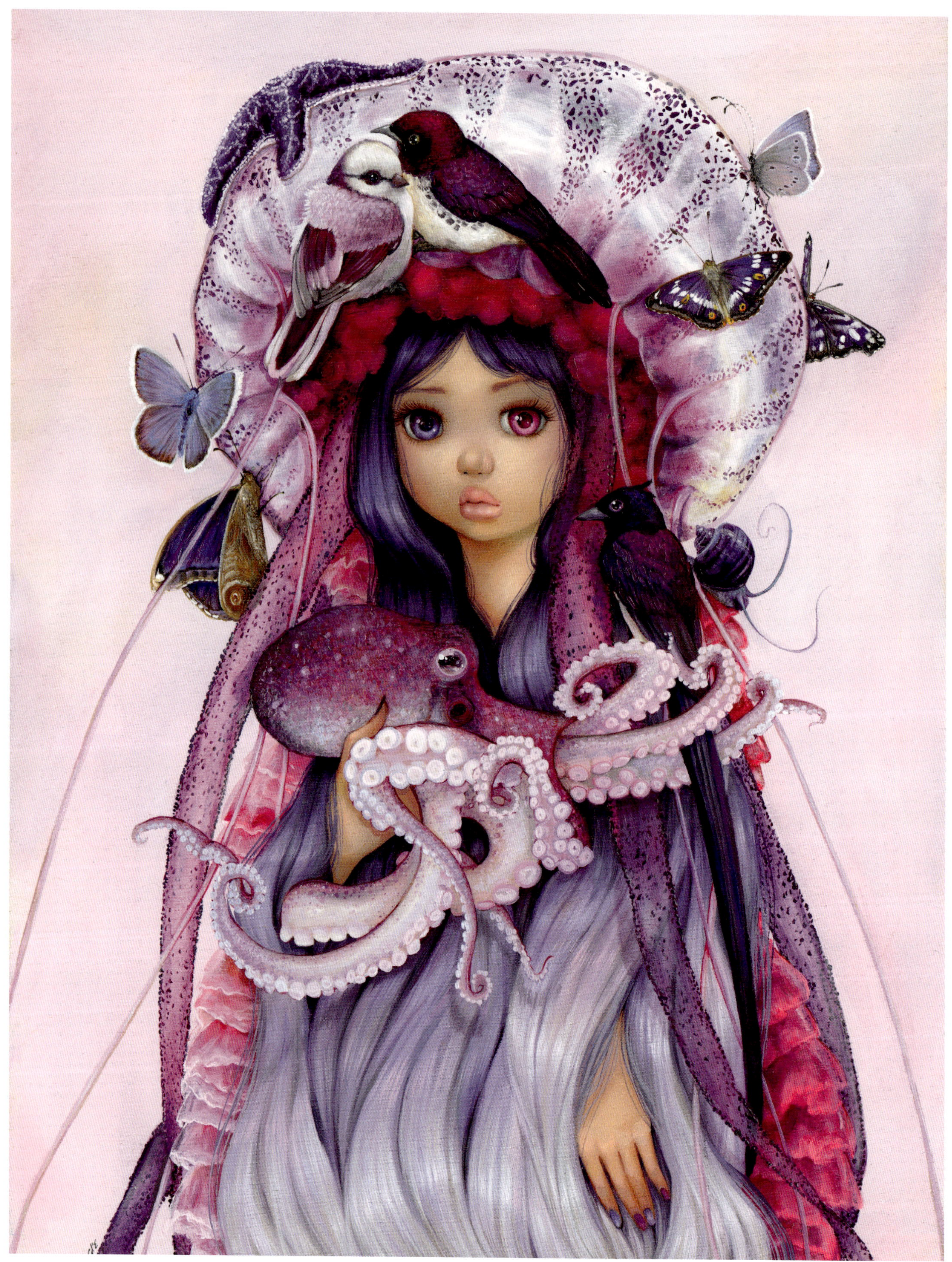

Lady Purpura | 18" X 24" | OIL | 2020

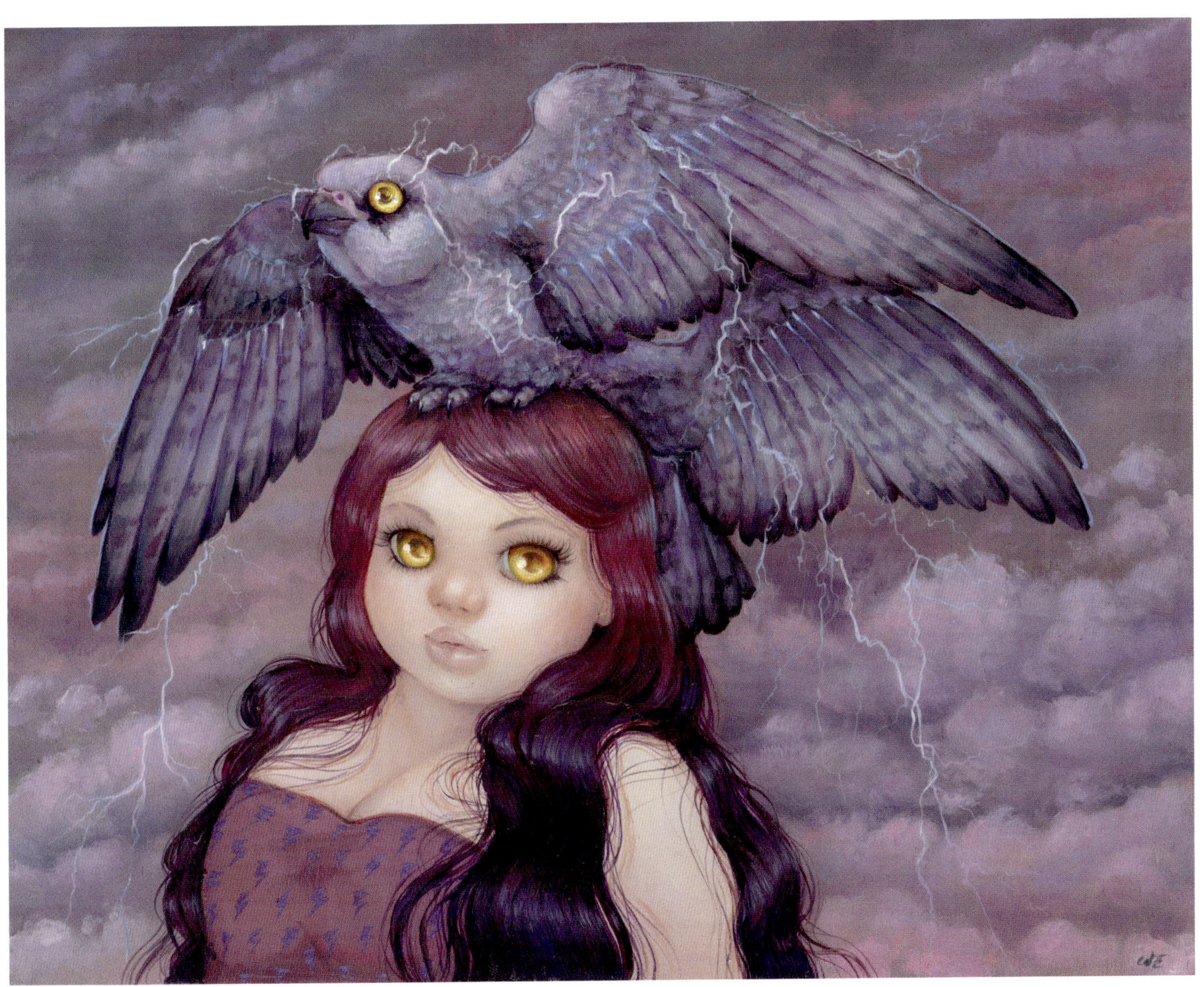

The Regent of the Storm and the Strike | 11" X 14" | OIL | 2021

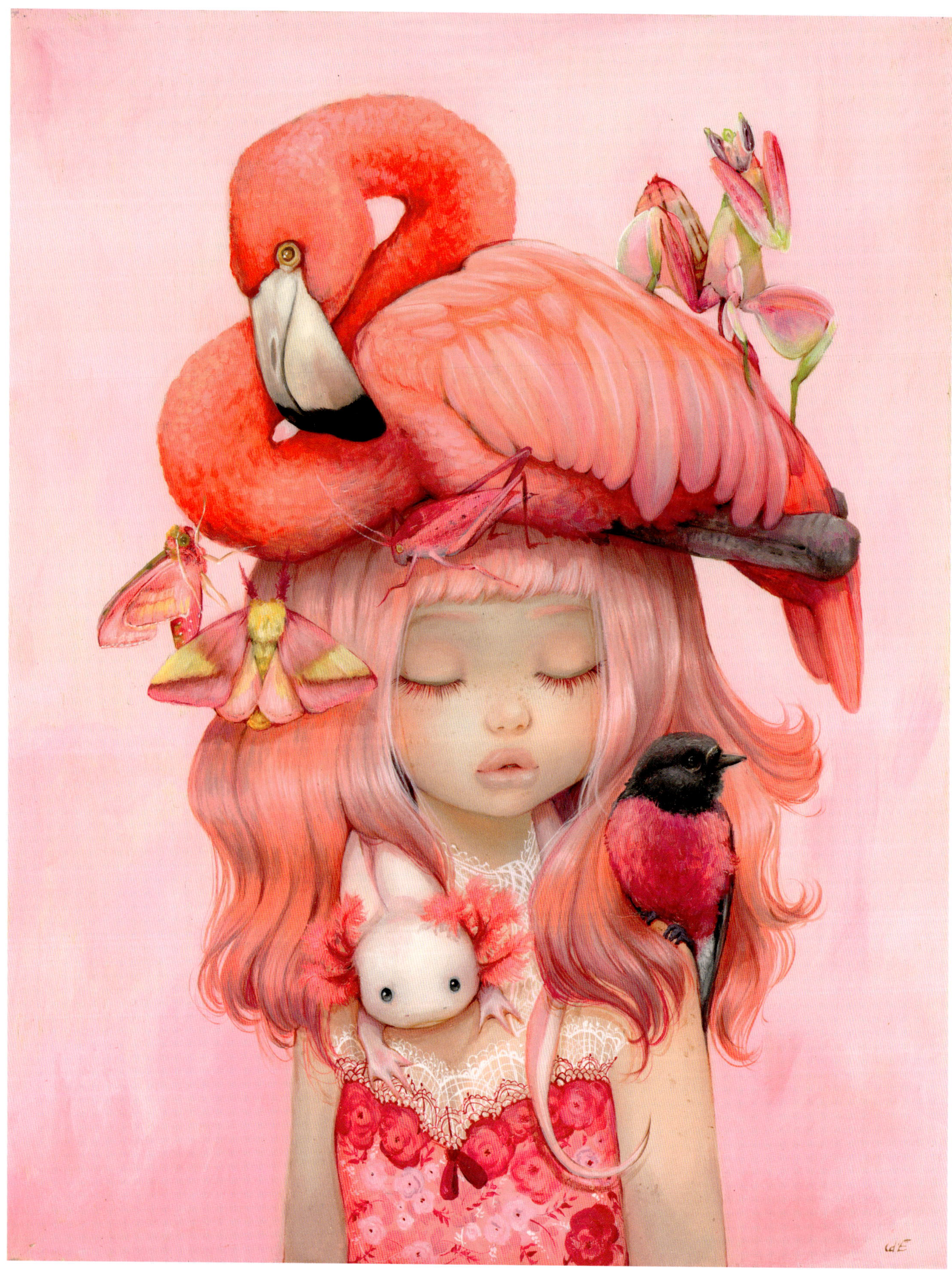

Rosea | 14" X 18" | OIL | 2020

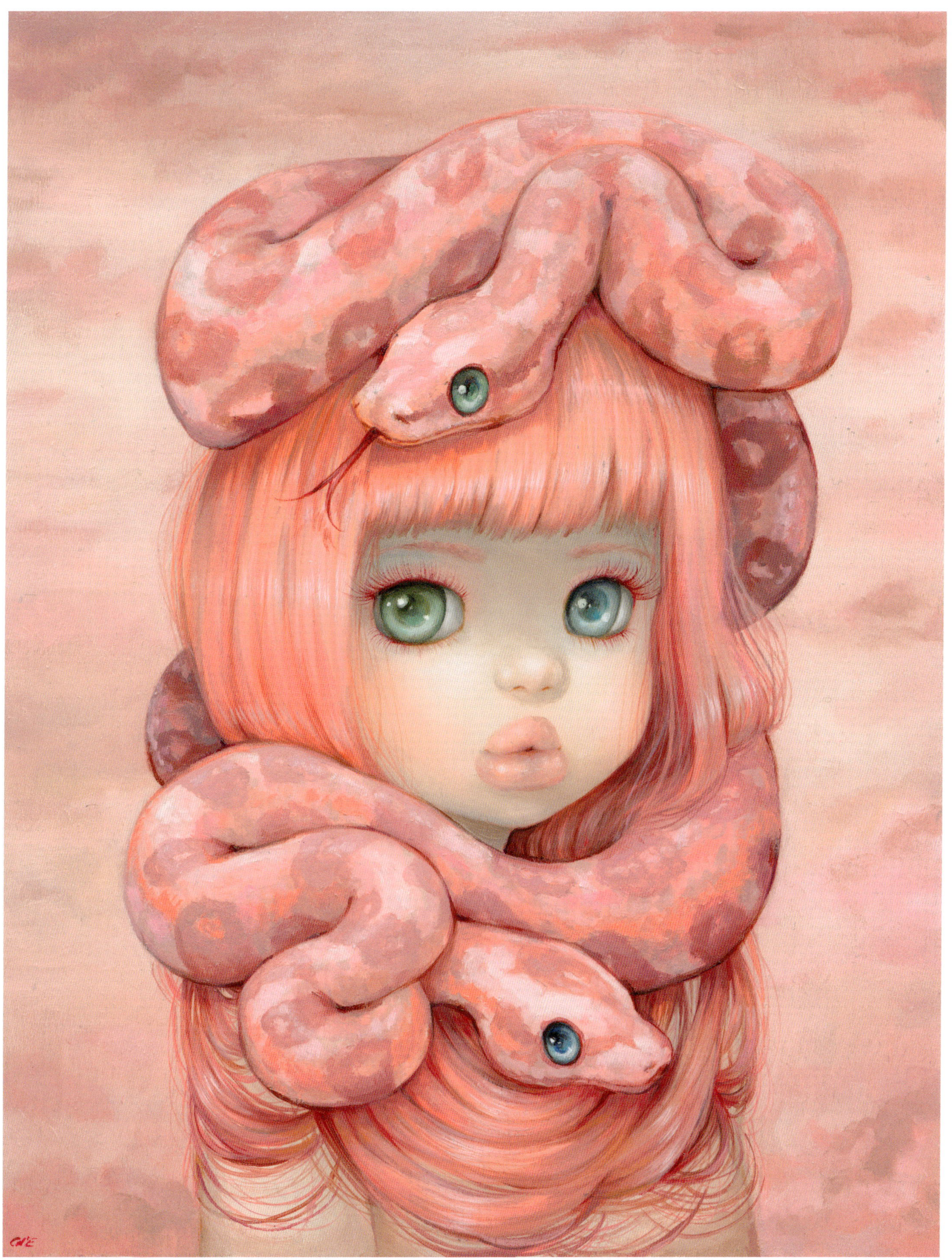

The Beginning and the End | 11" X 14" | OIL | 2021

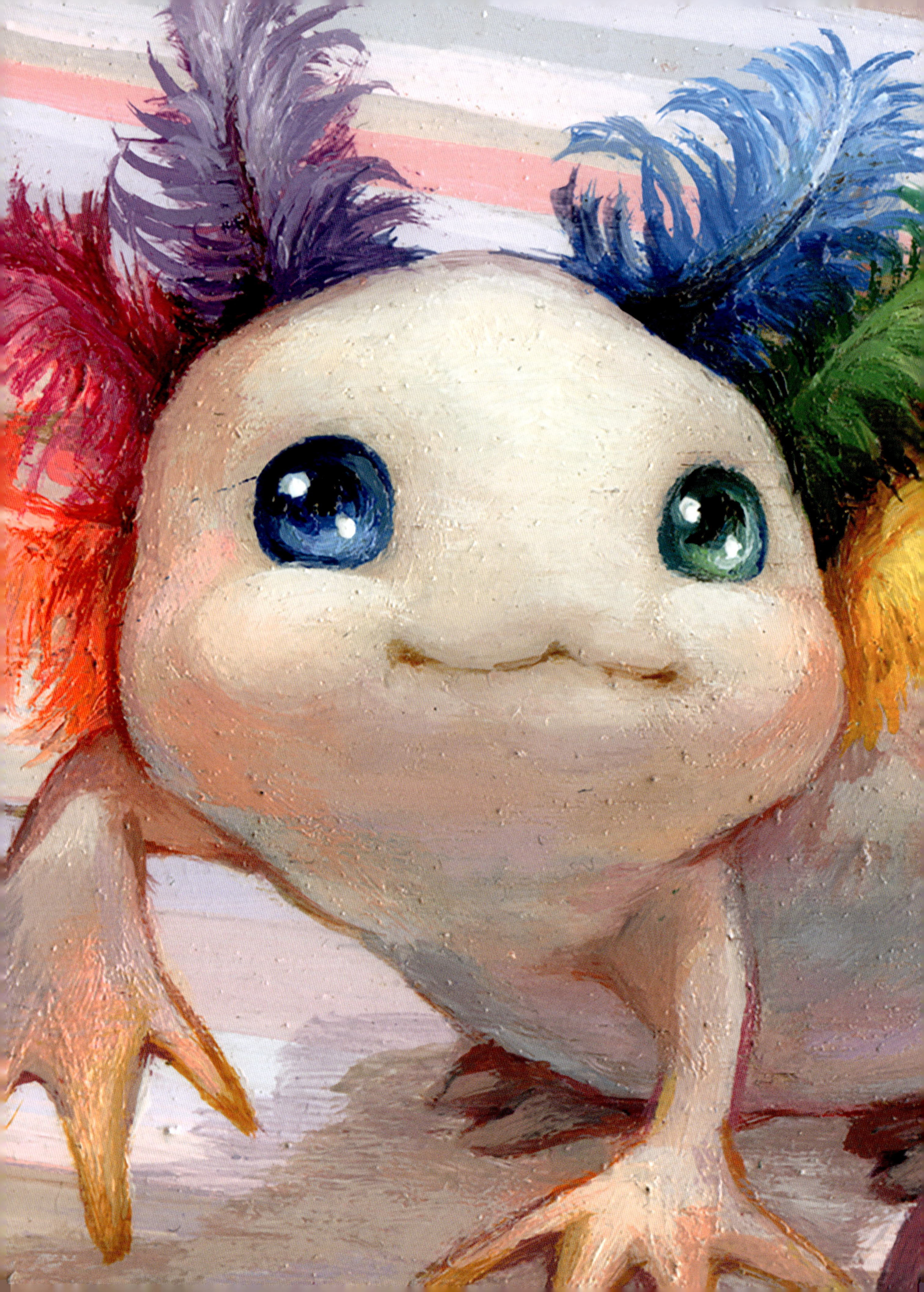

KINDRED KINGDOM

Facing page:
Pinkie Pie | 4" X 6" | OIL and ACRYLIC | 2017

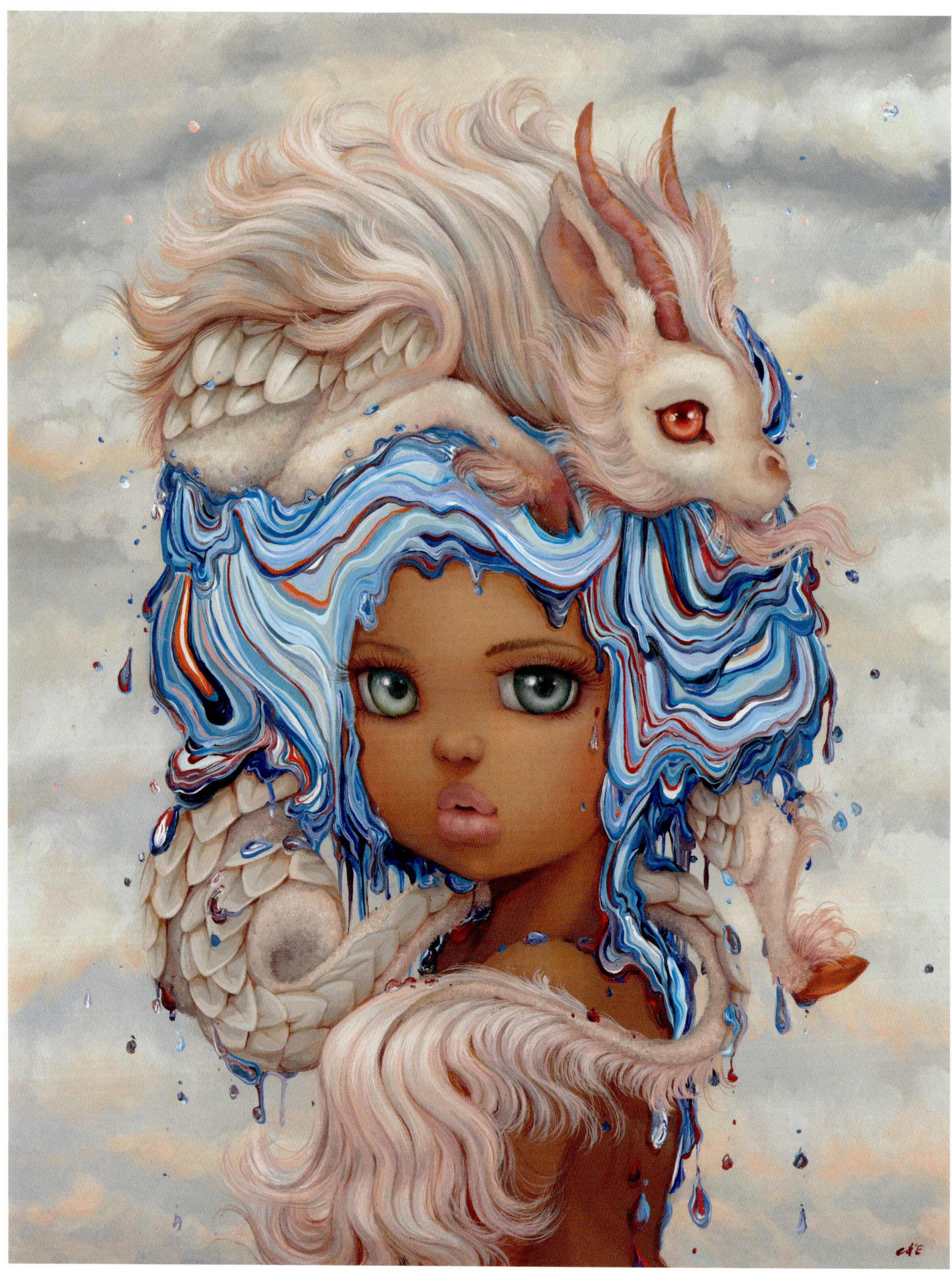

Little Miss Goo | 16" X 20" | OIL | 2018

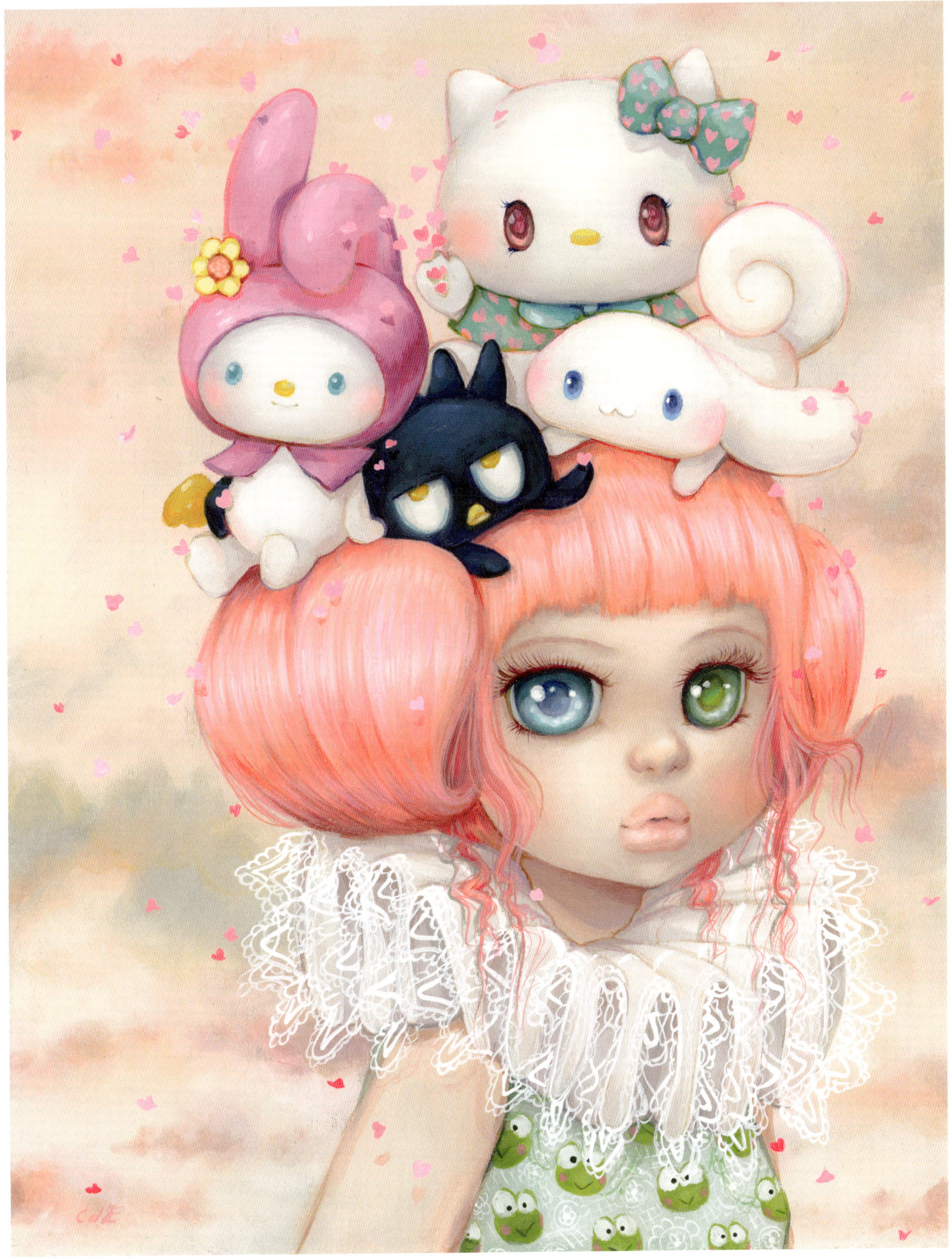

Hello My Love | 9" X 12" | OIL | 2019

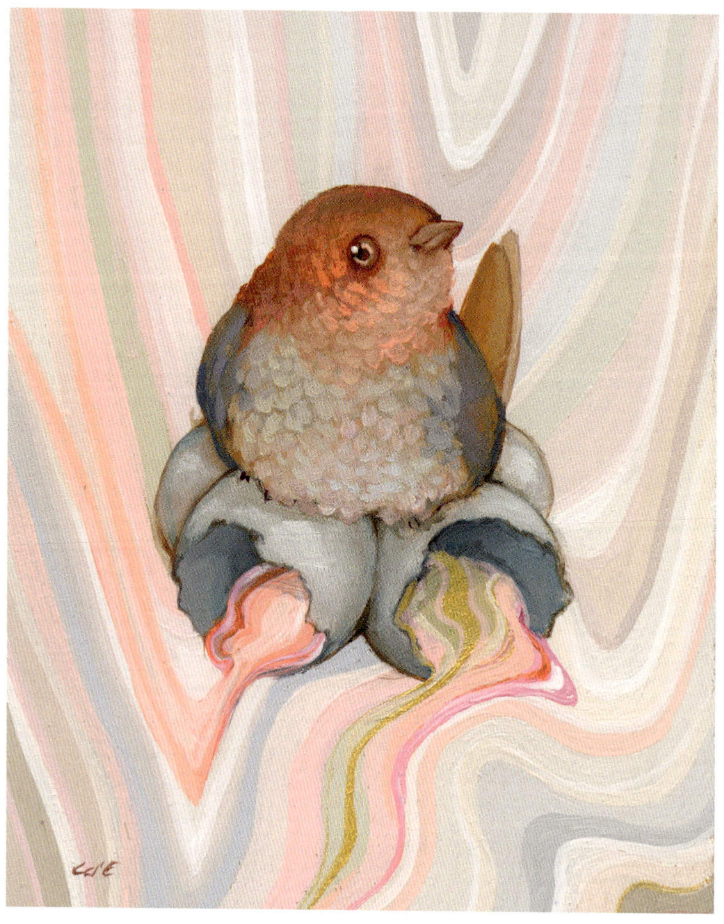

Avem Ovum | 5" X 7" | OIL and ACRYLIC | 2020

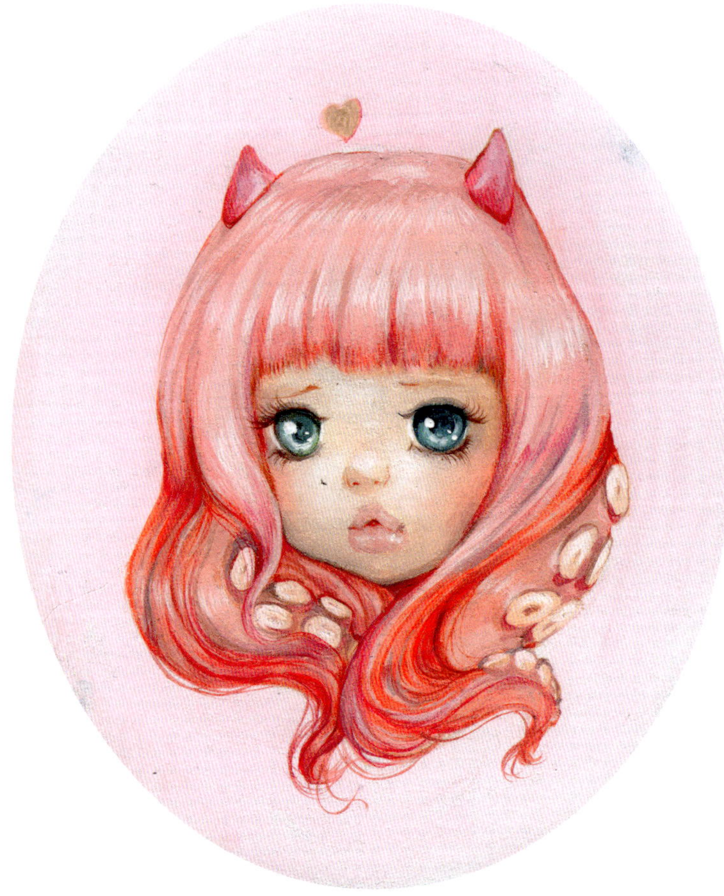

Rose Parfait | 5" X 7" | OIL and ACRYLIC | 2019

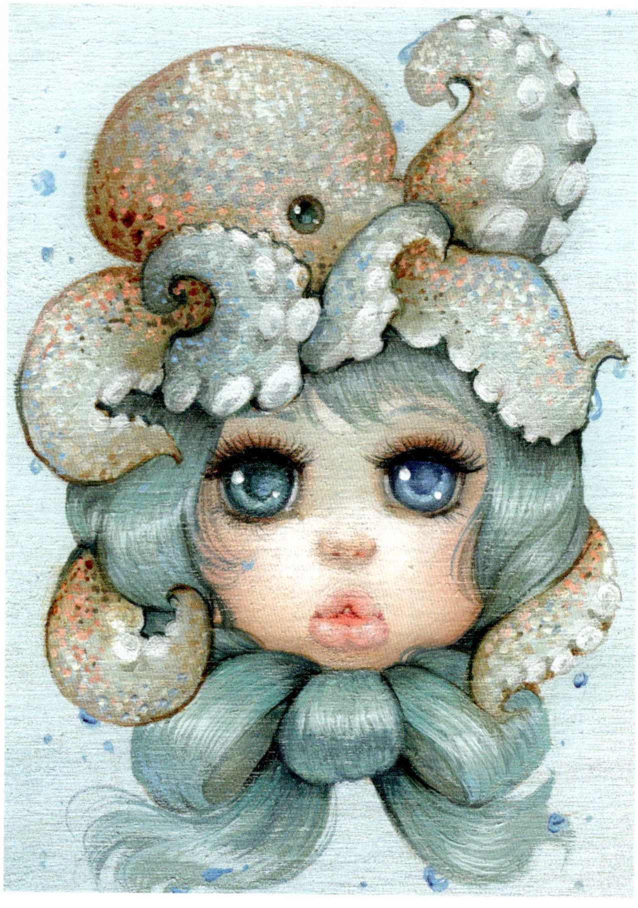

Tie It with a Bow | 16" X 20" | OIL and ACRYLIC | 2019

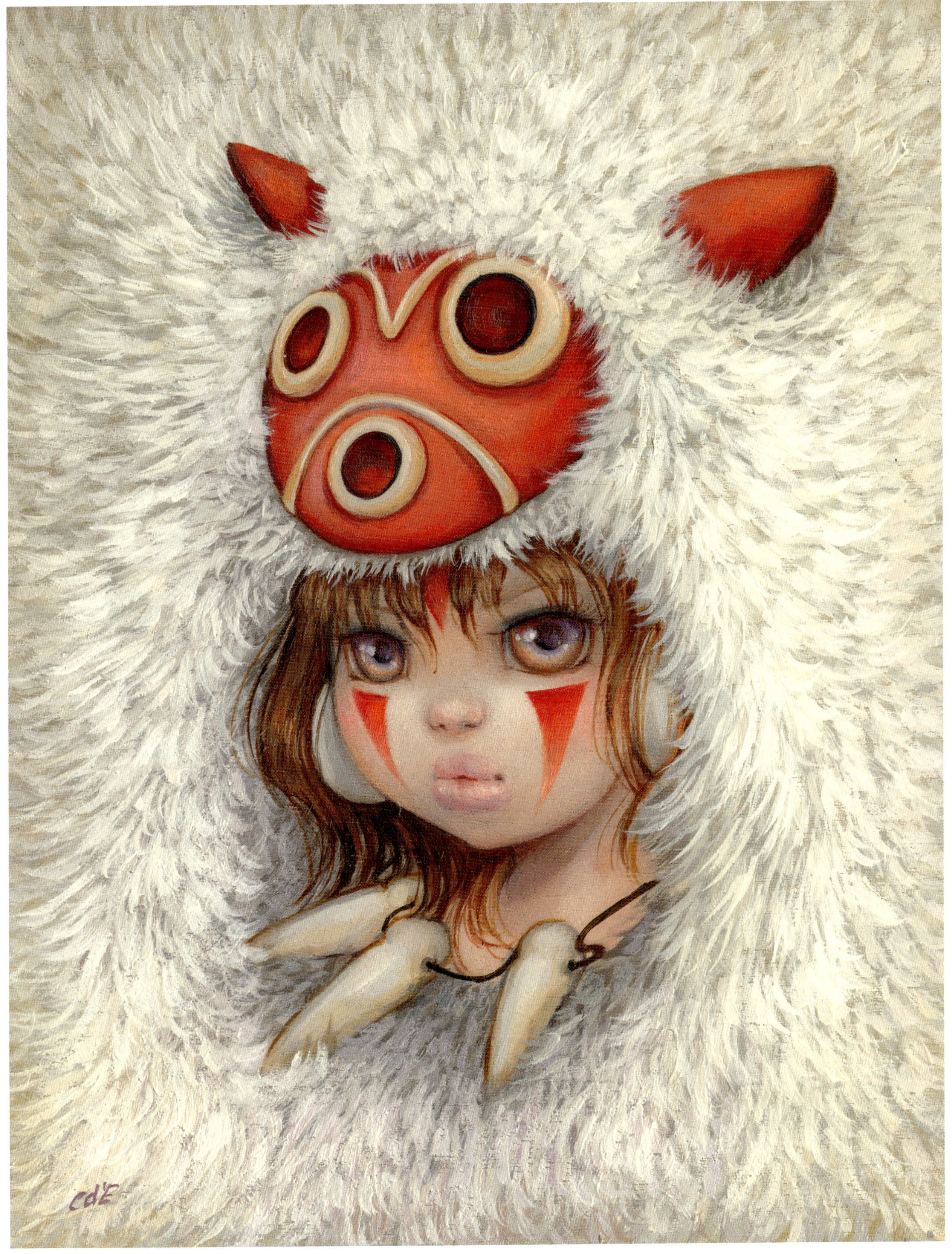

Like Mother Like Daughter | 8" X 10" | OIL | 2018

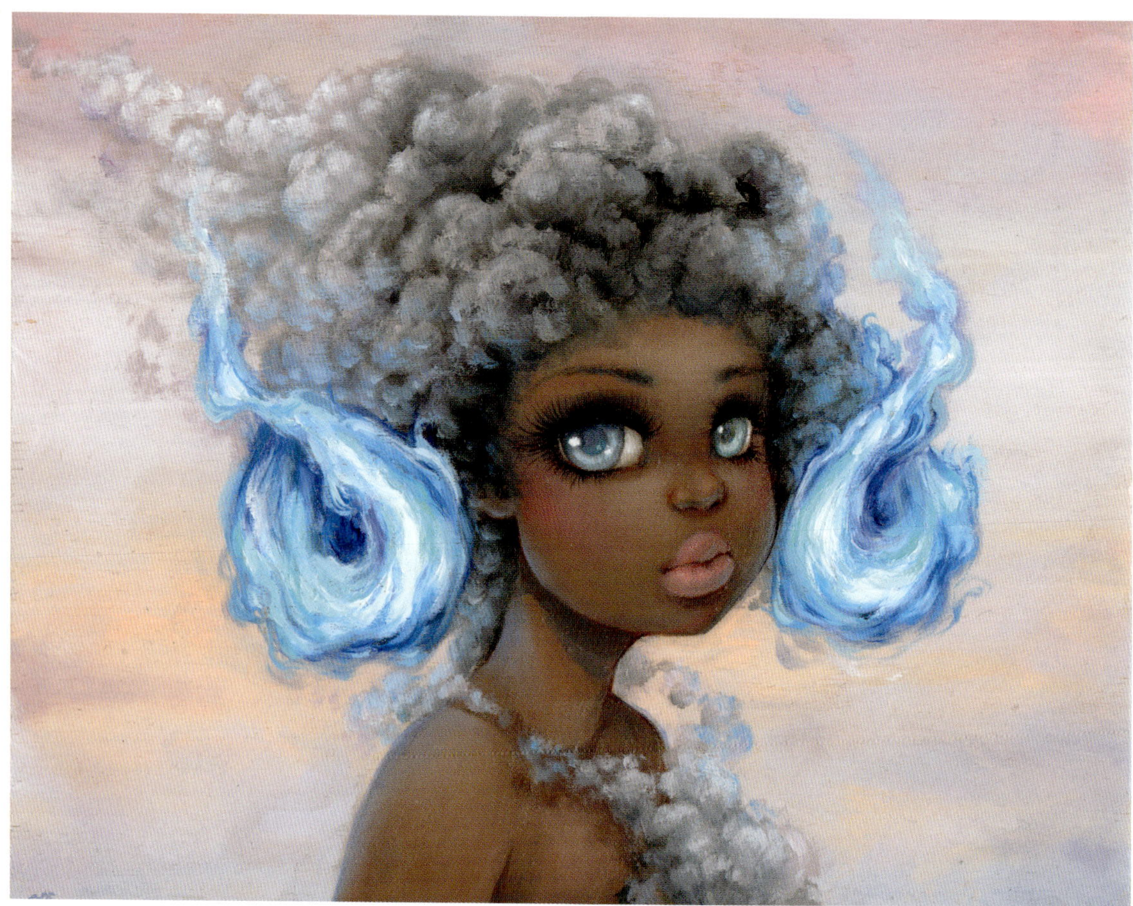

The Guardian Mazerunner | 8" X 10" | OIL | 2021

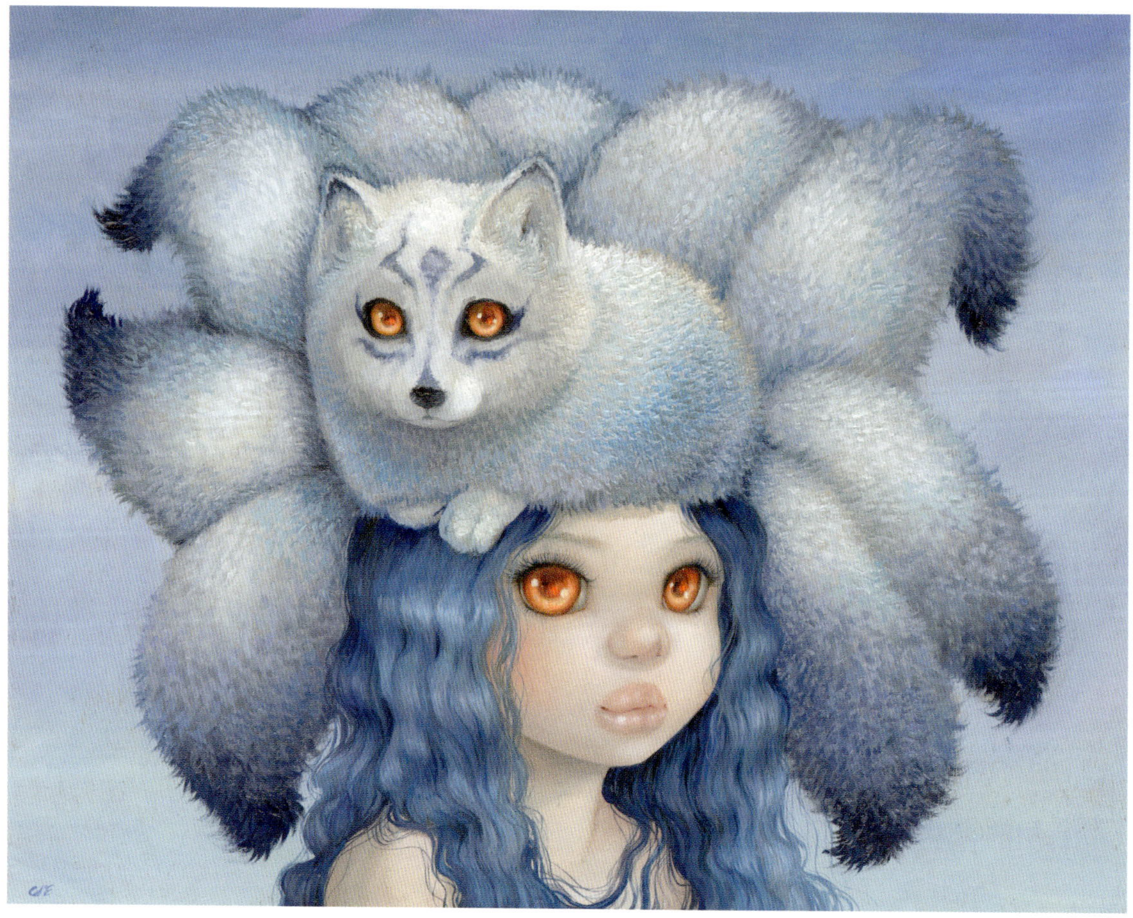

Kibbles and Nips | 11" X 14" | OIL | 2021

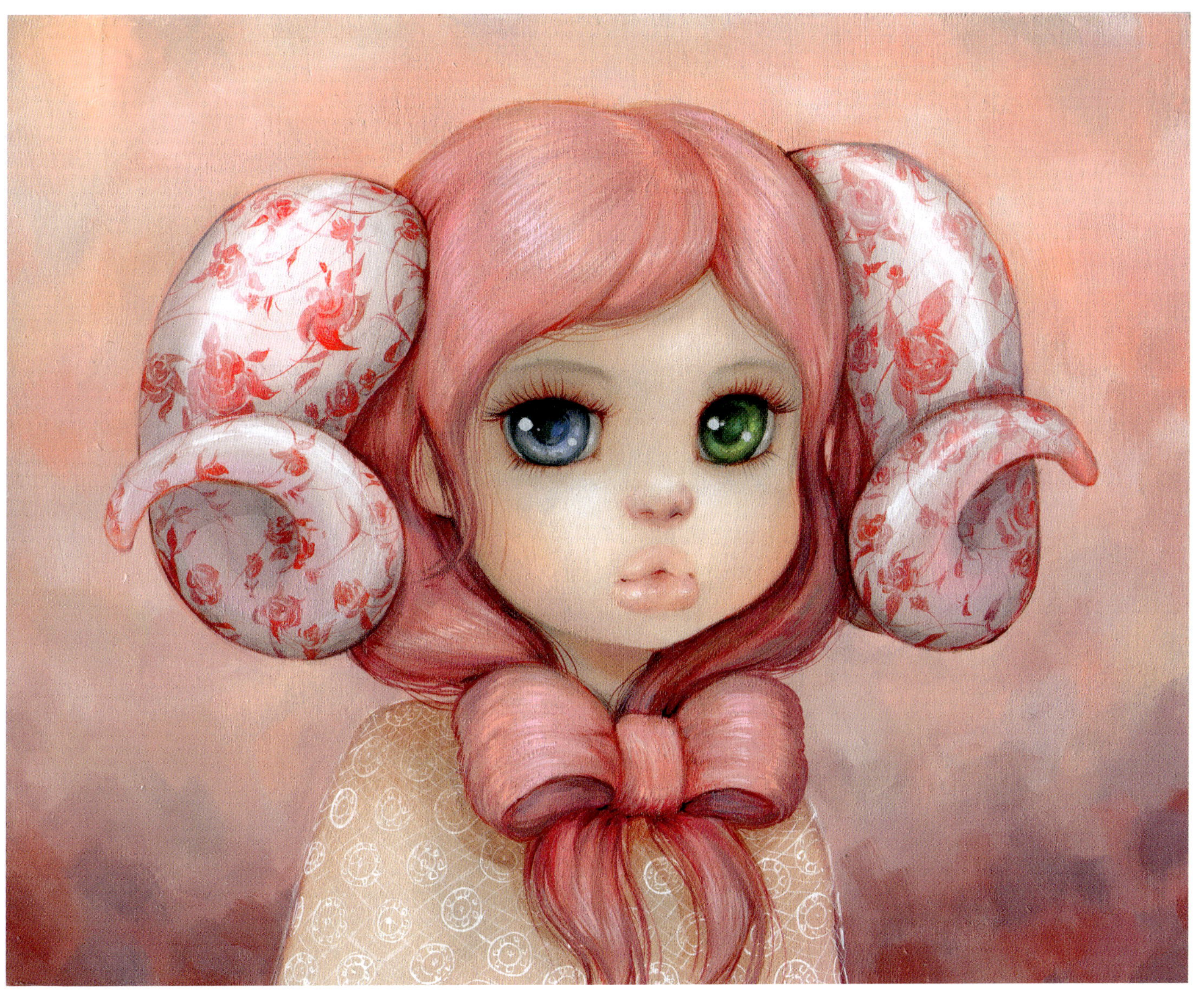

Fayette | 8" X 10" | OIL | 2019

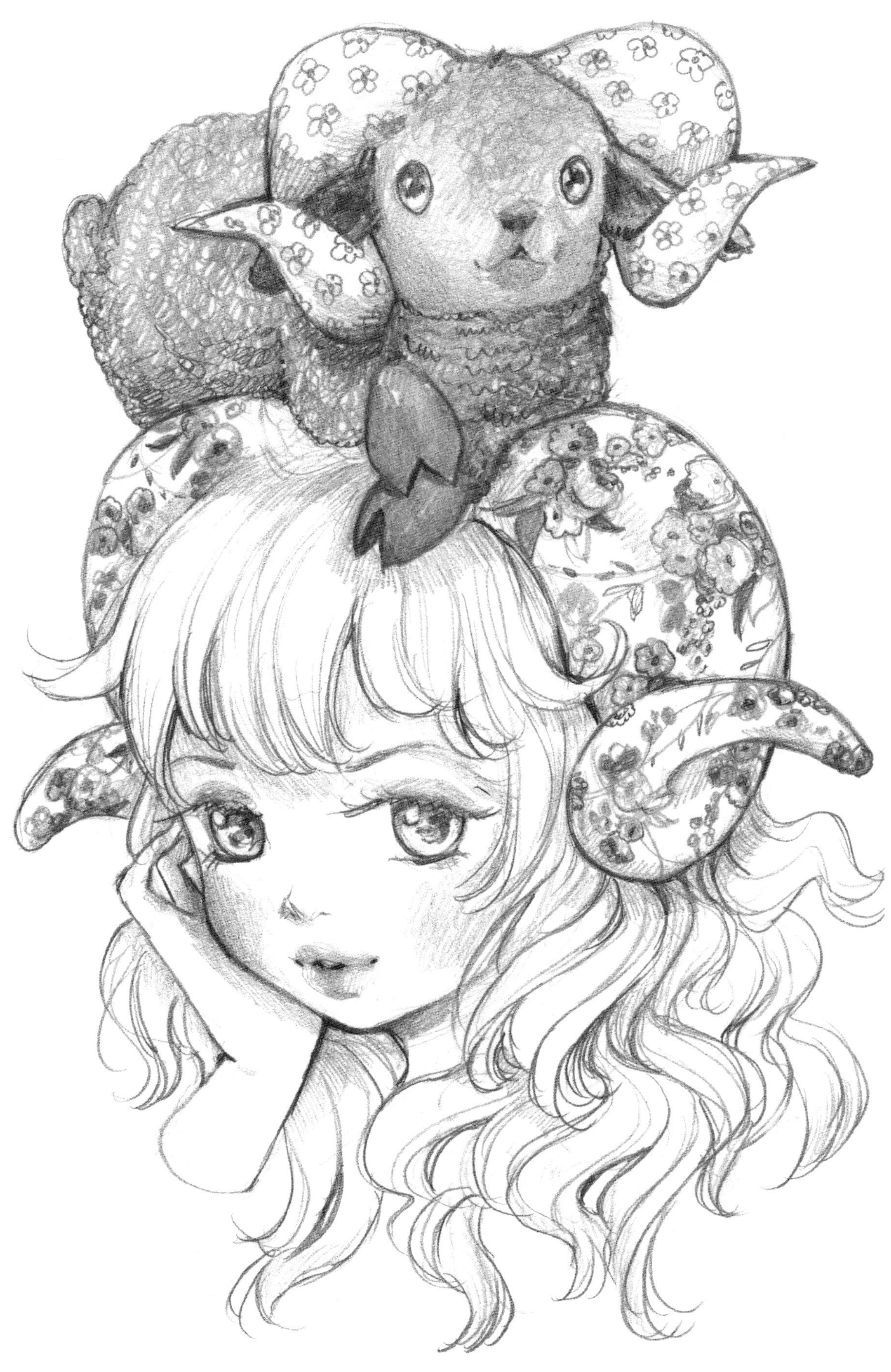

Aries Rising | 5" X 7" | GRAPHITE | 2020

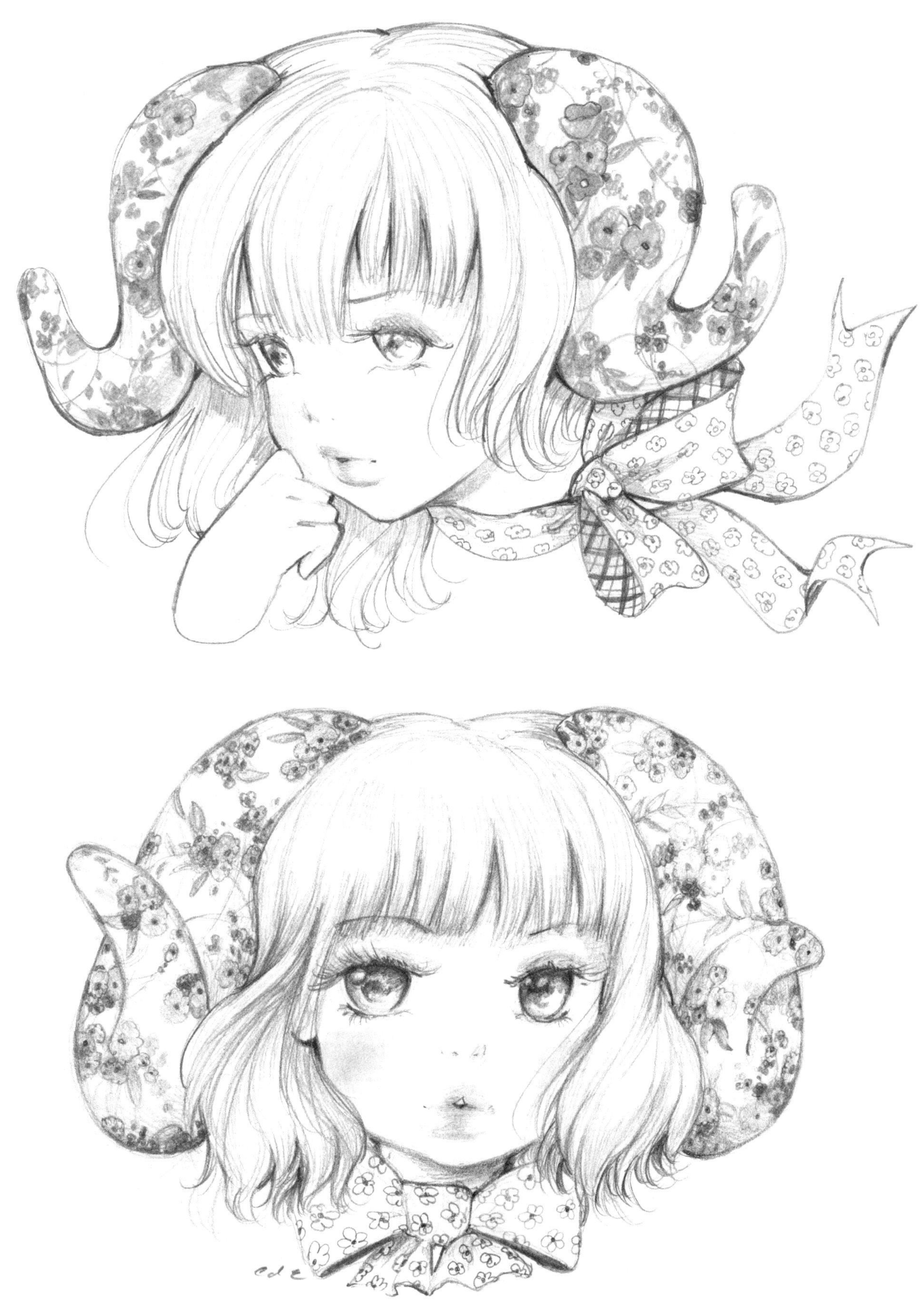

Fleur | 5" X 7" | GRAPHITE | 2020
Florette | 5" X 7" | GRAPHITE | 2020

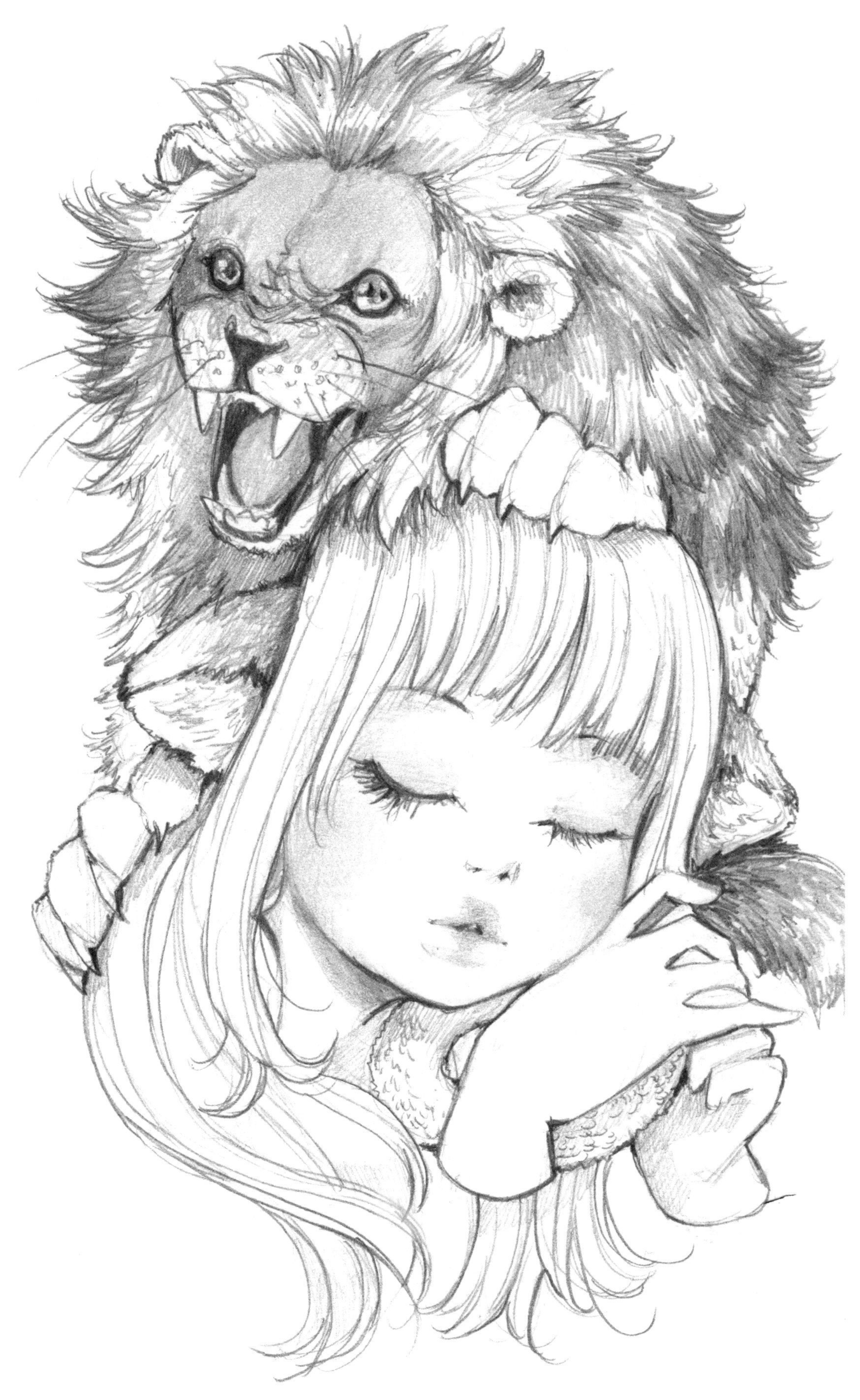

Daughter Of The Pride | 5" X 7" | GRAPHITE | 2020

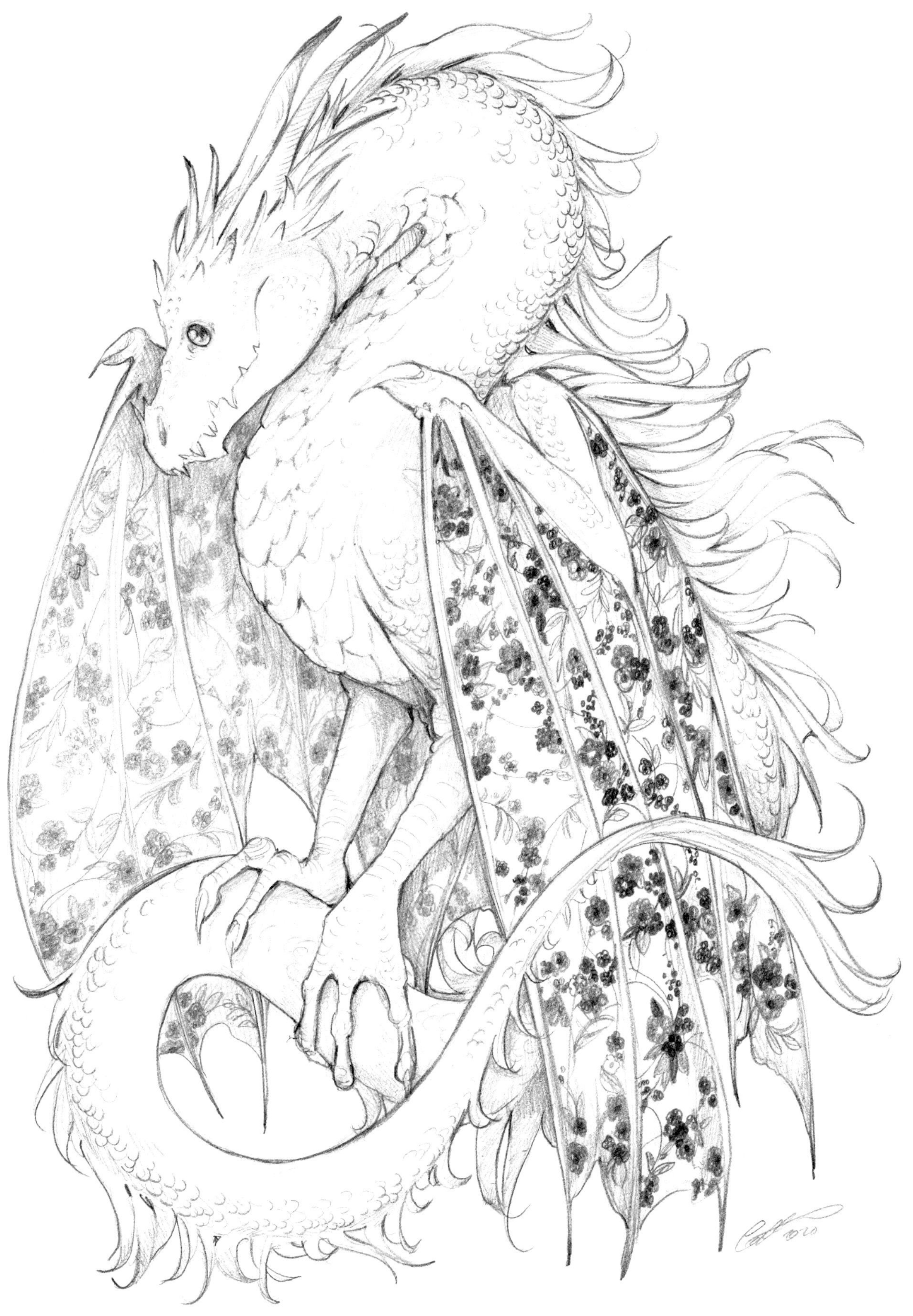

Victoria | 8.5" X 11" | GRAPHITE | 2020

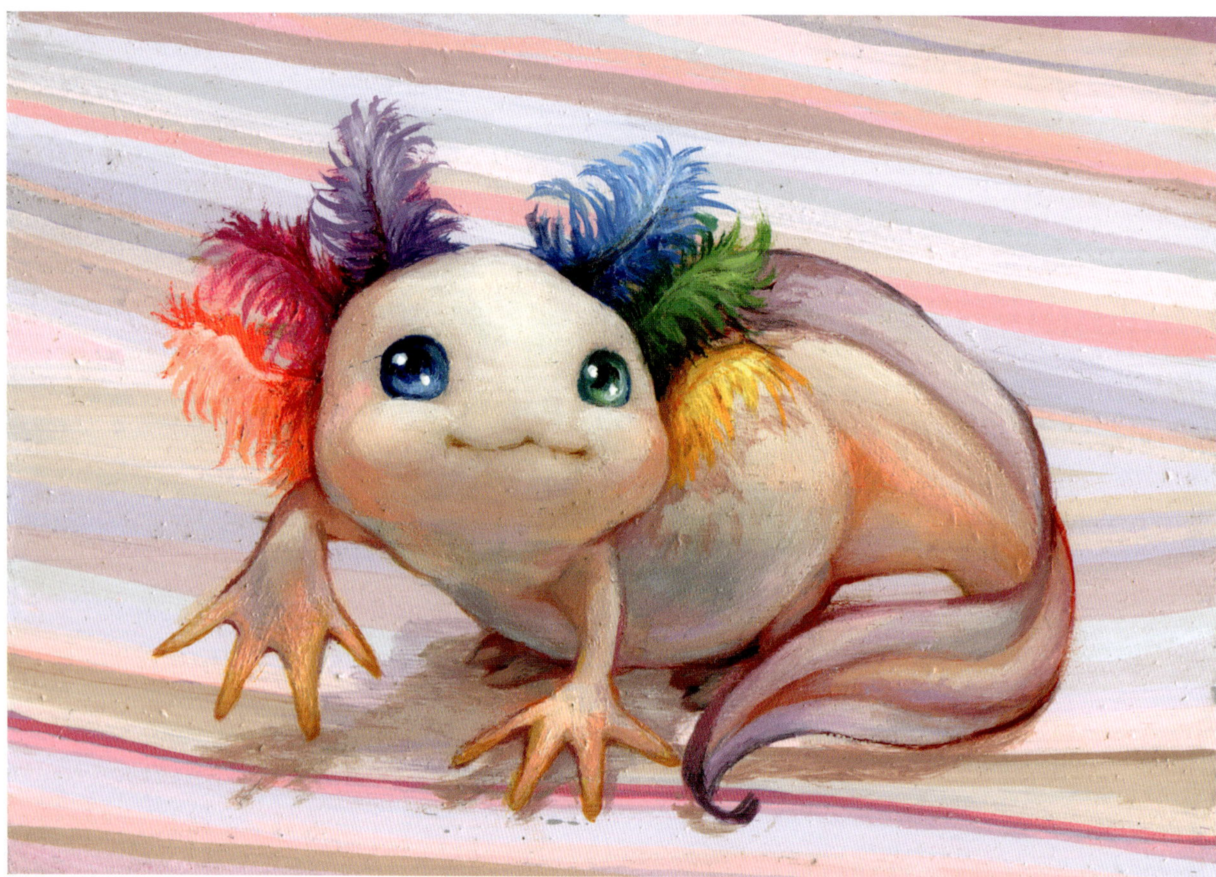

Pinkie Pie | 4" X 6" | OIL and ACRYLIC | 2017

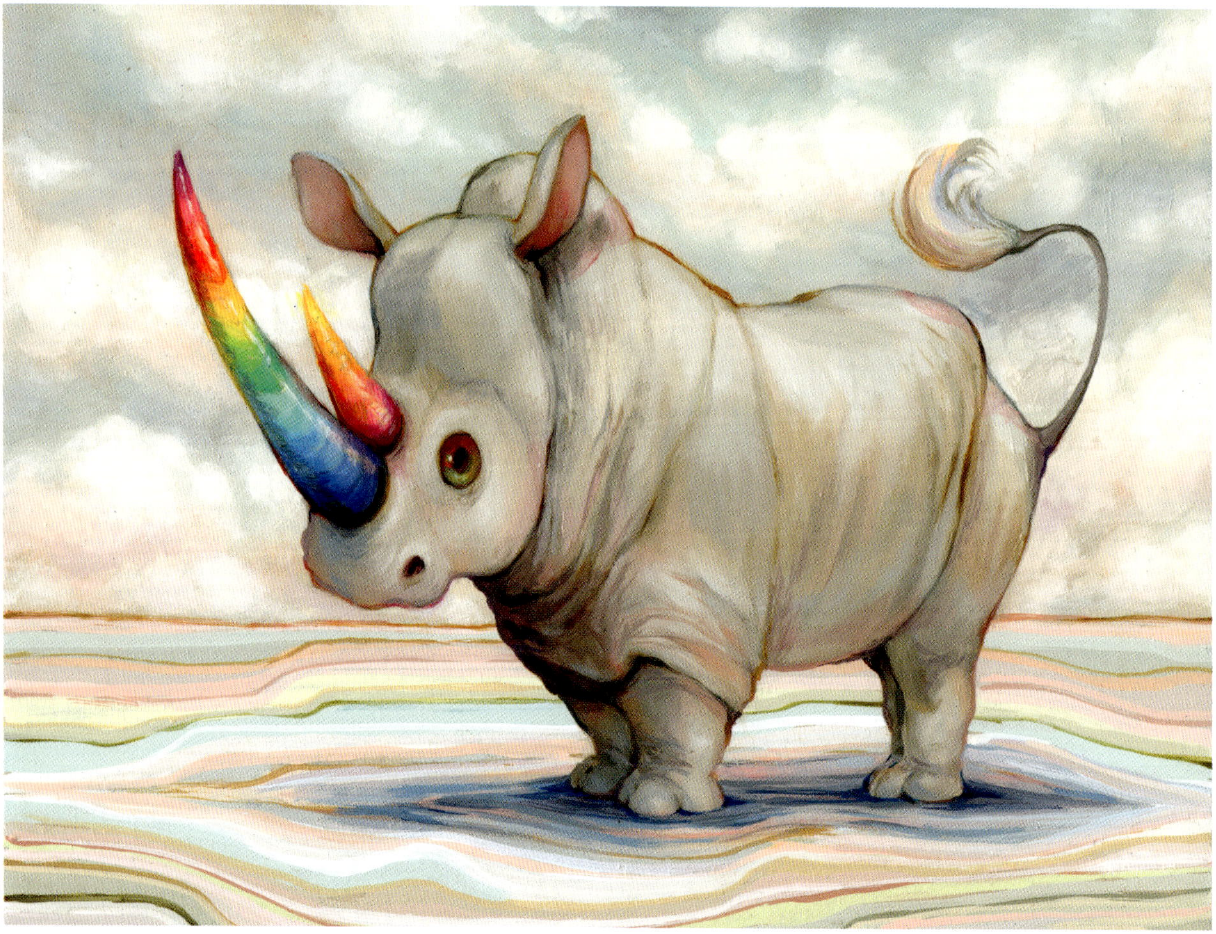

Albinow Rhinow | 8" X 10" | OIL | 2017

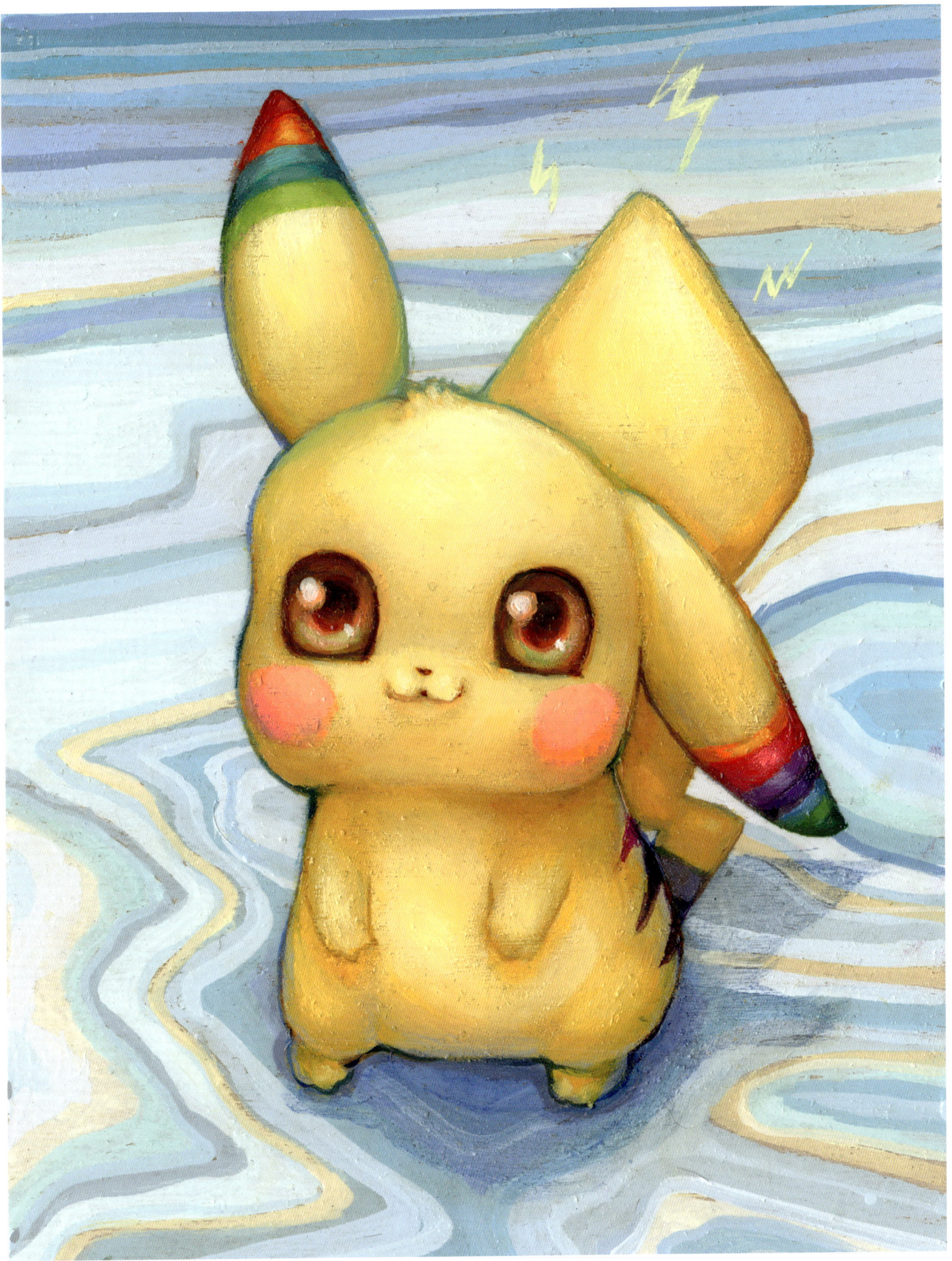

Pikabow | 5" X 7" | OIL and ACRYLIC | 2017

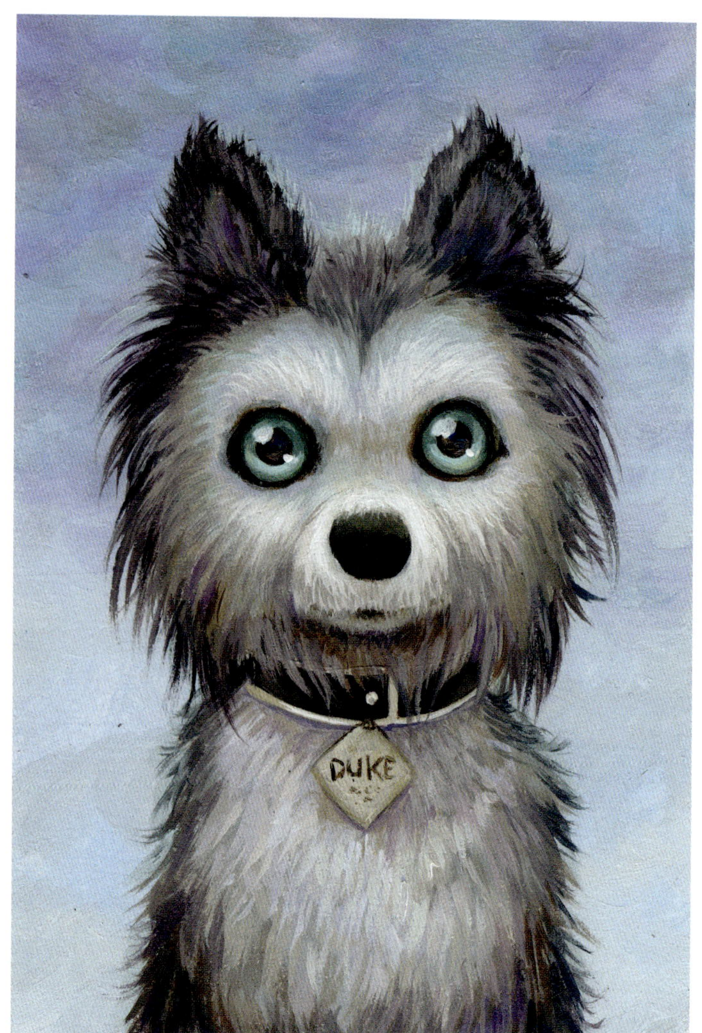

Jeff | 5" X 7" | OIL AND ACRYLIC | 2018

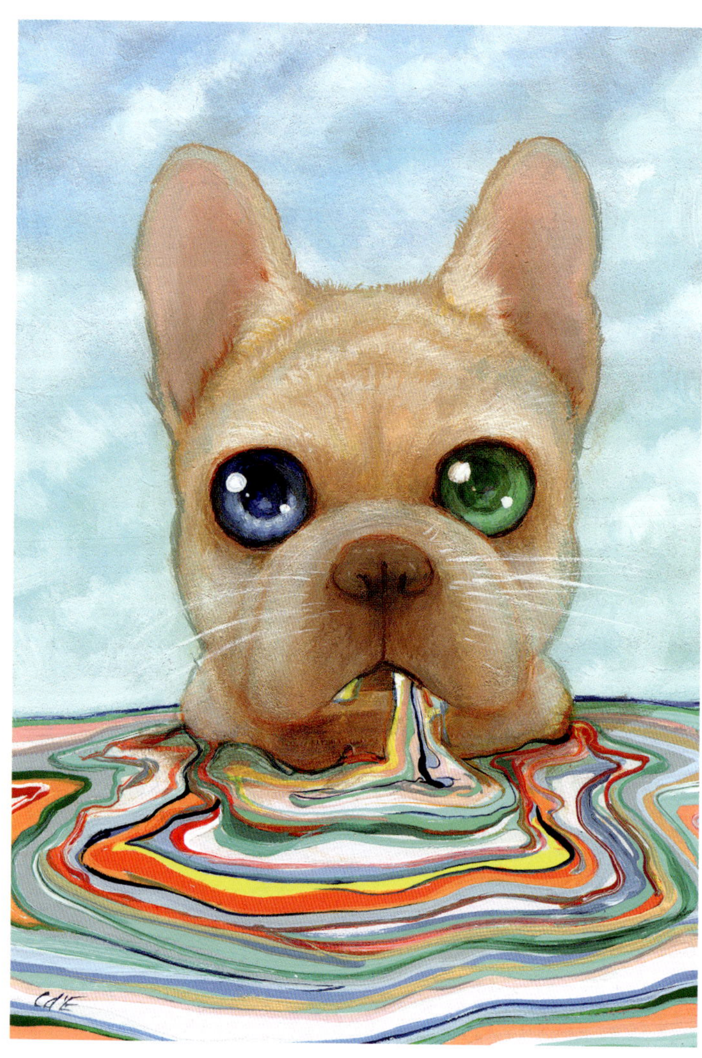

Sputum | 5" X 7" | OIL and ACRYLIC | 2020

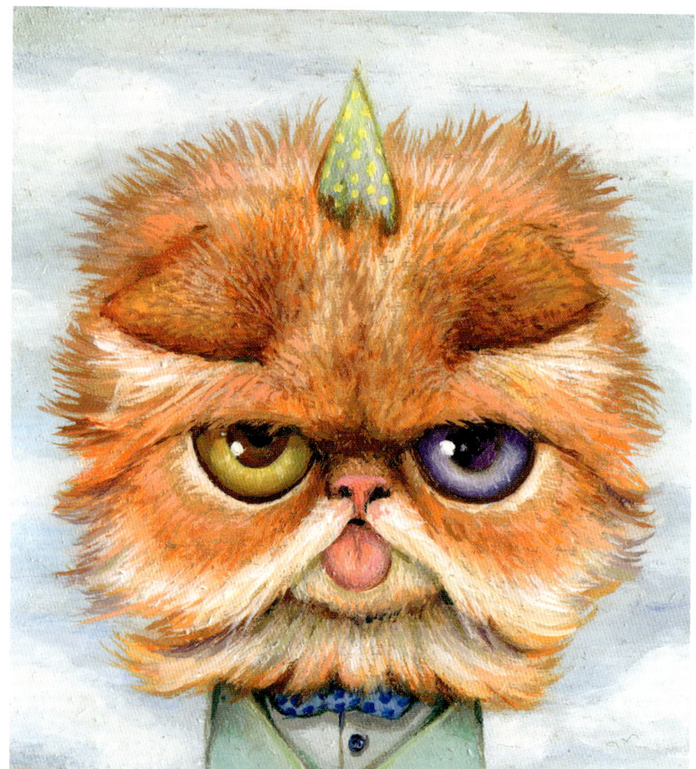

Bowie | 4" X 4" | OIL and ACRYLIC | 2017

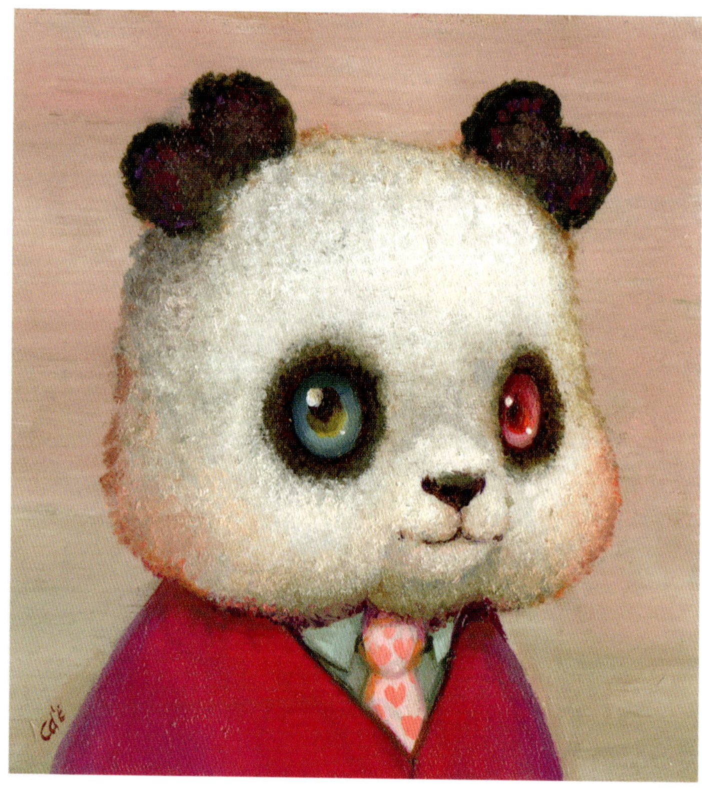

Professor Love | 4" X 4" | OIL and ACRYLIC | 2017

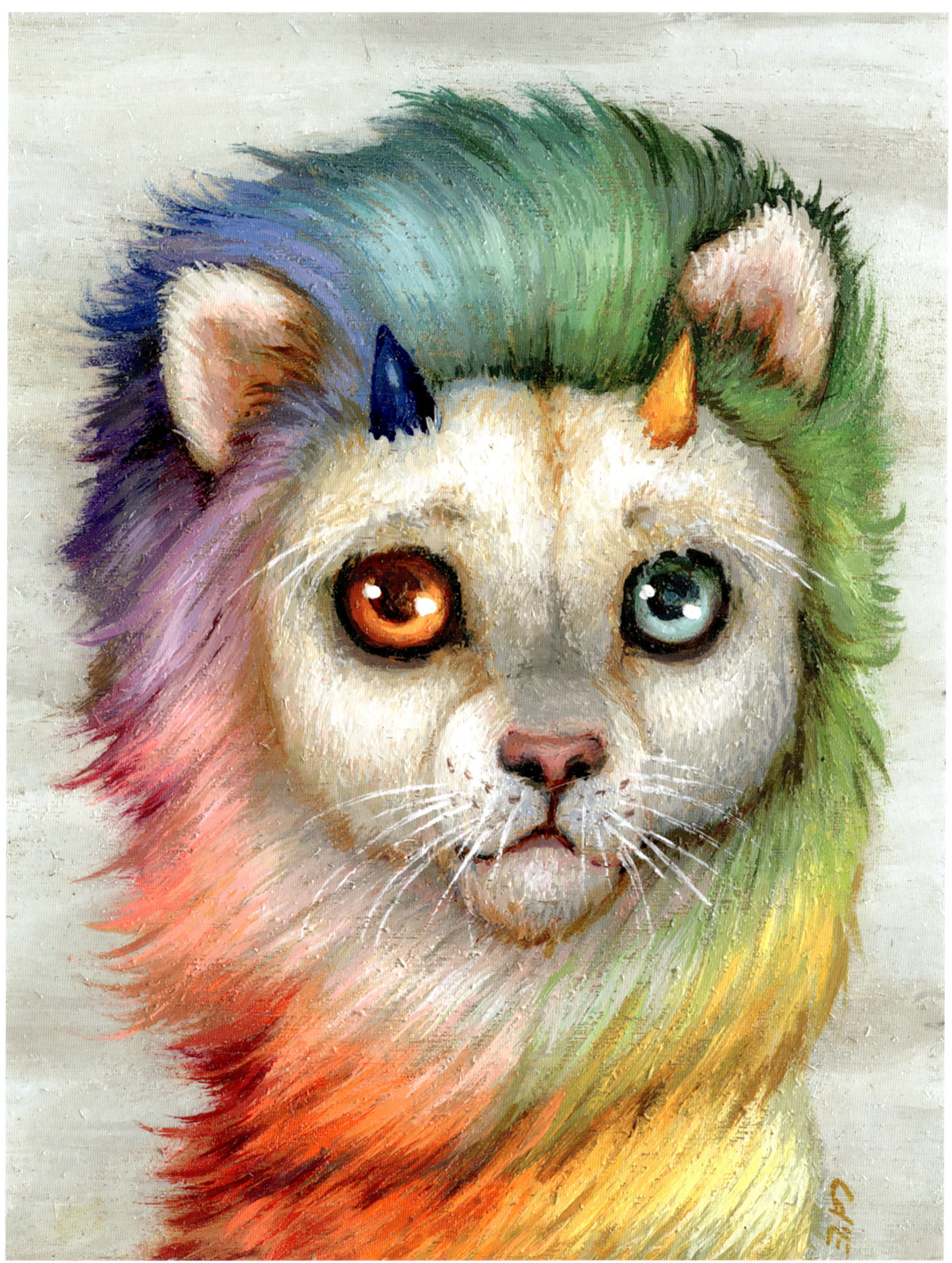

Dandylion | 4" X 5" | OIL and ACRYLIC | 2009

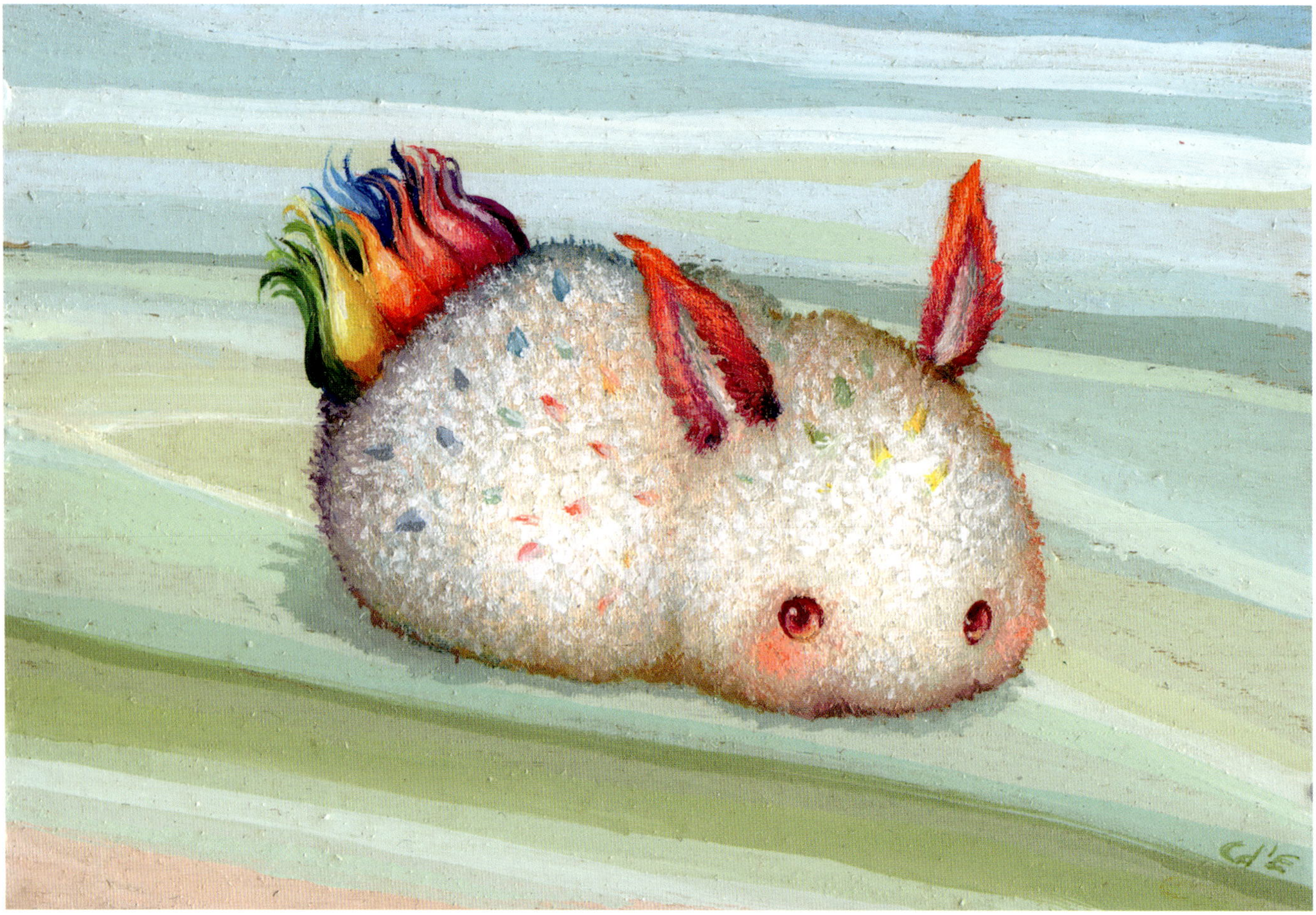

Sea Bun Bun | 4" X 6" | OIL and ACRYLIC | 2017

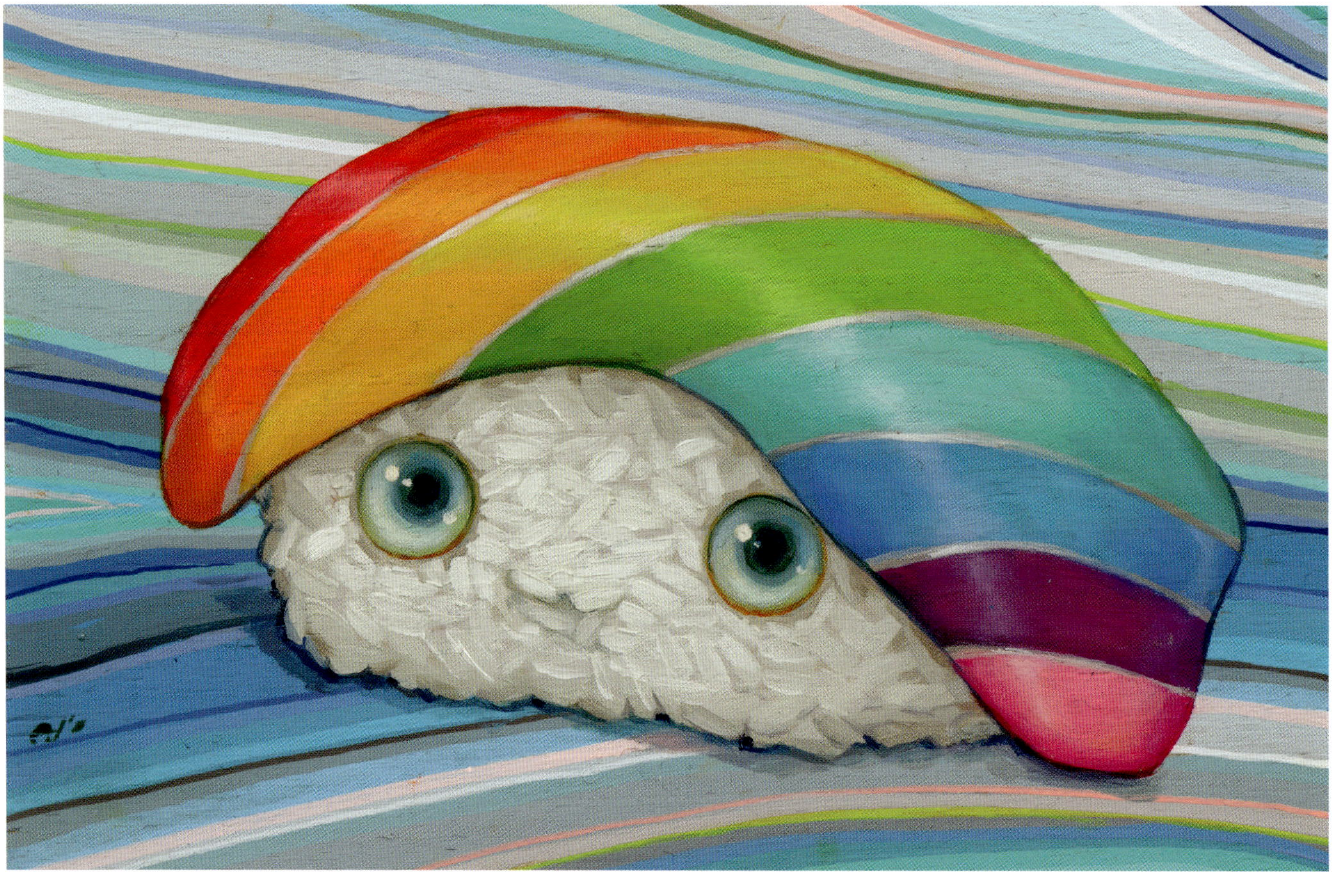

Rainbow Roll | 5" X 7" | OIL | 2016

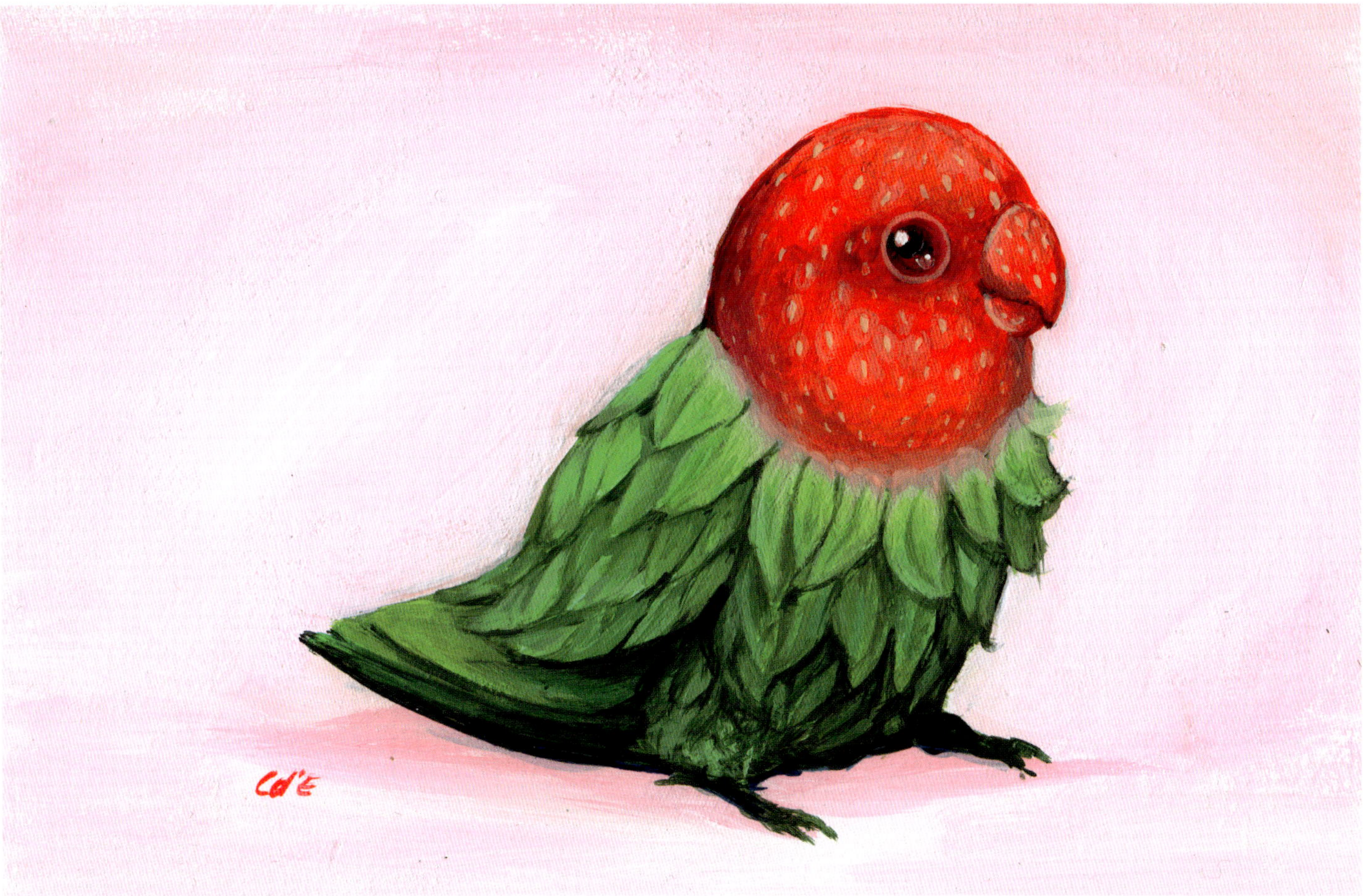

The Loveberry | 4" X 6" | OIL and ACRYLIC | 2020

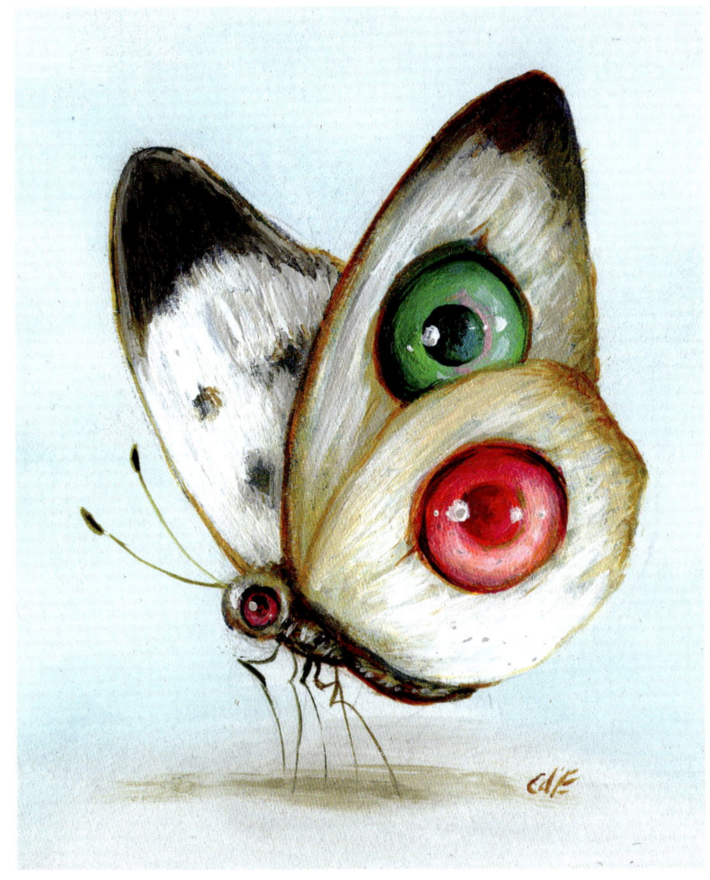

Fluttereyes | 4" X 6" | OIL and ACRYLIC | 2018

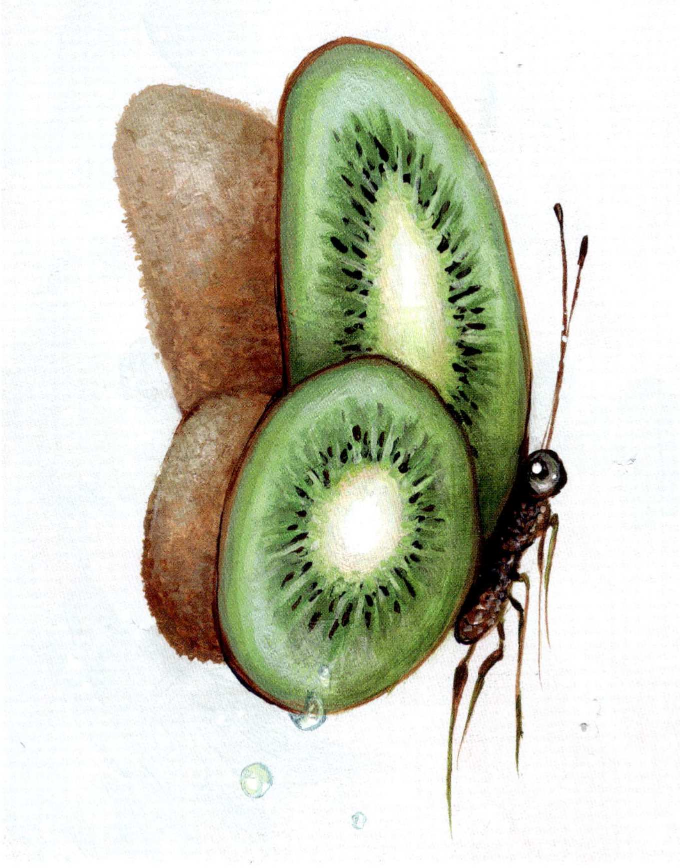

Midsummer Morsel | 5" X 7" | OIL and ACRYLIC | 2019

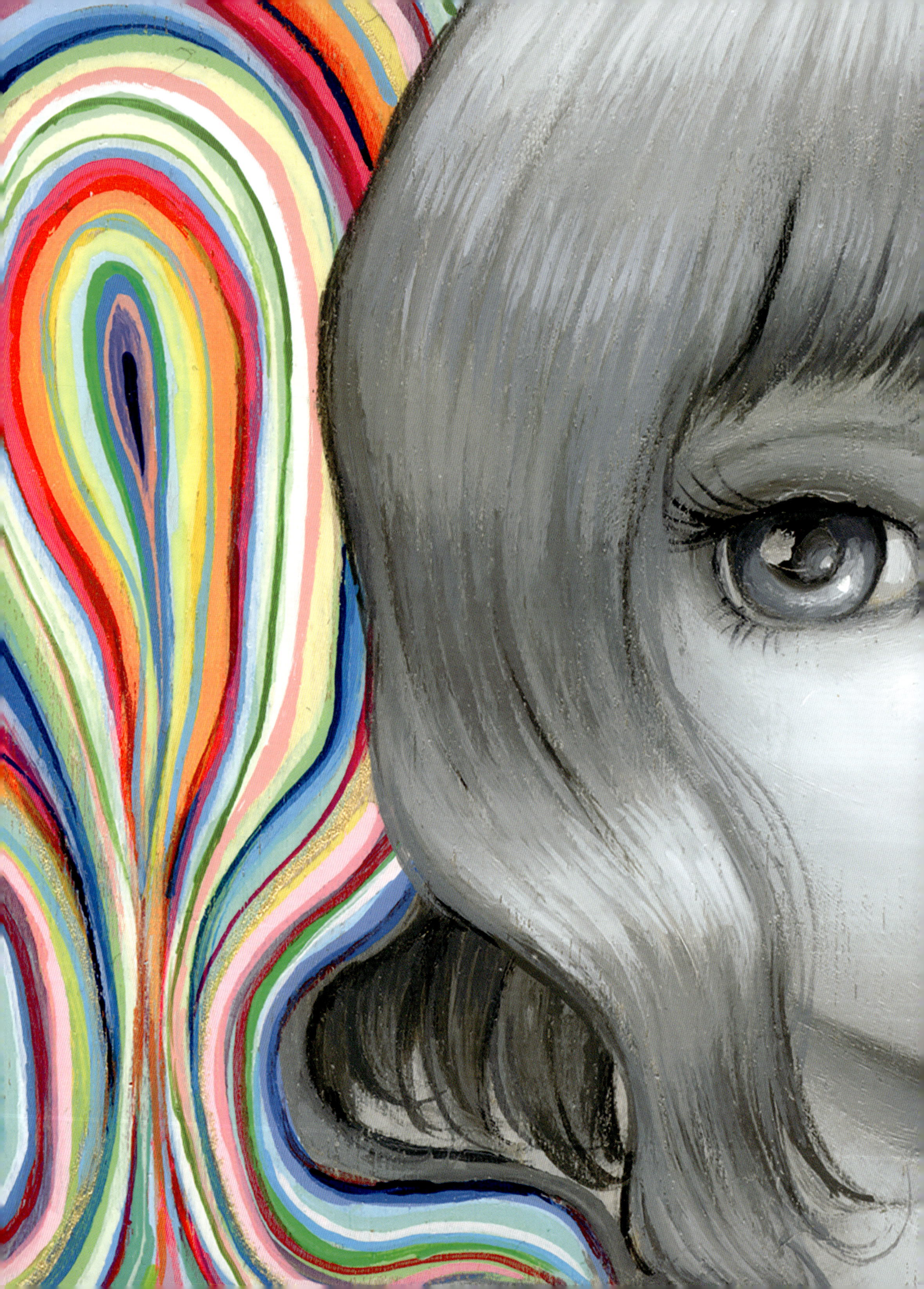

SOLO SHOW:

THE HUMAN ODYSSEY

This show opened in November 2020 at Dorothy Circus Gallery's London location. It featured over a dozen new paintings and drawings exploring the difficult journey humanity embarked on in 2020 and the emotional ties that bound us all together. Joy and despair dance around each other, illustrating the artist's emotional journey as well as the dualities of the human experience.

Facing page:
Interna | 8" X 10" | OIL | 2020

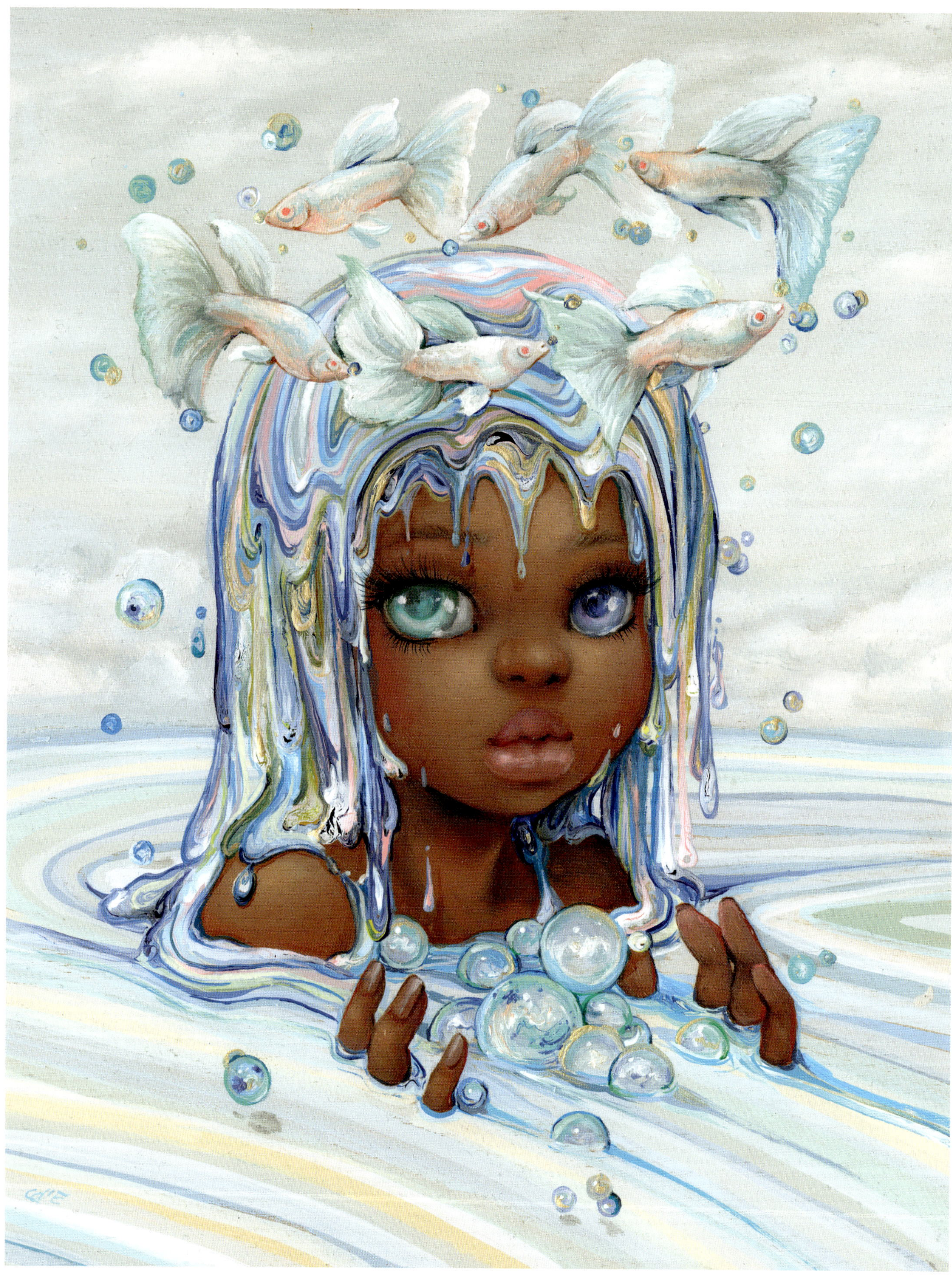

Agent of Reflexivity | 8" X 10" | OIL | 2020

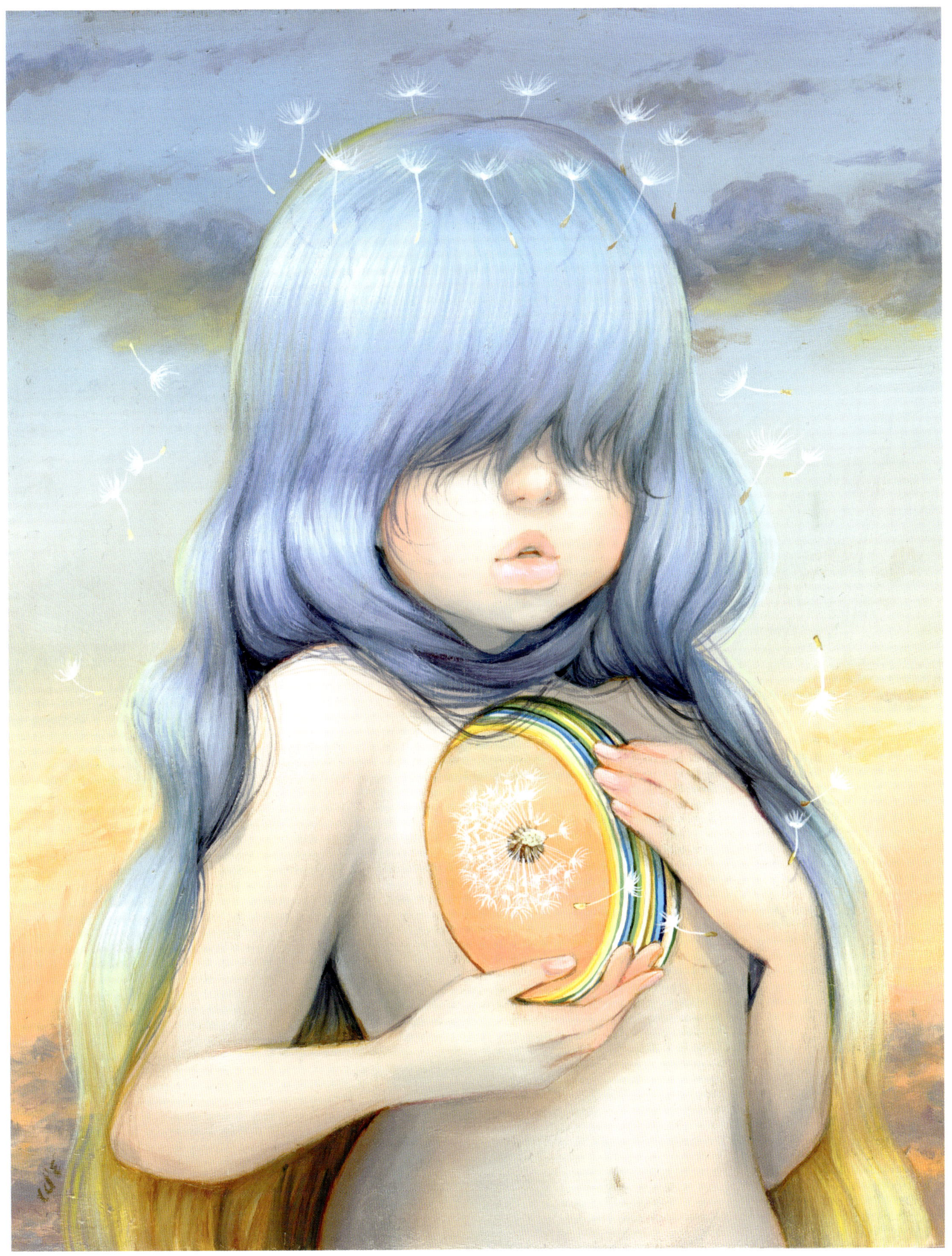

Diaspora | 8" X 10" | OIL | 2020

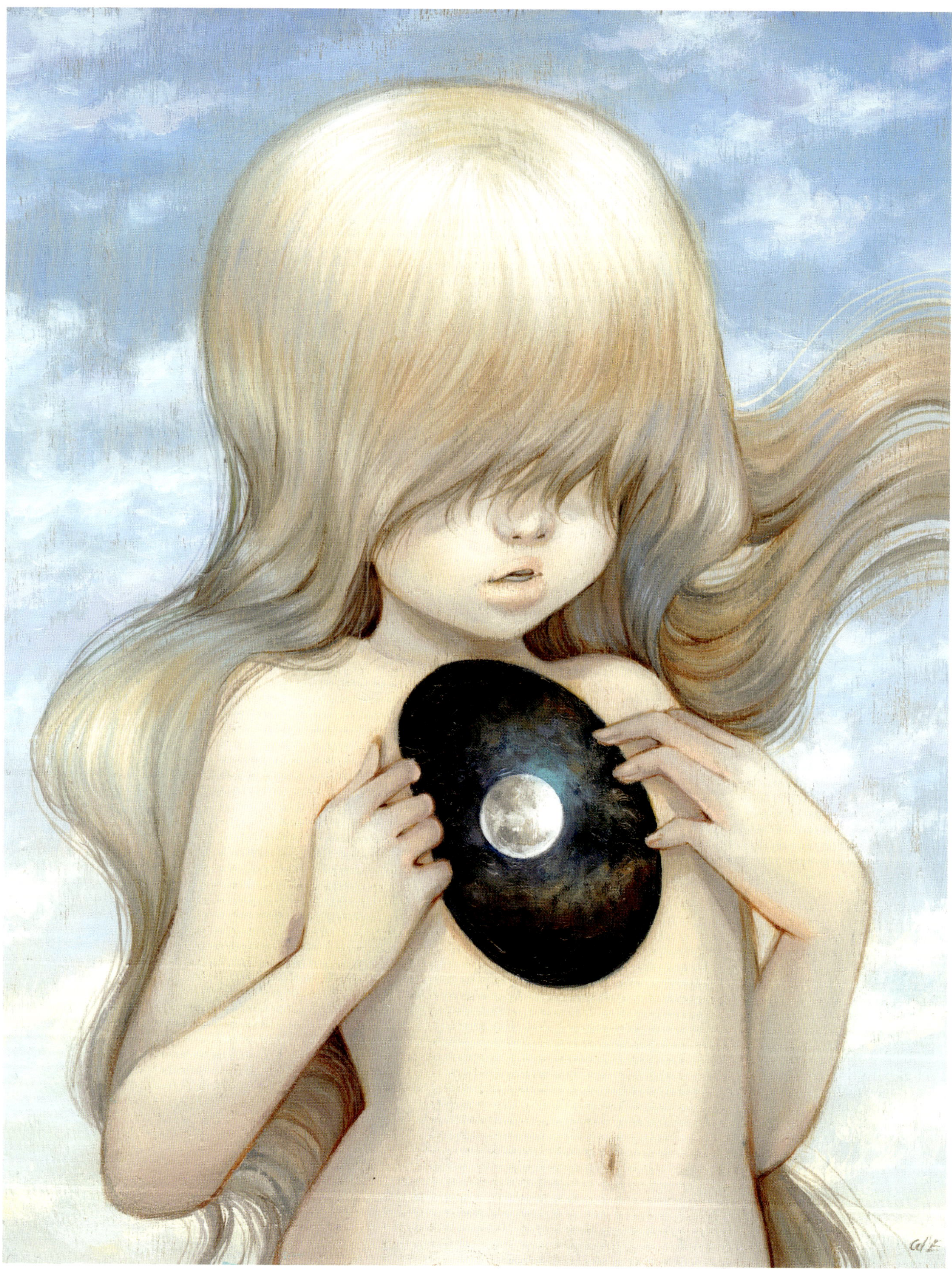

La Luna | 8" X 10" | OIL | 2020

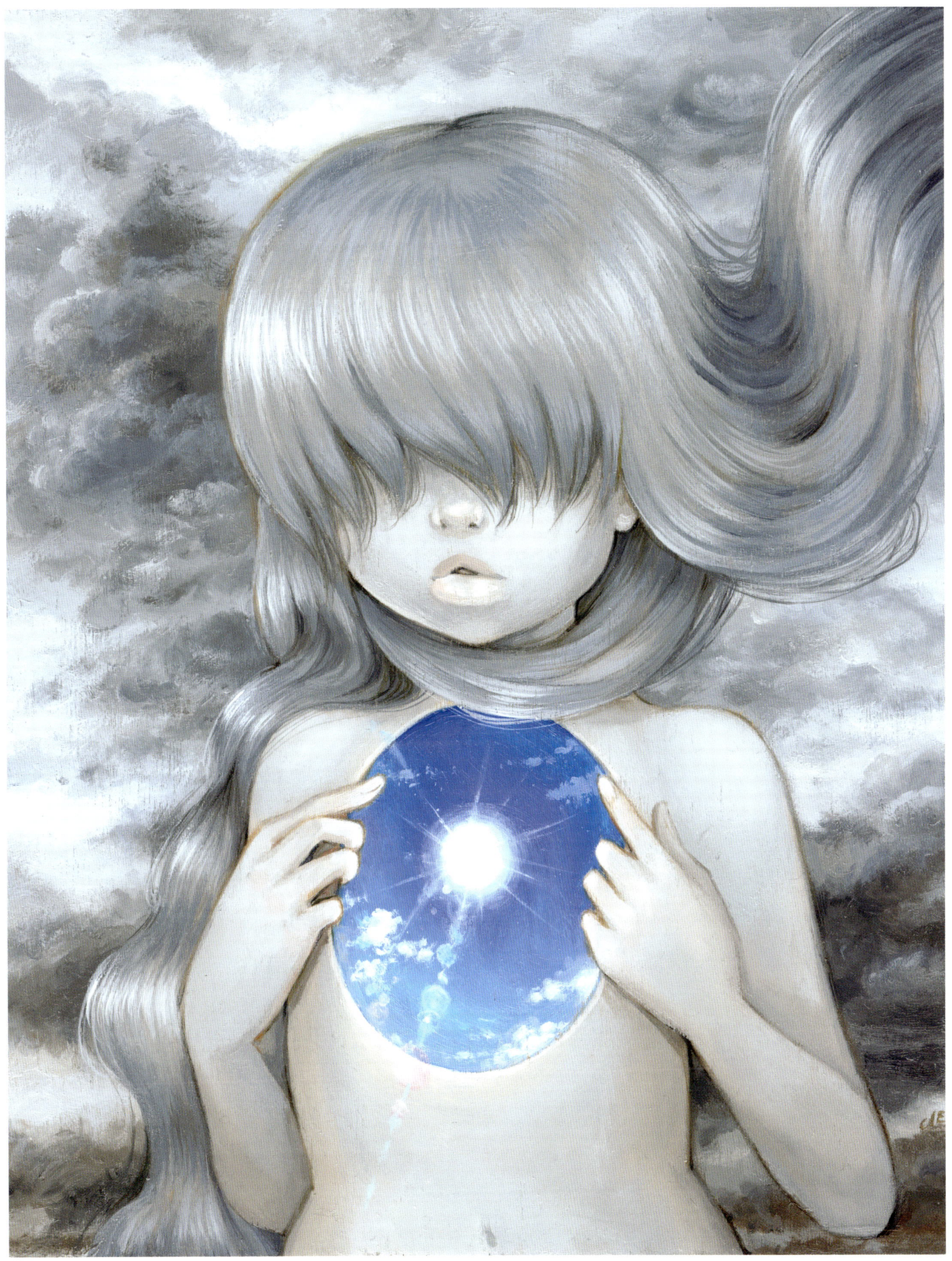

The Lighthouse | 8" X 10" | OIL | 2020

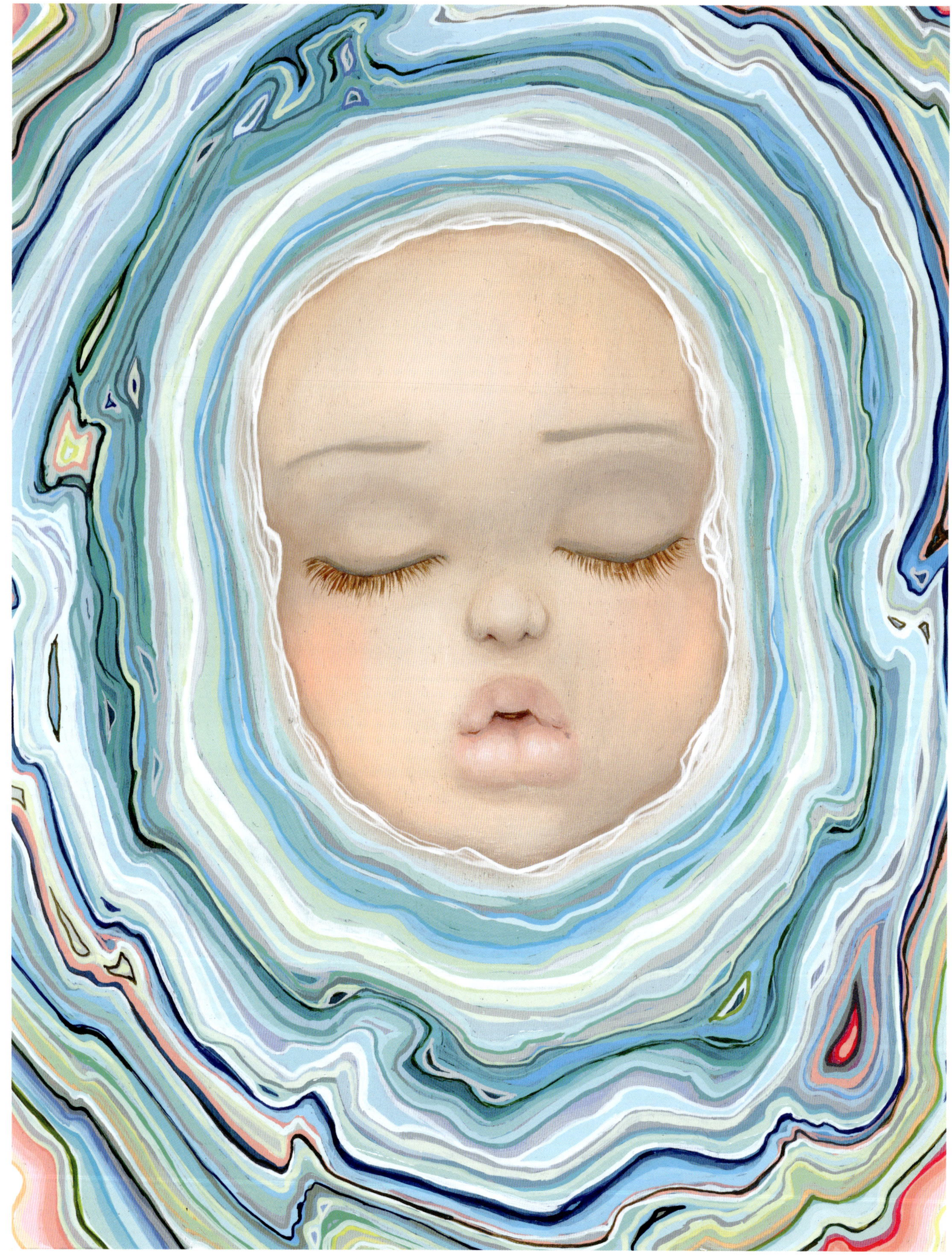

Pacifica | 8" X 10" | OIL | 2016

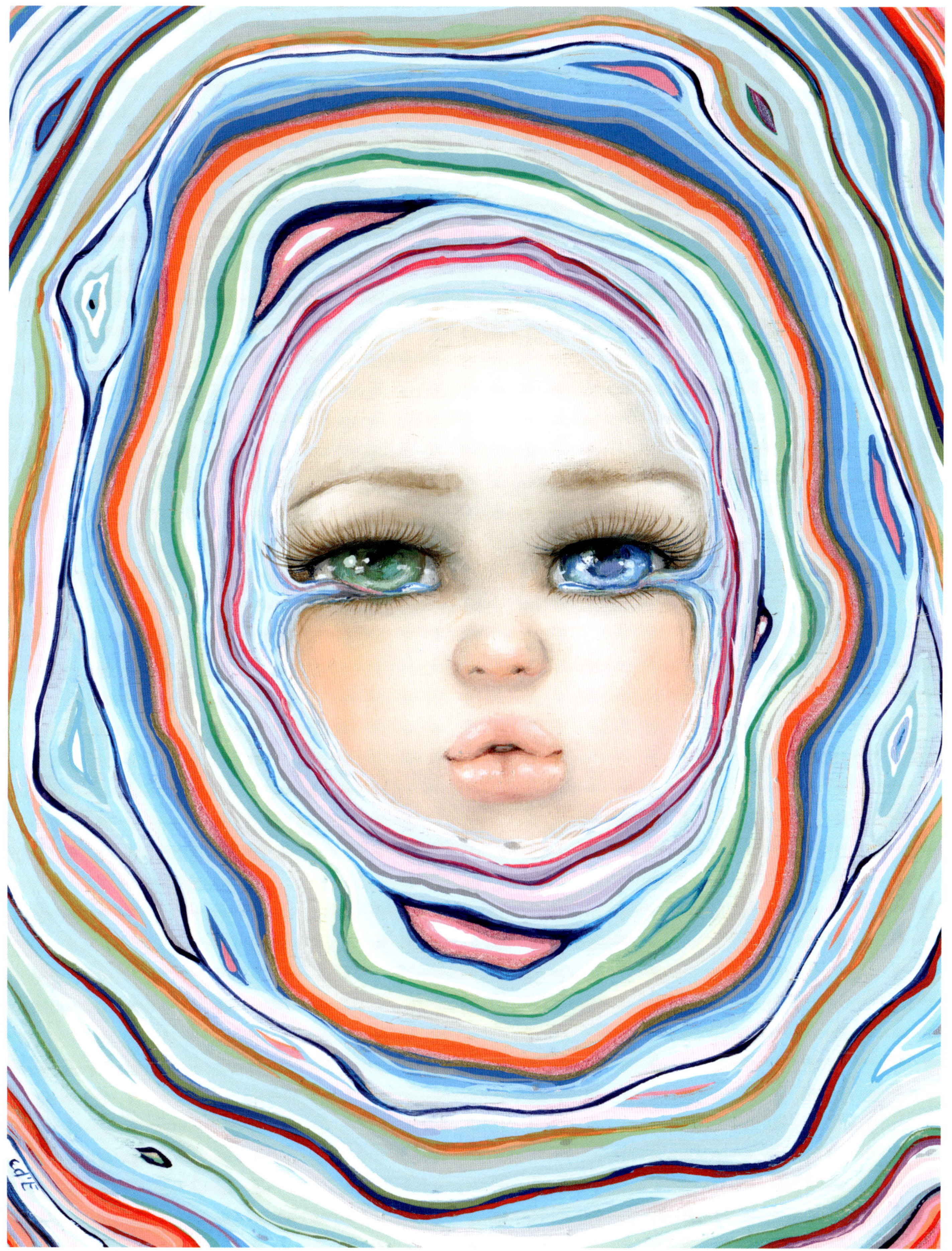

Atlantica | 8" X 10" | OIL | 2020

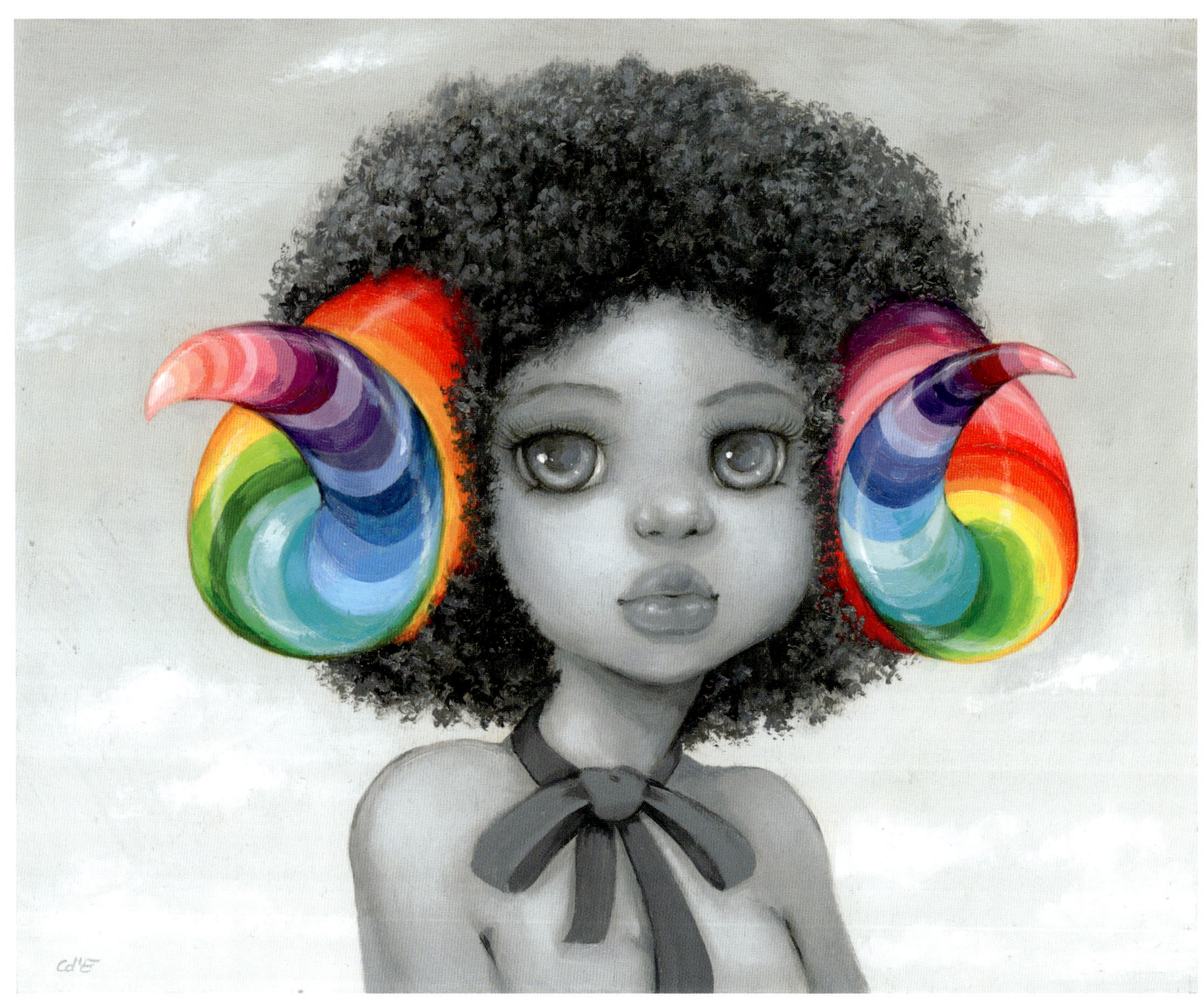

Spectra | 8" X 10" | OIL | 2020

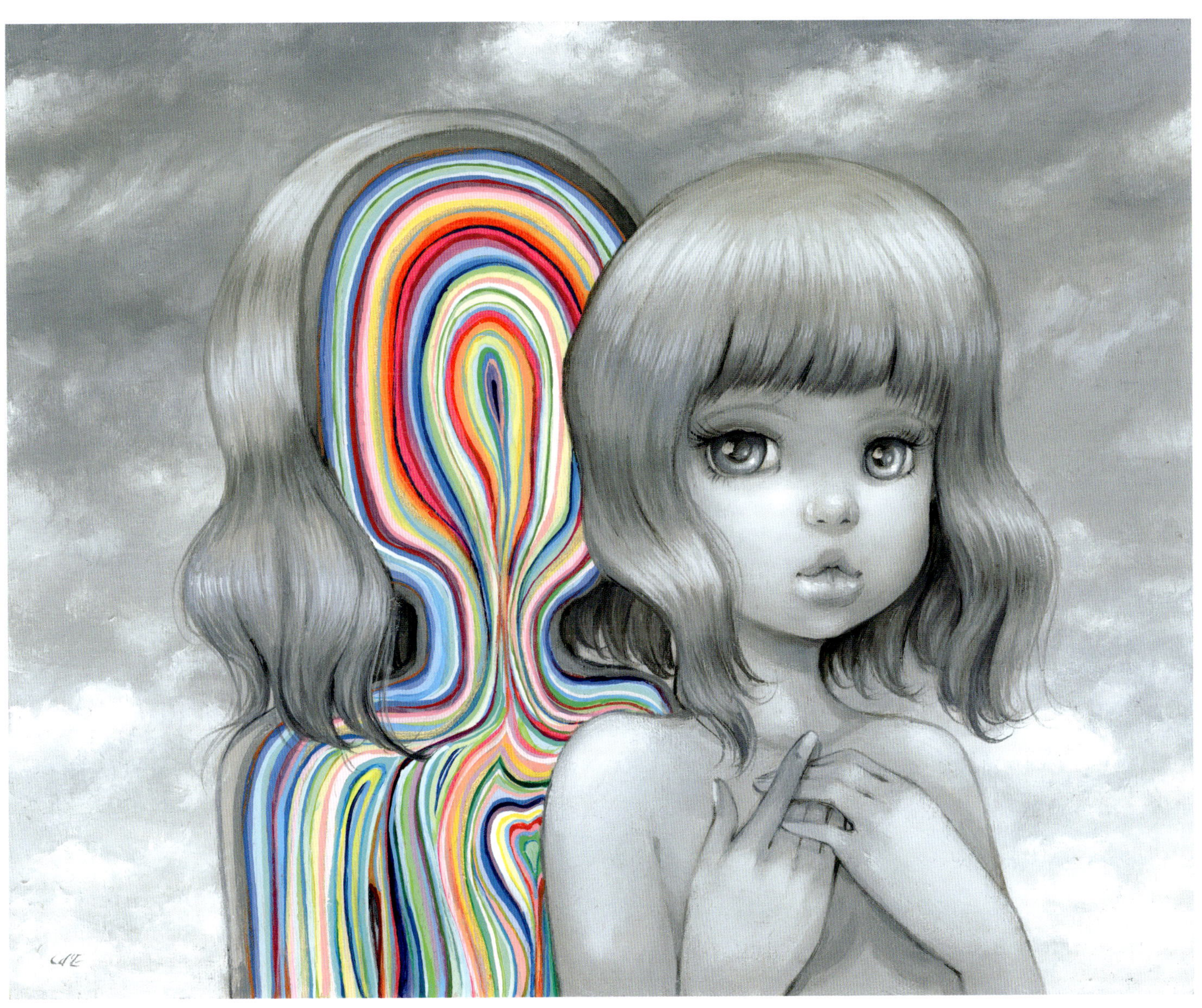

Internal | 8" X 10" | OIL | 2020

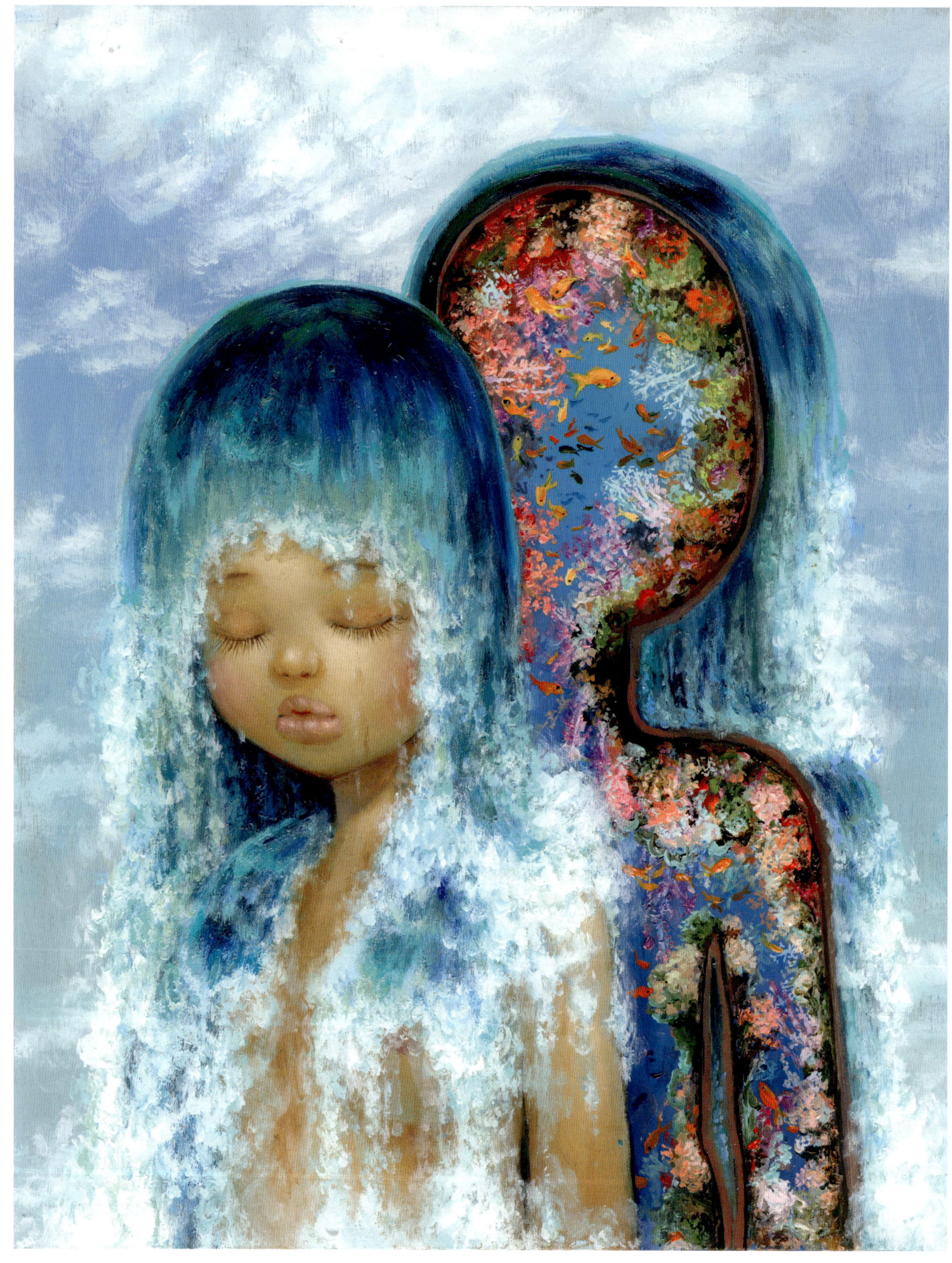

Mariana's Tide | 8" X 10" | OIL | 2020

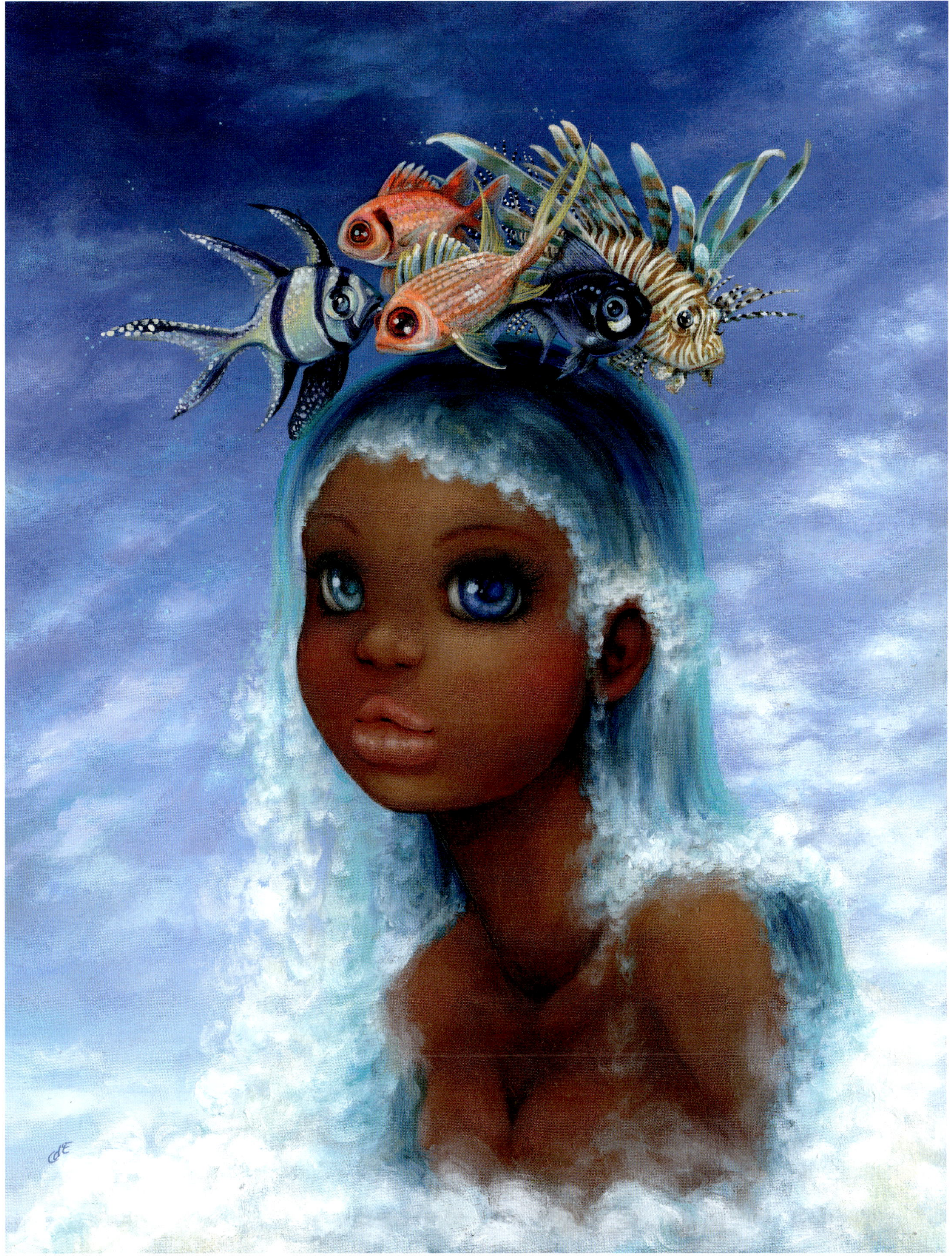

Nocturna | 11" X 14" | OIL | 2020

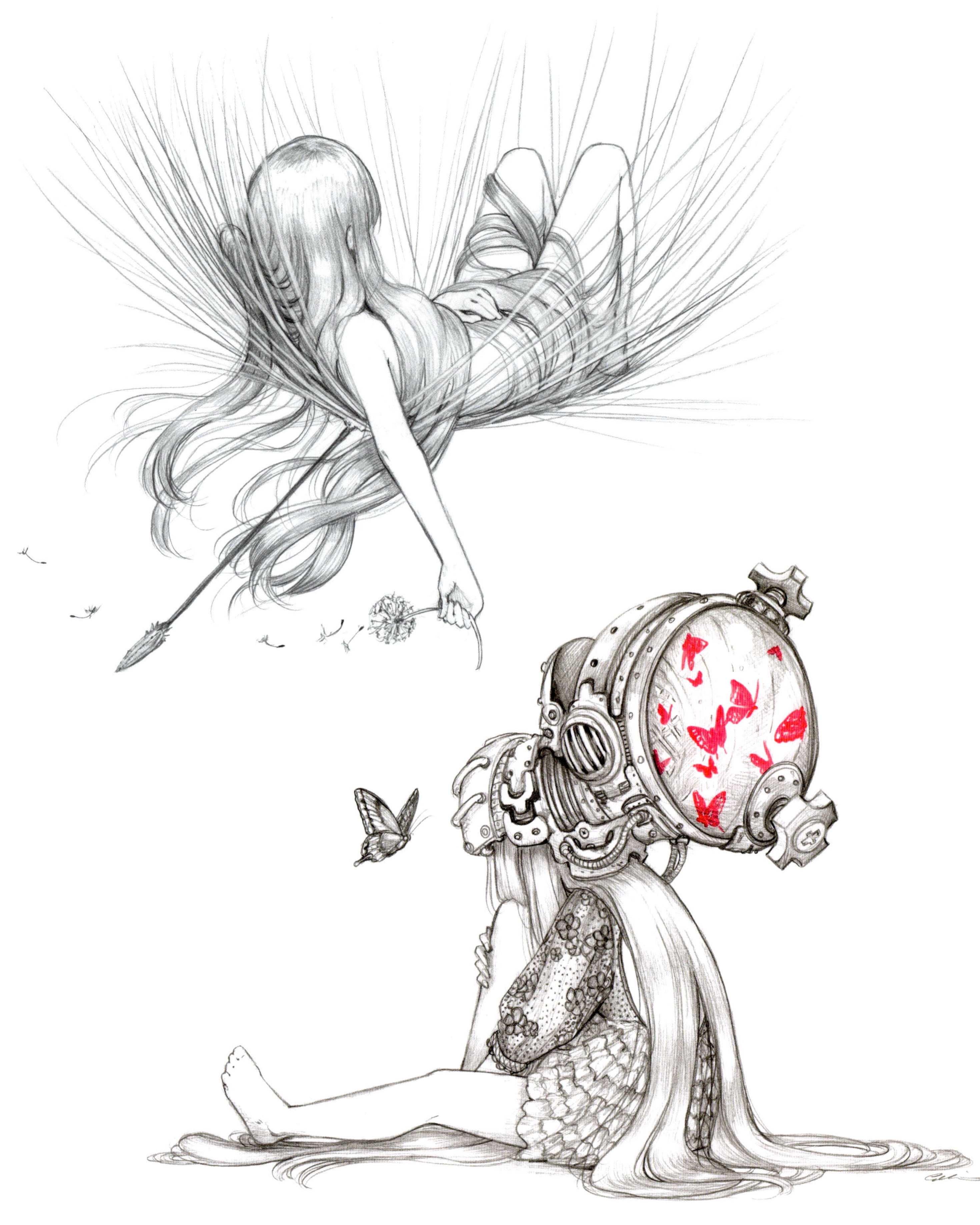

The Newborn | 8.5" X 11" | GRAPHITE | 2020
The Daydreamer | 8.5" X 11" | GRAPHITE | 2020

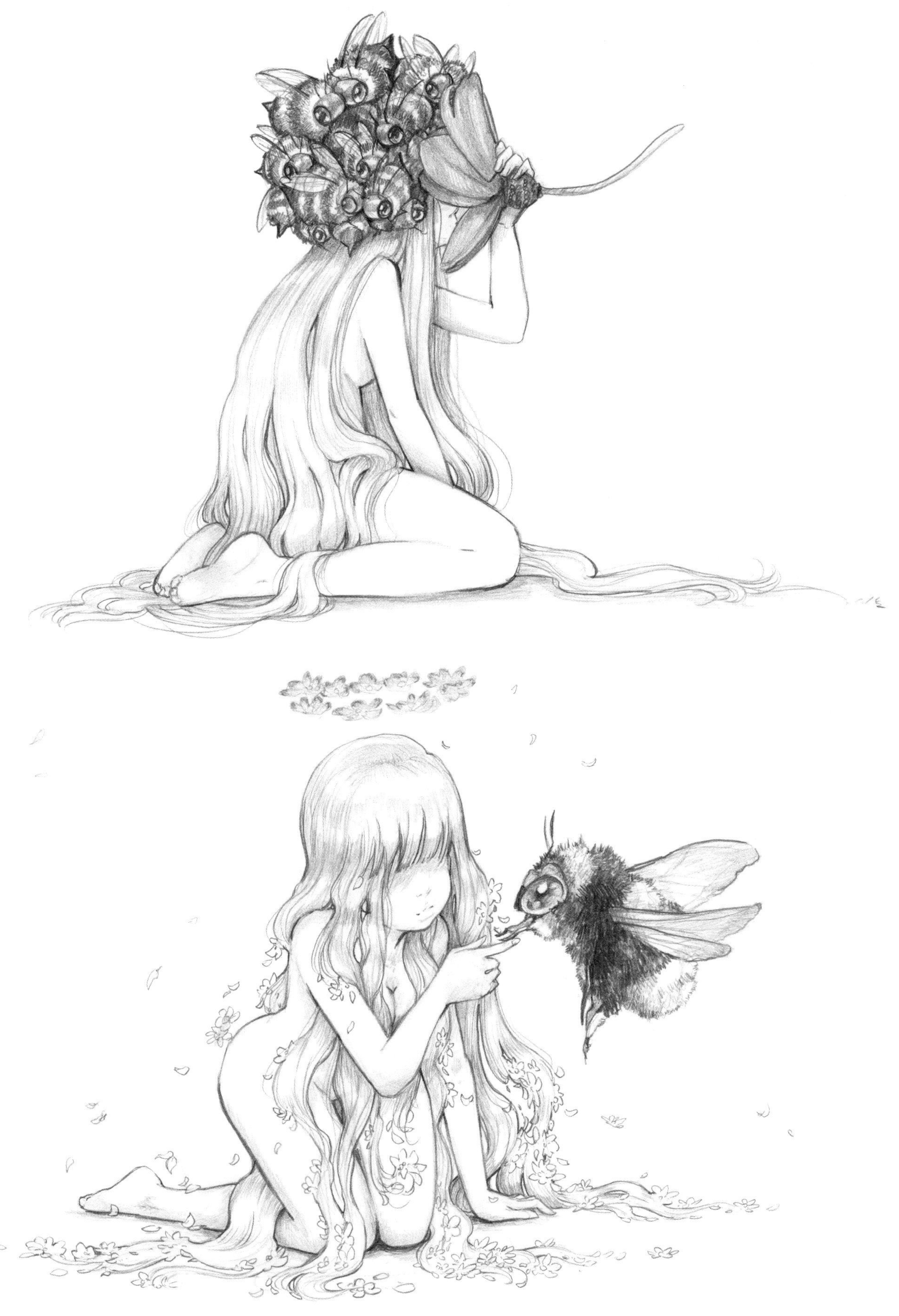

The Buds and the Bee | 8.5" X 11" | GRAPHITE | 2020
Amicizia | 8.5" X 11" | GRAPHITE | 2020

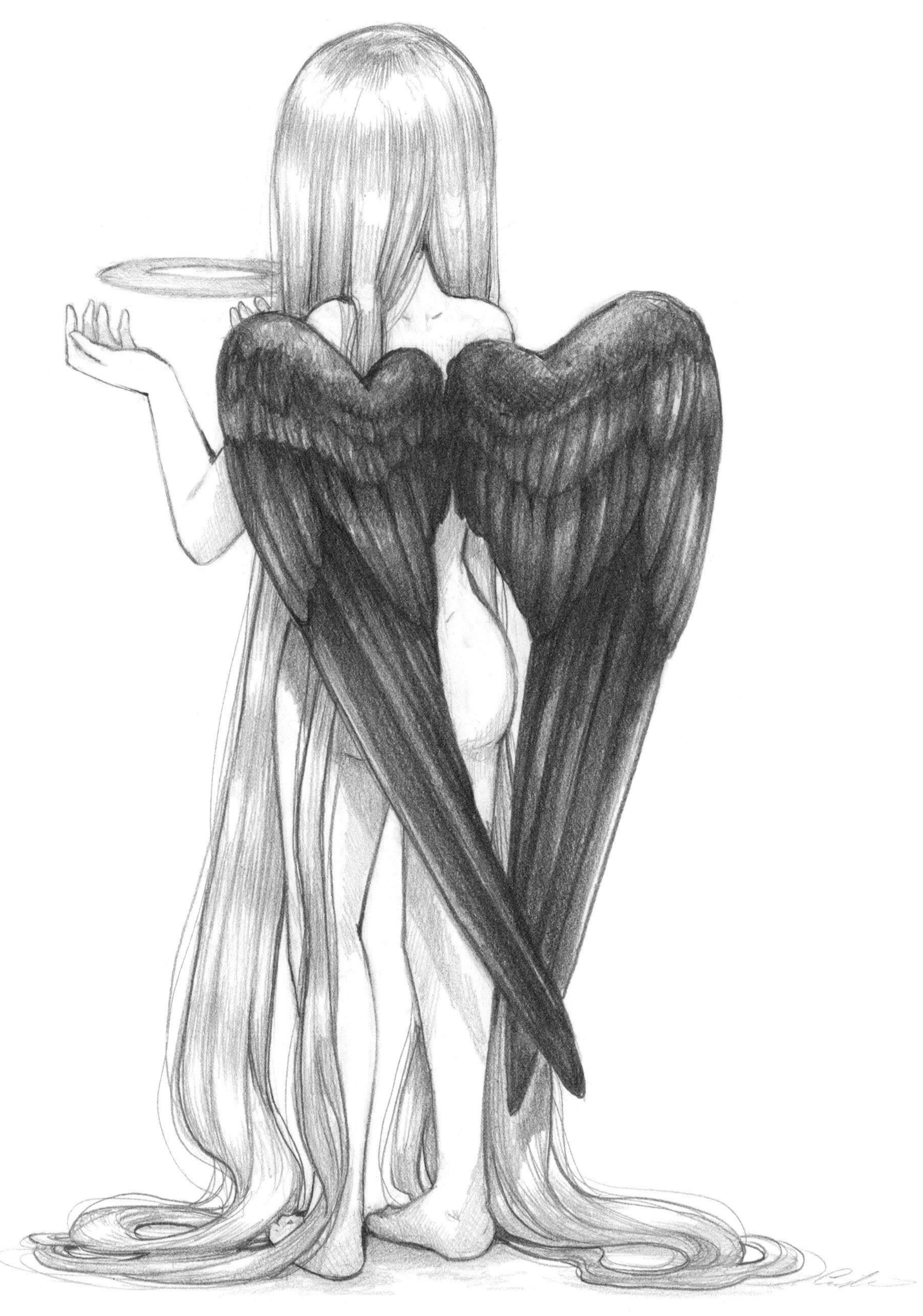

The Decision | 8.5" X 11" | GRAPHITE | 2020

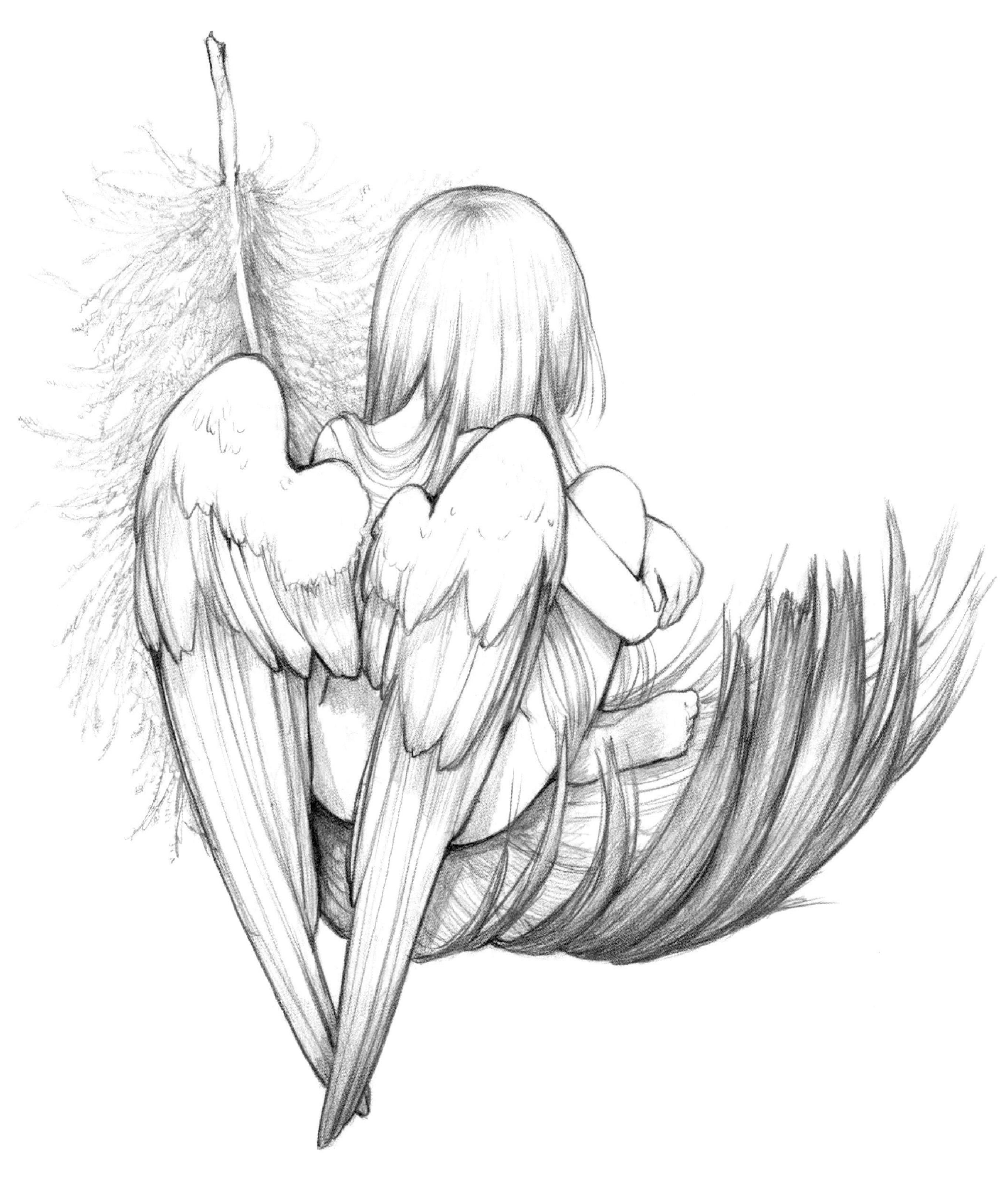

Impact | 8.5" X 11" | GRAPHITE | 2020

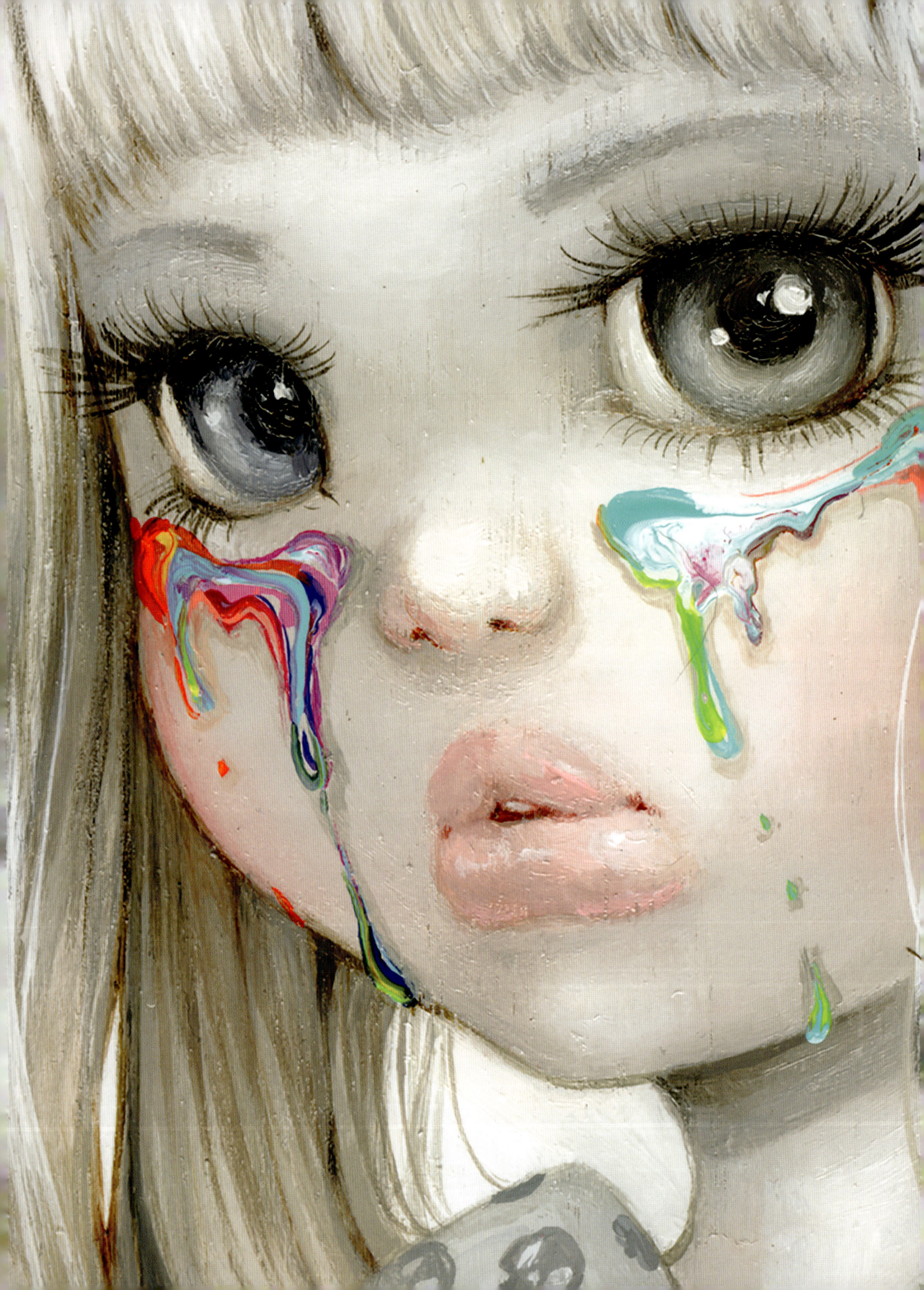

PROCESS

PAINTING BELLATOR

White and gray. Polychromatic. Mechanical. Organic. Helmetgirl. Rainbow child. Bellator is the amalgamation of all of these details, aesthetic staples of Camilla's oeuvre both past and present melting together in a painted liminal space. The explosion of rainbow color in the otherwise grayscale work evokes feelings of imagination, creativity, and beauty, as well as a push and pull between the living and inanimate. Despite the multitude of color focused there, the painting is expertly balanced; the mystery girl stands firmly as the main focus, daring the viewer to come in for a closer look. What could she be thinking about? What secrets does she share with you?

This section details the lengthy process of bringing a work like this to life, from sketch to final piece.

Facing page:
Bellator | 11" X 14" | OIL | 2020

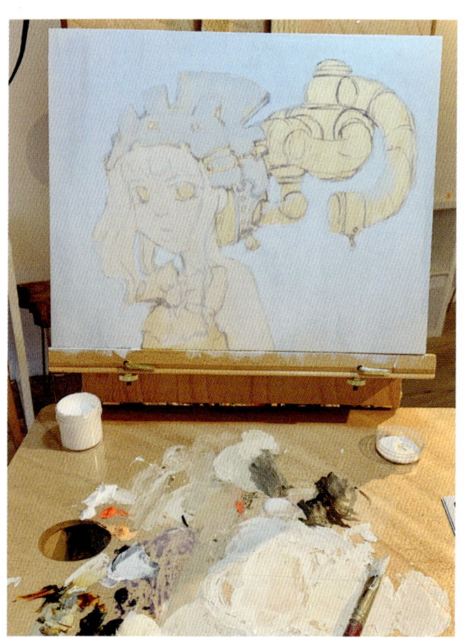

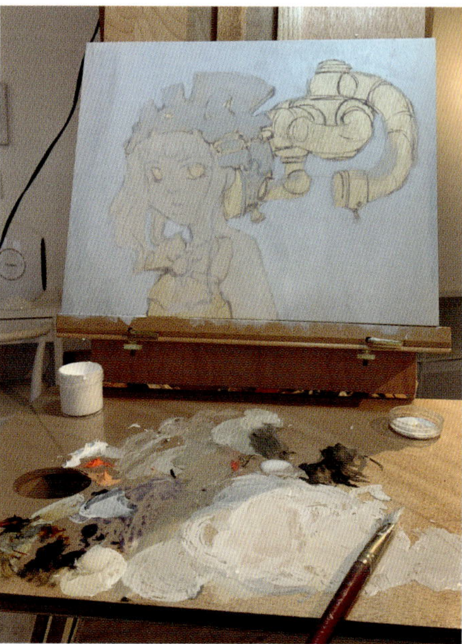

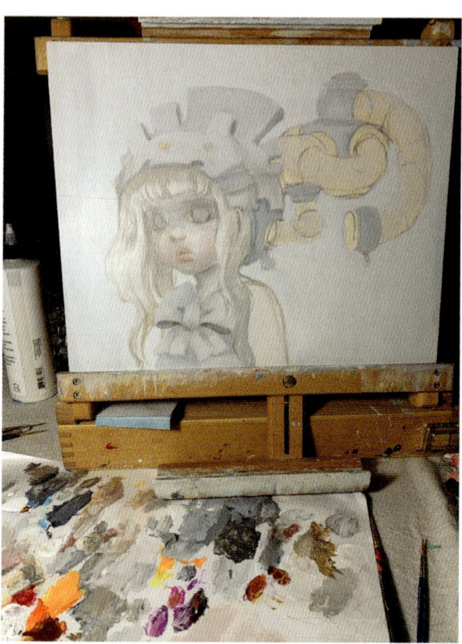

All creative endeavors start with a single seed of inspiration before sprouting into a draft, and eventually growing into a fully realized work. *Bellator* is no different; it starts with a sketch over a birch plywood base. The sketch is further refined and detailed. At last, the first layers of paint are applied and the Helmetgirl starts to appear.

The first swaths of color are added, defining not only the tube protruding from the helmet, but also the liquid texture of its contents. The addition of dark irises balances out the color.

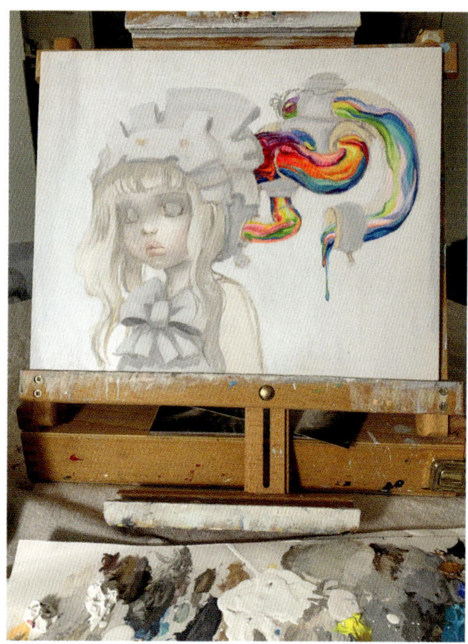

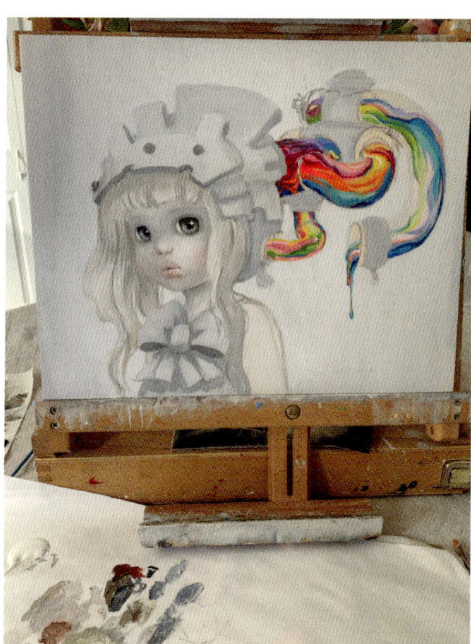

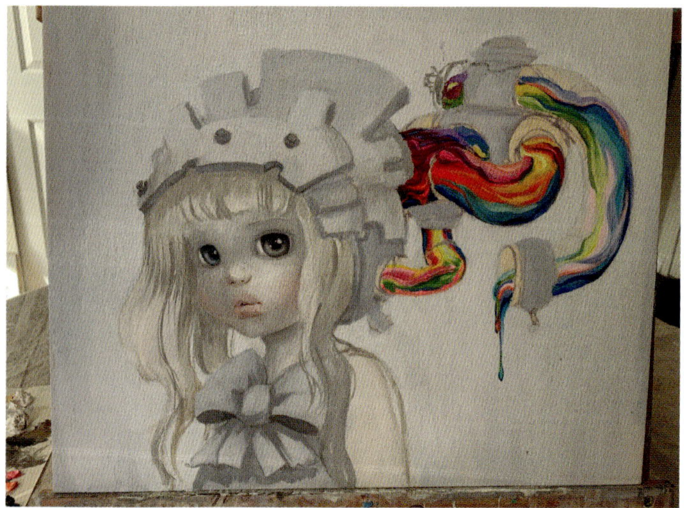

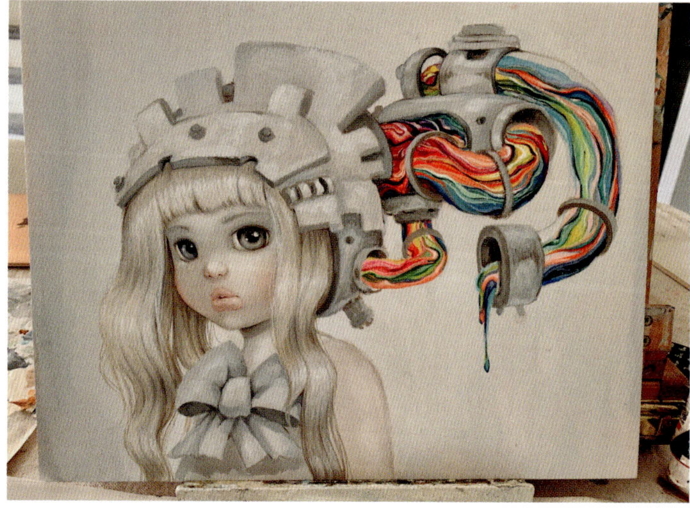

As work progresses, the finer details start to become more apparent, and the subject's personality starts to shine through. The layers of paint are built up until they create the desired tones and density. Additional values are added, and the shadows and highlights give the painting depth and texture. The shine added to her eyes and the blush to her cheeks makes her come alive.

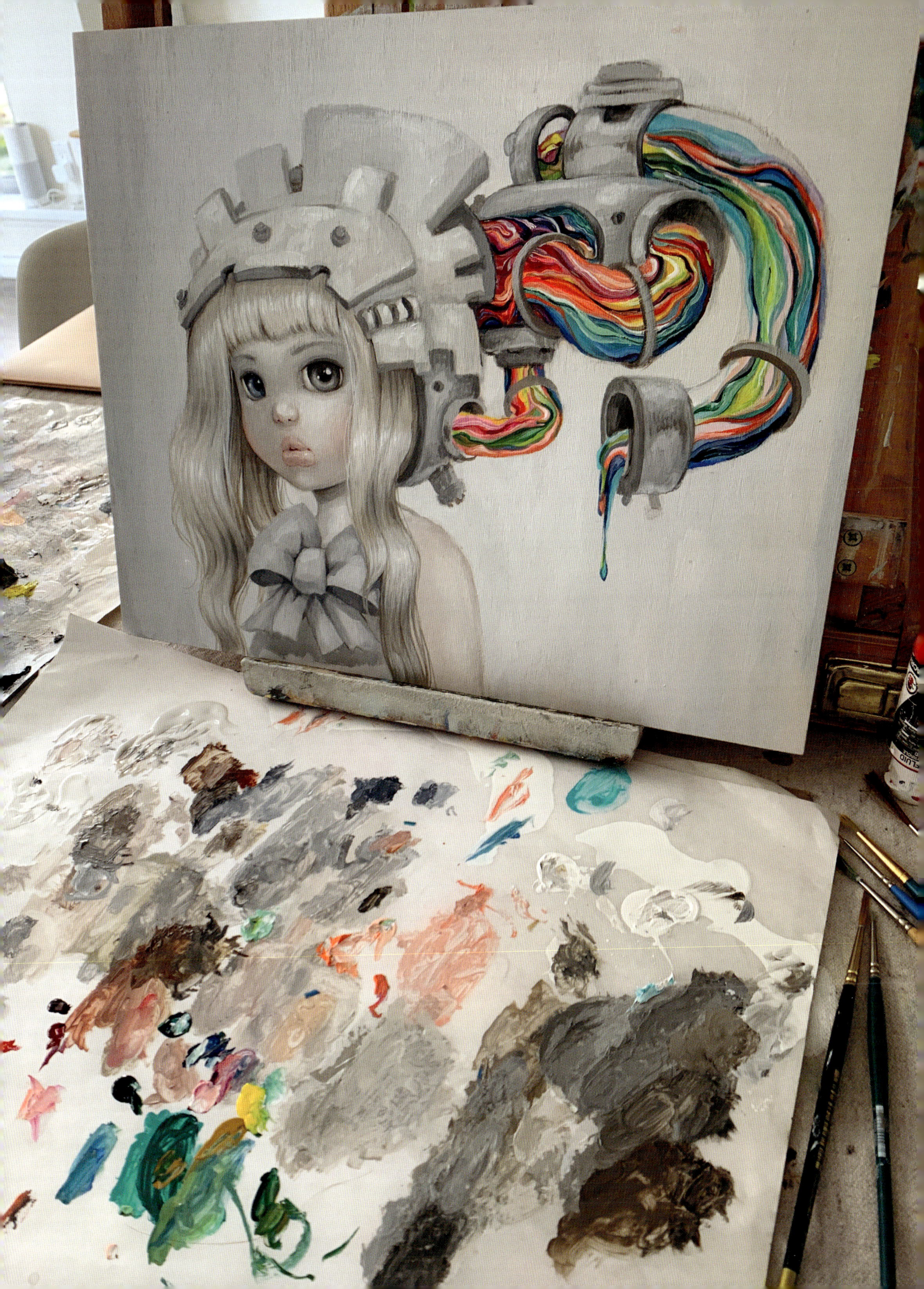

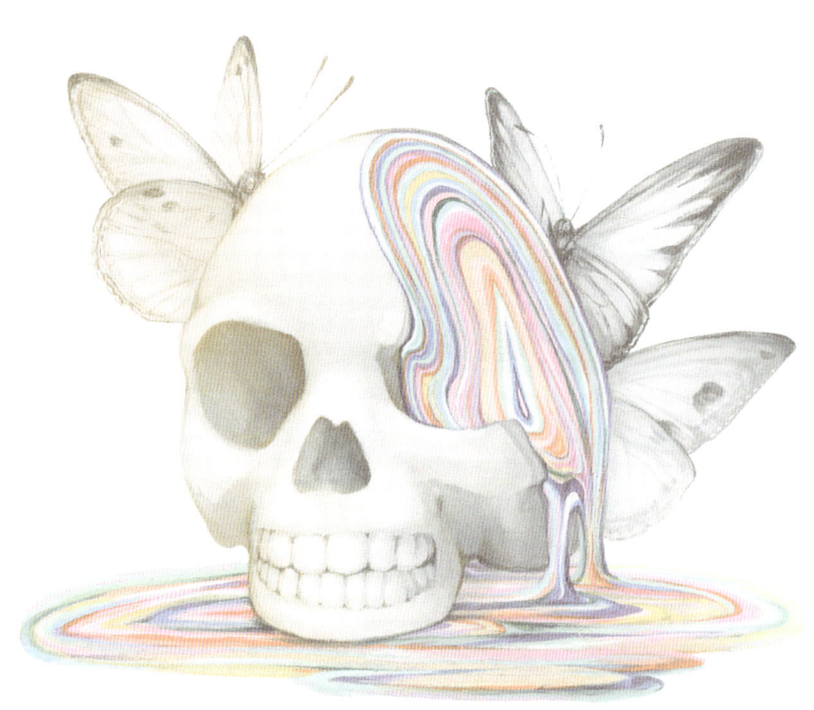